AF737739

Aid Donor Collaboration, Organizational Behavior, and Aid Flow Predictability

Aid Donor Collaboration, Organizational Behavior, and Aid Flow Predictability

Not Your Father's Bureaucracy

David Bell

Foreword by Harvey L. White

LEXINGTON BOOKS
Lanham • Boulder • New York • London

Epigraph to chapter 9 from "The Study of Administration," by Woodrow Wilson from *Political Science Quarterly*, vol. 2, no. 2 (1887): 197–222. Used with permission.

Published by Lexington Books
An imprint of The Rowman & Littlefield Publishing Group, Inc.
4501 Forbes Boulevard, Suite 200, Lanham, Maryland 20706
www.rowman.com

6 Tinworth Street, London SE11 5AL, United Kingdom

Copyright © 2020 The Rowman & Littlefield Publishing Group, Inc.

All rights reserved. No part of this book may be reproduced in any form or by any electronic or mechanical means, including information storage and retrieval systems, without written permission from the publisher, except by a reviewer who may quote passages in a review.

British Library Cataloguing in Publication Information Available

Library of Congress Cataloging-in-Publication Data Is Available

ISBN 978-1-4985-6894-4 (cloth)
ISBN 978-1-4985-6895-1 (electronic)

Contents

Foreword

Bureaucracy continues to be an intricate aspect of public service. While certainly not limited to government, bureaucratic administration is caricatured by academics and by politicians as an endemic problem in the delivery of public goods and services. The resulting tendency of characterizing public servants as incompetent, indifferent, bloated, malevolent, and paper-shuffling petitioners is cause for concern. The current demonization of individuals who work for government as the swamp, deep state, alt-government, rogue bureaucracy, secret government, and traitors is even more disconcerting.

As Charles Goodsell points out, however, "bureaucracy is neither a generalized failure nor sinkhole of waste as mythologized by anti-government ideologues." It is indispensable for the effective implementation of the social contract citizens have with their government. Moreover, it is the most reliable and dependable mechanism for providing the goods and services citizens deserve.

Researchers from Weber to Simon to Goodsell demonstrate the essentialness of bureaucracy for good governance in Western democracies. Bell's work in this book extends this recognition to countries with emerging economies as well by looking at the collaborative role bureaucrats play in international development activity. As he makes clear, however, this is not your father's bureaucracy; it is new.

The new bureaucracy emerges from global public service organizations that are central to the work of administering foreign assistance. Some are government entities; others are foundations, international nongovernmental organizations, and religious charities. The service, ethics, and trust that inform the nomenclature for organizational and individual behavior in this arena constitute high professional standards to earn the "public trust," which these new bureaucrats are expected to protect.

As Bell reveals through his "behavior-volatility linkage framework," the new bureaucracy has structures and processes to serve the public effectively, efficiently, and responsively, and with accountability. Determined by the interactions of collaboration, accountability, effectiveness, efficiency, and responsiveness, the new bureaucracy is embedded in responding to a need for capital investment delivery mechanisms. Financial transactions, human development, credit, and entrepreneurship are employed to help understand the functions of this new bureaucracy.

Although different from its domestic-based counterpart, the new bureaucracy has several similarities and constraints. Similar to domestic public service organizations, new bureaucracy is expected "to produce quality outcomes at the least cost and is challenged by forces pursuing greater equality." Both types of bureaucracy must also compete for human talent. As astutely observed by Bell, public organizations in emerging countries, for instance, are unable to invest in human talent development. This limit on the availability of appropriate local talent often necessitates acquiring talent from the international workforce.

Financial constraints are also a challenge for both traditional and new bureaucracies. In each instance, financial resources are based on promises from another party, which are usually year-to-year appropriations. The prevalence of line-item appropriations or awards also represents a further constraint on both types of bureaucracy.

Even with these similarities and constraints, the new bureaucracy described in this work represents a very insightful contribution to the literature on public service organizations. The discussion of how power operates in the new bureaucracy and its unique attributes in this multinational donor collaboration is a much-needed addition to the study of bureaucracy. Consideration of how this power in the new bureaucracy operates to enhance or diminish the capacity and effectiveness of domestic public service organizations would be a significant contribution to literature in this area as well. Goodsell's advice, in this regard, continues to be relevant: bureaucracies should open themselves to closer research scrutiny by students and professors. Rather than fear the risk of exposing embarrassing flaws, administrators should welcome the opportunity to show that, in general, they have more to be proud of than ashamed.

Goodsell also encourages more comparative studies. Bell's research on Sierra Leone in this work is a very positive step in this direction. His research effort and the organization's willingness to open itself up to the author for study and analysis are commendable.

Harvey L. White
Professor and Associate Director
Joseph R. Biden, Jr. School of Public Policy and Administration
University of Delaware

Preface

We Understand Bureaucracy in International Development Collaborations through Observations of Practice

This book is about how bureaucracy serves and constrains the collaborative work of international development as seen in the relationship between organizational behavior and capital flow volatility (behavior-volatility linkage). However, it is not the bureaucracy of Woodrow Wilson, Frank Goodnow, Max Weber, Leonard White, Luther Gulick, and others from 1887 through mid-twentieth century. This volume excavates the distinctiveness embedded in the broad and deep effects of collaboration when examining the behavior-volatility linkage. Human development is deemed vital to global organization performance. It is accepted as one measure of organizational performance, generally considered essential in any definition of successful outcomes of development policy and practice. There is often a positive correlation between human development and foreign aid in low-income countries. Donor agencies are global public organizations central to the work of administering foreign aid. Understanding the new bureaucracy seen in this collaborative foreign aid work to advance human development is best introduced by considering financial transactions, human development, credit, and entrepreneurship.

History records how people and households in many traditional societies lived self-sufficiently. Food, clothing, housing, and security were provided at the household level. Then people discovered that not all people perform all tasks equally well, and people began to specialize, which led to individuals forming communities, which led to the exchange of goods and services via bartering. Money as an artifact served to address some weaknesses of bartering.

The value of money is not intrinsic, but its utility is in facilitating exchange. It allows the value of each good to be specified only in monetary terms rather than in relative values. Grain, cattle, salt, shells, tobacco, and various metals were used in societies of old as money. Metal coins functioned as the primary form through most of recorded history. Paper notes and currency, followed later by checks, were used to facilitate more efficient exchange transactions. Banking became central to facilitating efficient exchange transactions.

Money and credit are related, but different. For most people, money is *owned*, credit is *owed*; money is an *asset*, credit is a *liability*, and people are either savers or borrowers. Savers choose to hold savings as cash, use it to reduce debt, or rent out the purchasing power of their savings to borrowers. Borrowers create financial claims in the form of notes (i.e., evidence of borrowing and debt). Borrowers provide notes to savers, and savers in turn provide money to borrowers. Borrowers pay off the note through the payment of interest (rent) and the payment of principal (the notes' original face amount). In practice, people are usually neither exclusively savers nor borrowers, but both. People function in different roles based on the nature of a transaction. Servicing us in these different transactional roles is the function of banking, or financial intermediaries.

INTERMEDIARY ROLES: BANKS FACILITATE TRANSACTIONS

Exchange transactions between borrowers and savers occur through direct or intermediary markets. Investment banking involves institutions that bring borrowers and savers together in capital markets. The typical banking actors are brokers and dealers. Brokers bring parties together to facilitate transactions and receive remuneration in the form of a commission. Dealers, on the other hand, purchase notes from borrowers and then sell notes to savers. Dealers are compensated on the difference between the amount they pay for notes and the sales price. This difference emerges over some period of time, results from numerous factors, and is not always advantageous to dealers. In the capital market transaction, savers own the notes of borrowers as an asset, similar to currency.

In contrast to the capital market activity of investment banking, commercial banking involves borrowing through instruments that can be viewed as secondary notes. Savers obtain (purchase) secondary notes from these intermediary market institutions. For example, savings and checking accounts are secondary notes through which the bank owes the depositor. In turn, these institutions purchase notes from borrowers. For instance, when I obtain a car loan from the bank, the bank is purchasing the loan note from me. Intermediary institutions facilitate two exchange transactions that occur practically simultaneously. Money flows from savers to intermediary institutions and then money flows to the borrowers.

Centuries ago commercial banks provided safe storage of precious metals such as gold and coins. Two things resulted from this transaction. First, people were given receipts (secondary notes) by commercial bankers for depositing their precious metals and the receipts facilitated exchange transactions. In essence, the receipts functioned as currency. The holders believed they could go to a commercial banker and exchange the receipt for precious metals. That is, there was a credible commitment that the receipt was backed by the bank. Second, commercial bankers learned that notes could be purchased from borrowers with receipts rather than actual precious metals. In other words, bankers could make loans without actually giving the borrower precious metals from storage and use receipts instead. Not only did receipts have transaction value, but more receipts could be issued than were represented by actual precious metal stores in the bank. This was because only a portion of receipts representing all precious metals at the bank would be presented to the bank for payment in the form of precious metals at any given time.

The result from the notes-receipts transaction relationship is understood as the money multiplier effect of fractional reserve banking. Multiplication of money resulted in an abundance of resources for development based on promises—that is, credible commitments—rather than precious metals. The ability to trust and act based on promises became integral to economic systems. Commercial banks, however, are only one financial intermediary form. Another form is designed to operate in both direct and intermediary financial markets.

Finance companies are a form of financial intermediary that operate in direct and intermediary markets simultaneously. Finance companies raise capital by selling short- and long-term securities in direct financial markets. Securities function similar to notes. They are obligations and borrowings of finance companies. Finance companies are normally understood in terms of the customer segments they serve, generally either businesses or households. The history of the small loan company goes back many years and shares the focus of serving a population described in a manner very similar to the population served by the modern-day microfinance institution (MFI).

THE ROLE OF CREDIT IN HUMAN DEVELOPMENT: HISTORICALLY AND MODERN-DAY MFIS

Historical lending practices in Ireland dating to the 1830s created lending products for the poor. These products focused on pledged loans in the form of pawning, and loan-fund contracts that served as character loans. The loan-fund product generally required a co-signer. The co-signer feature is associated not only with the social pressure to repay (to avoid humiliation) but also to facilitate a mentoring or coaching type relationship between co-signer and borrower. The loan funds were not a panacea for addressing all the ills of the working classes, but a device to be given careful consideration. The relationships and power that emerged from access to Ireland's loan-fund financial services were believed to be more than just a tool of economic development, they also benefited human development.

There are similarities between modern microcredit institutions and the loan-fund program in Ireland. In 1976, Professor Muhammad Yunus began experimenting with making loans to poor people. Yunus, founder of Grameen Bank, focused on the "landless poor," and those who had skills in weaving, husking rice paddies, cattle tending, and rickshawing (pp. 42, 140).

Also in 1976, Milton Friedman, in his address upon receiving the Nobel Prize in Economics, said "The poor stay poor not because they are lazy, but because they have no access to capital." Sir Fazel Hasan Abed, founder and chairman of the Bangladesh Rehabilitation Assistance Committee (BRAC),[1] characterizes Friedman's connection as involving capital and personal empowerment: "The poor remain poor because they are powerless. Once empowered the poor are able to change their lives" (2006, p. vii).

In this book, I describe the problem of lack of access to capital by first drawing on a statement by Alex Counts, president of the Grameen Foundation USA, at the 2010 Africa-Middle East Microcredit Summit in Nairobi, Kenya, who said "there is no lack of capital . . . [but instead] the lack is delivery channels for capital." The new bureaucracy described in this book is embedded in responding to a need for capital investment delivery mechanisms.

An innovation at Grameen Bank that facilitated rapid growth seems to be a variation of the Ireland loan-fund program's sponsor-co-signer feature. Rather than a single sponsor with greater financial strength, early results indicated that borrowers were being helped a great deal and repaying predictably without providing collateral. Yunus employed a group lending contract that provided for the poor to, in-effect, co-sign for each other. He explained that economically empowered poor people are determined fighters of the problems of population growth, illiteracy, and ill health.

Another distinctive microfinance feature that empowers people in poor countries is a specific target market. Before Yunus and the Grameen Bank, BRAC pioneered the idea of targeting women as microfinance borrowers. Also, BRAC took a client relations approach to microfinance that focused on customers' businesses as much as on loan terms and performance. BRAC's experience supports the view that benefits of microfinance go deeper than economics to include health, education, and family planning (Smillie, 2009). Contemporary microfinance has significantly expanded the portfolio of loan products available (e.g., individual loans) and is impacting the institutions' credibility, earning them a seat at the table where development agendas are shaped and strategies designed. Collected microfinance data reflect a capital delivery mechanism serving a diverse income group, including the poorest people.

HUMAN DEVELOPMENT, ENTREPRENEURS, AND CAPITAL DELIVERY

Entrepreneurship is about more than economic development; it is also about human development. Entrepreneurship provides individuals the opportunity to guide their own destinies through work. Entrepreneurship that is supported by nongovernmental organizations that serve as MFIs has been effective at assisting the poor in achieving sustainable livelihoods. Microfinancing is preferred over donations as an alternative approach to development. Entrepreneurship offers poor people the power to decide their own financial fate and to reap the associated dignity that comes with trying and success. As banking intermediaries, MFIs serve as a capital delivery mechanism to empower people in their quest to alleviate poverty. Money is seen by entrepreneurs as providing freedom, contributing to confidence, and enabling choice. In addition, it provides a sense of camaraderie with business colleagues. Efforts to alleviate poverty by public organizations such as those that support entrepreneurial ventures are illustrated in global multicultural cooperation activities of microcredit as a capital delivery mechanism.

Entrepreneurship is celebrated both for its innovation in responding to needs, and as a valuable mechanism for its ability to advance national development agendas. Entrepreneurship is a cross-cutting field of study that has been used to explain several societal phenomena in various disciplines of social science. Development economists contend that entrepreneurship provides a comparative advantage at both micro- and macrolevels. Individual entrepreneurship is reflected by employable skills or business ventures. National entrepreneurship results are manifested in exportable products.

A common question involving entrepreneurship is how to generate sufficient financial capital to promote innovation that permeates all societal levels in the face of volatility. Capital flow volatility, as will be explained later, involves disbursement variances in the amount and timing of capital, including foreign aid. This aspect of the problem—capital delivery mechanisms experiencing capital flow volatility—is a serious concern because volatility has demonstrated dramatic devaluing effects on capital.

MICROFINANCE IS BANKING AND IS INTEGRAL TO HUMAN DEVELOPMENT

MFIs in countries affected by conflict and state fragility find it difficult to access capital and market mechanisms. It is not hard to understand that customers and capital investors perceive there are high risks associated with doing business in a setting that might be destroyed overnight by ongoing or resumed conflict. These concerns directly affect access to capital.

Researchers have examined capital flow access by focusing on factors such as capital market characteristics, access to external financing (e.g., foreign investment), rule of law, and investor incentives. There is a positive relationship between government infrastructure and foreign direct investment.

Whereas investors in Western economies usually obtain investment capital through markets, investors in postconflict and fragile states cannot because the state lacks the capacity and institutional structure to support healthy markets. Challenges to viable capital markets are exacerbated by the absence of both institutional infrastructure (e.g., institutionalized formal rules) to support a viable capital market, and insufficient financial incentives to attract private capital. In effect, postconflict nations are dependent on foreign aid as a primary source of capital. Consider that development financial institutions[2] account for more than 50 percent of the more than $4 billion in foreign aid microfinance capital investment in 2007 (Cull, Demirguc-Kunt, & Morduch, 2008). Foreign aid is a vital capital source for poor countries, and so are capital delivery mechanisms for MFIs engaged in battling poverty. Therefore, one response to the need for capital delivery channels is organizational rather than market focused.

Foreign aid provided by organizations and government agencies takes the form of money (e.g., grants, subsidized loans), commodities, and technical assistance. To be considered foreign aid, two criteria are to be satisfied. First, the main goal should be the promotion of economic development and welfare. Second, aid may be in the form of a grant or subsidized loan (which may be restricted to purchasing commodities, technical assistance, and so forth). Most foreign aid has been in the form of bilateral assistance. Donor countries also provide aid through multilateral mechanisms in which resources are pooled with the participation of institutions such as the World Bank, United Nations Development Programme (UNDP), and United Nations Capital Development Fund (UNCDF).

Foreign aid is capital that has proven to be an effective tool in human development.

Effectively employing aid has increasingly required collaborations among organizations with a variety of diverse personnel. Organizational performance is a measure of human development and has long been considered an important measure in development policy and practice. Its importance is embedded in the belief that people possess measureless potential to achieve good. Human development is often positively related to foreign aid in some of the poorest nations in the world. Donor agencies as global public organizations are central to the work of administering foreign aid. As such, global organization performance is affected by the degree to which multicultural staff can be assembled in a competitive global hiring context.

A COLLABORATIVE RESPONSE TO THE NEED FOR CAPITAL DELIVERY

In 2004–2005, the United Nations undertook a project to identify capital access barriers. The project included multistakeholder consultations, input from a 2005 global e-conference, material from experts via an on-line questionnaire, and in-depth interviews. One output was a published report, "Building Inclusive Financial Sectors for Development." A year before that, in 2003, UNCDF implemented a new strategy to respond to the need for capital delivery mechanisms in Sierra Leone. The strategy, known as the Microfinance Sector Development (MITAF) initiative, had three key features: financial sector assessment; development of national strategy and action plans to promote the development of an inclusive financial sector; and capital investments in MFIs. Most importantly, it was a collaborative approach that functioned at a time when the Commission for Africa noted that such arrangements are a principal device for meeting development goals and when the heads of the Group of 8[3] countries agreed to a 100 percent increase in foreign aid (Eyben, 2012). As a capital delivery mechanism, the strategy was designed ultimately to give poor people access to financial services, including capital in the form of credit.

Programs such as MITAF in Sierra Leone are an organizational response to the need of poor countries for capital investment mechanisms when markets cannot provide an adequate response. They also represent collaborative capital delivery mechanisms that address a major constraint to the poor having access to the financial sector. Yet programs such as these also experience capital flow volatility, which reduces the value of capital.

There are several reasons it is important to understand the volatile properties of capital flow to poor economies and to MFIs. First, aid volatility can indirectly offset some direct beneficial aid effects, such as loans for entrepreneurial ventures. Second, matters relating to aid volatility are receiving increased attention due to their impact on achieving the Sustainable Development Goals. The number and strength of external shocks (e.g., the gross domestic product effect) on poor countries tend be larger than those experienced by industrialized nations. Third is the large amount of aid provided to poor countries and MFIs. Finally, uncertainty about aid flows has a detrimental effect on economic growth; volatility of aid is an aid value determiner. As a result, knowing the characteristics of bureaucratic structures and processes linked to capital volatility is important to providing value in public service finance foreign aid.

THE PROBLEM REDEFINED AND ITS EFFECTS: CAPITAL VOLATILITY AND DELIVERY MECHANISMS

Capital flows at the macroeconomic level normally coalesce with business cycles and economic growth or contraction. Economic crises over the last twenty-five years have demonstrated that business cycles are closely correlated with short-term capital flows. Instability in these capital flows negatively affects the growth of macro economies. For example, capital quickly leaving a country in large amounts can be devastating. Beyond economic slow-down, the risk of capital instability is an impediment to investment. At the microlevel, capital instability affects livelihoods, nutrition, education, and health. For a business, opportunities for sales and staff development are missed, for households a decision must be made between paying school tuition and food. Numerous other tradeoffs also occur when capital is not reliability and consistently available.

There are important macroeconomic cycle impact differences between African and industrialized countries as measured by the consumption welfare cost of fluctuations. A study of thirty-three African countries over twenty-two consecutive years found welfare costs of cycles to African countries are large multiples of the cost to the United States. For example, consumption fluctuations in one model had a welfare cost of 1.36 percent of U.S. consumption, but the median was 5.11 percent in Africa (Pallage & Robe, 2003). Welfare gains occurring as a result of eliminating volatility are so substantial that they could add 1 percent to annual growth indefinitely. Important insights emerged on the economic effects of capital flow following financial liberalization (Celasun & Walliser, 2008; Honohan & Beck, 2007). For example, one study (Demir, 2009) of Mexico and Turkey found a relationship between financial liberalization, imperfect capital markets, and capital flow volatility. Capital flow volatility increased after liberalization, and reductions in growth and trade were significantly related to capital volatility. These findings are of particular interest because capital market mechanisms influenced by financial liberalization are generally viewed as the inevitable source of capital for a sustainable microfinance sector.

At the microeconomic level stable capital flows enable effective strategic planning and budgeting by individuals, firms, and even governments. Planning guides and promotes strategic activity. Conversely, microlevel capital instability constrains this type of activity. For example, a by-product of credit contractions is capital volatility, which can create economic shocks with negative impacts on poor people. Public organizations in poor countries, for instance, are unable to pay workers and delay human capital investments. Restricted access to credit, savings instruments, and insurance products constrain the poor's ability to exploit new farming opportunities, educational and skill development, medical care, and entrepreneurial initiatives. While MFIs are put forth as a mechanism to promote human development in poor countries, their effectiveness depends on reliable capital flow used to provide financial services.

Postconflict fragile states experience greater volatility in foreign aid compared with other developing nations. Some research has found that aid volatility costs far exceed the costs attributed to business cycles. For instance, approximately one-third of armed conflicts that reignite do so within ten years of declaring peace. A key risk factor for reigniting armed conflict is the lack of economic opportunities. Economic opportunity—defined as per capita income, per capita income growth rate, population growth, and schooling of young men—has been found to significantly affect the risk of resuming conflict (Bigombe, Collier, & Sambanis, 2000). With this understanding, it is sobering to note that 50 percent of 2007 foreign aid benefited only five of forty-eight postconflict fragile states.

Embedded in numerous transactions, descriptive statistics on institutional performance, and official processes of training and technological improvements was extensive evidence of the ongoing struggle among the competing issues of collaboration, organizational imperatives, and the dual goal of public benefit outcomes and performing in a financially sustainable manner.

This struggle represents the linkage between organizational behavior and capital flow volatility. Value of capital is affected by linkages between organizational behavior and capital volatility. Capital flow volatility is determined by the interactions of three properties of bureaucracy: (i) collaboration; (ii) accountability; and (iii) effectiveness, efficiency, and responsiveness (or impact). Capital value is a function of the level of volatility and MFI condition at disbursement.

This book examines the struggle through a case study of how organizational behavior and capital flow volatility are linked in one specific context: a multidonor collaboration in Sierra Leone during the period 2004 to 2010.

Cooperation in multicultural teams is central to both governmental and nongovernmental organizations facing human development challenges. One formulation of these problems is reflected in the seventeen U.N. Sustainable

Development Goals. The first goal is ending poverty in all its forms everywhere. The behavior of public organizations in attacking poverty, expressed as strategies and tactics, is an important component of achieving this goal. Strategies and tactics employed by public organizations in responding to difficult problems such as alleviating poverty include the need to establish an effective collaboration. These strategies and tactics also include access to and use of money. As such, knowing the characteristics of bureaucratic structures and processes linked to capital volatility is important to providing value in foreign aid as a public service.

With this background in mind, this book examines how bureaucracy serves and constrains the collaborative work of international development as seen in the relationship between organizational behavior and capital flow volatility.

ORGANIZATION OF THE BOOK

The period reported on in this book is during the ten-year window following Sierra Leone's brutal ten-year civil war. Slow progress toward achieving the development goals contributes to spillover effects felt throughout the global community, such as volatility, illicit activities, war, and public health concerns. Given the tremendous amount of capital investment aid, stakeholders are demanding explanations for shortfalls in development performance. The explanation, in part, is the devaluing effect experienced due to aid capital volatility.

The book excavates the new bureaucracy through examining the problem of not sufficiently understanding volatility in capital flow from delivery mechanisms to MFIs used to provide financial services to poor people. Capital flow volatility involves variances in the amount and timing of capital. During this examination a new bureaucracy was excavated to explain the linkage between how organizations behave and the volatility of capital. However, a study involving MFIs and capital flow processes necessitates a basic overview of the role and development of money and banking. That overview is provided in this Preface.

The point of departure is individuals engaging in financial exchange transactions. Increasingly without regard to what nation a person calls home, or an economy's sophistication level, this basic starting point undergirds a financial framework within which services and institutions can be placed. I provided a primer on the origins, structure, and basic functions of the financial services sector, money, and banking. Microfinance entities are institutions that facilitate poor people engaging in financial transactions using services that otherwise would not be available to them. I explained that the behavior-shaping power of promises (credible commitments) are central to a healthy, robust financial services sector. Human development is examined with a focus on the devaluing effects of capital flow volatility with the aim of understanding the relationships between organizational behavior and capital flow volatility. In a word that understanding bureaucracy, but not your father's bureaucracy.

Chapter 1 describes the UNCDF project in Sierra Leone. I used Sierra Leone as the case study because it captured the attention of world microfinance leaders. Moreover, employing a case study of MITAF within a particular theoretical framework provided for a robust, versatile analytic device. Case study methods facilitated a deep exploration of the complex activity occurring in capital delivery mechanisms. Case study approaches are able to incorporate numerous forms of evidence such as reports, artifacts, and interviews.

Data sources included MITAF quarterly narrative reports detailing MFI performance and donor activity, spreadsheets containing financial data on deals, meeting minutes, and policy documents. Quantitative data included financial information on all seventy-five capital investments.

Obtaining explanations directly from donors and borrowers in their own words, as opposed to imposing a structured survey instrument, was important to excavating behavior-volatility linkages (there were twelve focus group interviews with twenty-six individuals representing ten organizations, including MFIs, all MITAF donors, the technical service provider, and the central bank of Sierra Leone). Using NVivo, a computer qualitative analysis system, a hierarchical coding process of open coding, axial coding, and selective coding was employed.

Chapter 2 describes the components of the bureaucratic structure and process in this donor collaboration. The complexity and detail are investigated using the Institutional Analysis and Development (IAD) framework created by Nobel Laureate Elinor Ostrom. IAD served three primary functions:

- It identified components to be considered in my investigation.
- It provided patterns of component relationships that represent assumptions about order, attributes, and context. The assumptions are based on theoretical and empirical analysis.
- It accommodated numerous and varied theories employed in the investigation.

IAD is robust and effective in analyzing complexity because it provides a basic structure to a complex array of considerations. It makes sense and brings order to a dizzying array of important, interconnected components. IAD made it possible to incorporate and make explicit the linkages between organizational behavior and capital flow volatility including MFI regulation, the informal economy, and rules as key environmental factors.

Chapter 3 contains a description of the formal bureaucratic structure and process of the donor collaboration. The capital flow process from investment decision until all money is accessible to the MFI is described in terms of the design of the MITAF program. This description is embedded in the view that public policy administration is the actual expression of policy in attacking societal problems, whereas MFI sector development using a program project rather than aid directed to the Sierra Leone government is a fundamental distinction in my investigation compared with much of the capital volatility literature. The chapter describes capital investment agreements with MFIs as not only a key investment document. It is also integral to understanding linkages between behavior and capital volatility.

Chapter 4 provides insights on bureaucratic collaboration. The key components of completing and implementing a capital investment deal between the collaborator and an MFI are related and intertwined. For instance, a formal agreement is required to officially and legally implement a foreign aid investment deal. Certain provisions of the agreement are particularly important, such as performance targets and schedules for when capital will be disbursed to the MFI, conditions for disbursement, and reporting requirements for the MFI. In practice, the program proved to be imperfect, loosely structured, and deeply embedded in complex historical and human factors. The chapter concludes by discussing capital disbursement issues.

Chapters 5 and 6 continue the reporting of analysis results by examining the linkages between organizational behavior and capital flow. The benefits and challenges of the new bureaucracy are examined. The focus is on linkages between behavior and capital flow. How capital investment contract terms were interpreted and implemented by the project were perceived to be different after a North-to-South leadership change. The chapter explains how power operates in the new bureaucracy and the unique attributes in this multinational donor collaboration. Accordingly, the chapter describes interactions in a particular context and an intervening condition in the context of capital investment contracts with MFIs.

Chapter 6 further describes the linkages between organizational behavior and capital flow volatility as viewed through capital investment deals and disbursement activity in 2006. The importance of additional intervening conditions such as program evaluation are on efficiency, effectiveness, and reduced volatility. It is 2006 behavior that proved to be the touchstone that illuminated linkages with capital volatility. MFI perceptions of the project entity and donors were different and complex. Perceptions were more than individual opinions; they were a strategic assessment of business associations that had evolved according to history, information access, representations, and experience. As such, the new bureaucracy is viewed from a perspective shaped by global organizations serving human development and revealed through behavior-volatility linkages.

Chapter 7 describes the new bureaucracy and discusses the project's midterm evaluation as the intervening condition. It contains a discussion of the characteristics and measures that serve in applying the new bureaucracy to different organizations and environments. The chapter introduces a new lens to better understand relationship between organizational behavior and capital volatility, that of the Collaboration Bureaucratic Triad. Bureaucracy is helpful in making sense of the collaboration's complexities and interconnectedness. Bureaucracy, however, had special attributes in this donor collaboration project. Bureaucracy in the project took on attributes shaped by environmental factors. The uniqueness was primarily found in the broad reaching effects of collaboration. The new bureaucracy has structures and processes to serve the public effectively, efficiently, and responsively, and with accountability, whereas capital flow volatility is a collaborative outcome and is determined by the interactions of collaboration; accountability; and effectiveness, efficiency, and responsiveness (impact).

I found it a bit ironic, though perhaps intuitive, that assembling effective multicultural teams is affected by the success of human development work. Global organizations need this diversity to seize opportunities and attack global problems. Going it alone is less frequently an option, whether it be an entrepreneurial venture in a developing country, a U.S.-based human services nonprofit organization, or a fragile nation-state government. The importance of shared responsibility and collaboration was underscored in 2005 both by the Commission for Africa and the Organization for Economic Co-operation and Development's Paris Declaration on Aid.

Today's opportunities and problems place demands on countries and organizations beyond their capacity to respond alone. Forming and sustaining cooperation requires mutual benefit and encourages work that improves performance outcomes. Cooperation within and between global public organizations is reflected in the multicultural teams they assemble and is repeatedly affirmed as an effective organizational strategy. I have also found that this cooperation, especially at a high level of inter-organization commitment, involves a bureaucracy that is different from the simple organizational formulations of yesterday.

The project was an ambitious, adventuresome undertaking given environmental factors, a nascent microfinance sector, and administration required by this collaborative structure. The complexity and interconnectedness observed in capital investment deals held the key to making sense of linkages between behavior and capital volatility. As such, three properties of the new bureaucracy became evident:

- *Bureaucracy of Collaboration.* This property of bureaucracy provides for and challenges group commitment and individual organizational restraint.

Donors make investment disbursement decisions by working together to comply with collaborative commitments while remaining true to their respective organizational missions.

- *Bureaucracy of Accountability*. The attributes of simultaneously serving and resisting managerial oversight, governance, transparency, and stakeholders constitute the property of accountability. It often involves both top-down pressure and bottom-up pressure from stakeholders.
- *Bureaucracy of Effectiveness, Efficiency, and Impact*. Those features designed to produce quality outcomes at the least cost are challenged by forces pursuing greater equality and broader access to financial services. In this collaborative setting of shifting prevailing coalitions, whoever sets the goals determines the measurement of performance (e.g., effectiveness, efficiency, and impact).

Bureaucracy, as defined by these three properties, interacts with capital flow, shaping and being shaped like conglomerate rock in a river.

In chapter 8, the model now developed from the data is populated with the people who were involved, and their actions are described. Capital investment deals were part of a multi- faceted strategy to improve access to financial services for the poor and were in a context shaped by certain environmental factors. The Bureaucracy of Collaboration attributes were the basis for the espoused goals in commercial-based investment decisions where the project donors had political agendas. They also conflicted with those goals. The chapter explains how the overarching goal of poverty alleviation required project stakeholders (i.e., donors, the project entity, and MFIs) to cooperate. At the same time, each organization's mission was the primary compass guiding its work. The project's effectiveness was directly related to its ability to coordinate the complexity of various interests while working collaboratively. The collaborative property of the new bureaucracy is the distinguishing aspect that presents an alternative way of viewing bureaucratic authority relationships in the project, the new bureaucracy.

The Bureaucracy of Accountability and its various dimensions were evident within the organizations and the project participants. The project's contracted staff, for example, struggled to track and account for capital disbursements. Their effort was fraught with bureaucratic complexity between the staff's main office in Mexico and a difficult tracking mechanism in Sierra Leone. One donor, UNDP, had a decentralized, locally responsive bureaucracy that illustrated one dimension of accountability, whereas UNCDF had a centralized, multilevel review and approval process that demonstrated another dimension. Regardless, the project staff and each donor demonstrated a distinctive ability to consummate deals and disburse capital during the year when an accountability mechanism (i.e., the mid-term evaluation) was administered. Reporting data on outreach and financial performance constituted accountability for effective resource deployment. For instance, when expected capital was not available, MFIs answering credibility and representation questions for people in their community could be considered a type of implicit legitimacy accountability. MFI tactical decisions were observed to be directly tied to outreach and financial performance requirements for capital disbursements.

The dimensional epicenter for the Bureaucracy of Effectiveness, Efficiency, and Impact/Responsiveness is sustainability, and sustainability is about reliability and stability. The people of Sierra Leone needed (and still need) reliable access to financial services and the project aimed to fill that need by developing financially sustainable MFIs. However, the project struggled in developing strategies to enhance institutional capacity while incorporating industry standards rather than exclusively focusing on strategies for MFIs to reach industry performance standard targets. Actions within organizations, including tactics and strategies, are an important aspect of this property. MFI tactics and strategies (behavior) were in response to the incentives of performance indicators incorporated in deals as conditions for capital disbursement. For instance, one MFI had better financial self-sustainability, but it had an extremely high caseload per credit officer. This was a strategy employed to satisfy capital disbursement conditions.

The biggest challenge faced by the new bureaucracy, within and between organizational group types, was having a common perspective and the ability to rapidly implement an agreement such that outcome values were not diminished by capital volatility.

Chapter 9, the final chapter, outlines four strategic recommendations for collaboration optimization of the new bureaucracy so as to minimize the capital-devaluing linkages of organizational behavior and capital flow volatility. They are as follows:

1. Directly address exogenous variables, or environmental factors, to minimize delays in capital disbursements.
2. Employ the combined skill sets of a multicultural team to expeditiously assess the situational context, detect and assess contextual changes, and maintain a calculated action orientation while realizing changes in human behavior and life-style status are long-term propositions.
3. Provide sufficient funding and marshal sufficient resources to collect data and employ the rigorous processes required to guide the process and learn from it, and to make thoughtful, nuanced, strategic decisions as the program progresses.
4. Account for project commitments, because entering into a collaboration makes one-to-one transactions between donors and MFIs subject to the

additional commitments of the project; tracking money is only part of accounting.

In addition, the final chapter recommends an agenda for future research. The central theme is stable capital flow. Research should deeply explore the actors in the model that give rise to different linkages between organizational behavior and the desired outcome of the collaboration; in this instance, stable capital flow. In an arena where participants who represent different parts of the world interact to address societal problems, a better understanding of cultural factors can convert barriers to bridges in accomplishing common objectives. Moreover, understanding these factors and how they are linked to aid capital volatility is important in developing responses to minimize the capital-devaluing effects of volatility.

NOTES

1. BRAC's relief work evolved to development initiatives. The organization changed its name to Bangladesh *Rural* Advancement Committee. Later, in the 1990s, BRAC was deeply involved in urban poverty reduction. The acronym, BRAC, now represents a motto: Building Resources across Communities. Microfinance is central to BRAC's development model.
2. Development financial institutions are private sector development mechanism for government development initiatives (Reille & Forster, 2008).
3. The 2018 G7 plus Russia.

Chapter 1

The Actors Used to Understand the New Bureaucracy

Bureaucracy is a way of organizing both structure and process. I find it helpful to think of organizing as being about roles, relationships, and results. Sociologists studying bureaucracy think of roles as the structural characteristic of specialization or differentiation. I also include here an often-stipulated characteristic, competence, or qualification. Relationship is generally considered as the most important characteristic and referred to as hierarchy. Roles are embedded in relationships that have consequences and produce results. A mission is served by specific aims employing resources in activities to achieve success. Historically, bureaucratic hierarchical structures were deemed to be universally applicable to all organizational settings. Heady (2001) explains its prominence decades ago among researchers of public administrative structures. In fact, bureaucracy in its basic form is still the organizational skeleton preferred by organizations, public and private, all over the world. That is why it is so important to make sense out of how it serves or hinders efforts to address some of the most challenging societal problems facing public organizations globally.

I believe better understanding relationships between behaviors at the organizational level and capital volatility elucidates a substantial portion of what remains unexplained about the capital flow volatility problem. The capital delivery mechanism analyzed in this book, the first UNCDF sector development programme (Programme), was involved in many activities to produce outputs and outcomes selected and defined by its organizers. I narrowed in on activities that identified and explained linkages between organizational behavior and capital flow.

Investigating aid capital volatility is essentially an analysis of public organization behavior and donor foreign aid capital flows. Behaviors are actions/interactions, strategies, and tactics. This book is not about how microfinance institutions helped people emerge from poverty and enhanced their self-worth. Similarly, it is not focused on decision processes involved with foreign aid donors deciding to participate in the project nor on decision processes resulting in capital investment deals. My focus is phenomena associated with capital investment deals that serve identifying linkages between behavior and volatility. The focus is the actual disbursement, the flow of capital once the decision was made to invest. The focus also includes the associated behavior by organizations. Beyond identifying the linkages, bureaucracy helps makes sense of the linkages' occurrence. *Aid flows are operationalized in numerous ways in the literature; however, I demonstrate that participants in this case study understand it in terms of different time dimensions. Volatility is variability in disbursement timing of each payment from the time a capital investment deal was approved and as measured against the structure of the deal* (e.g., length of time to satisfy conditions, and length of time between satisfying conditions, technical service provider requesting donor disbursement/processing disbursement, project entity process/procedure).

This chapter provides insight on the organizations participating in the collaboration, including microfinance institutions (MFIs), as well as the structure of the collaboration. It is useful to keep in mind the characteristics of collaboration. The centrality of collaboration is beyond organizations to life itself, including the essence of human existence. Symbiotic collaboration ranges in levels of need, including sustaining life as seen in a mother's milk nourishing the gut microbes of her child who is unable to digest certain sugars.[1] Often, the terms partnership, network, coordination, cooperation, and collaboration are used as synonyms. When looking closely to understand the different types of relationships bureaucratic organizations have, it is important to make distinctions and measurements.

There are principal differences in the types of commitments that various relationships call for. Often, collaboration is viewed as a higher level of commitment between actors than simple cooperation. Collaboration actors are independent volunteers having a stake with the risk of meaningful loss, as well as the benefits normally ascribed to such arrangements. At a minimum, collaboration is distinguished by the degree of interdependence or formality. It involves a mission of change or increased capacity through shared resources that is bigger than can be achieved by acting alone. It is less than coordination required by a powerful authority and greater than implied cooperation, beyond a loosely coupled view (Gazley & Brudney, 2007; Guo & Acar, 2005). Although some view cooperative arrangements like collaboration as pushing aside bureaucratic hierarchy as the primary way to address challenging societal problems (Eyben, 2012), I explain how bureaucracy is a tool employed and very present in collaborations.

THE CASE STUDY AND THE QUESTIONS

The case study approach is well suited for this close, detailed analysis of capital investment deals. Case study analysis is appropriate for relatively current phenomena where a controlled intervention cannot be administered. My investigation of a U.N. Capital Development Fund (UNCDF) Programme involved the years 2004 through 2009,[2] which did not lend itself to experimental controls as the project was near completion at the commencement of this investigation. Case study techniques have the capacity to incorporate numerous forms of evidence such as reports, interviews, and artifacts. For example, observations, interviews, and archival and document analysis data collection procedures are appropriate for the case study approach I used in this investigation.

The book does not attempt to generalize to all MFIs nor all flows of donor aid. Rather, it develops a lens, a substantive theory, applicable to Programmes and other collaborative arrangements to create inclusive financial sectors. The book also adds to current understandings and theory.[3] These are appropriate aims for case study research.

This book adds to both aid volatility and bureaucratic organizational understandings by answering three questions as applied to the Programme case:

- How do different actors account for variances in capital disbursements?
- What responses do different actors recommend to reduce variances?
- How are organizations' behaviors linked to volatility in disbursements?

The resulting substantive theory (lens) represents the actors in the Programme case and is applicable to that collaboration; it focuses on the population from which it was developed (Strauss & Corbin, 1998). That is to say, I discovered an explanation believed by the people and organizations involved. This theory—this explanation—can also be applied to similar settings as set forth in this chapter. I call this theory Collaboration Bureaucratic Triad (CBT). It states: *Value of capital as a project outcome is affected by linkages between organizational behavior and capital volatility. Capital flow volatility is determined by the interactions of three properties of bureaucracy: collaboration; accountability; and effectiveness, efficiency, and responsiveness (impact). Capital value is a function of the level of volatility and MFI condition at disbursement.*

The explanatory power of the theory and model was found in the specific external variables shaping capital investment deals, particulars of a deal, organizational behavior, structure of the collaborative, and related capital volatility. In other words, CBT's ability to explain what may occur in certain situations is the framing of conditions that give rise to capital disbursement and the actions/interactions employed and explaining the volatility affect. It is important to understand certain conditions in collaborations that give rise to bureaucratic behavior and outcomes in discrete situations, as well as the outcome variances affect. Outcomes—results—are what public organization bureaucracies are about. They are about performance in an accountable fashion. I explain why the characteristics of this case study make it a good selection for gaining this understanding.

CASE SELECTION: WHY MICROFINANCE, SECTOR DEVELOPMENT PROGRAMME, AND SIERRA LEONE?

Capital delivery mechanisms are needed at various levels of societies in poor countries and for numerous development instruments. Capital volatility at these levels and for these instruments devalues the foreign aid disbursed. I explain in this section that microfinance is a valuable instrument, Programme a valuable mechanism, and Sierra Leone a valuable setting for examining linkages between organizational behavior and capital volatility. The structure and processes for delivering capital provided a space to identify and understand the important properties of bureaucracy in collaborative work.

Why Microfinance?

The need for capital delivery mechanisms and the challenges of capital volatility are vivid when viewed through MFIs. MFIs are a ubiquitous development device in poor countries. They have demonstrated the potential to be an effective capital delivery mechanism for poor people.

The problem of volatility experienced by aid capital delivery mechanisms is better understood by examining capital investments in instruments that provide capital directly to poor people in poor countries. Microfinance is one of many development instruments and is intriguing because it demonstrates that the poor are bankable.[4] Access to financial services such as savings, insurance, transaction instruments (e.g., checking accounts, debit/credit cards, and mobile phones), and credit help poor entrepreneurs and households improve their welfare and manage economic shock. Although rigorous research on the role of microfinance in improving the lot of the poor is sparse, encouraging work has shown that better financial institutions and private credit both grow aggregate output through an increase in savings and improve income dispersion (Beck, Demirguc-Kunt, & Levine, 2007; Clarke, Xu, & Zou, 2006; Gries, Kraft, & Meierrieks, 2009; Karlan & Morduch, 2009; Joseph Stiglitz, 1988). Given the futility often connected with efforts to establish statistically significant relationships and causation to development interventions, it seems to be more important that microfinance is a development instrument with the potential to be self-sustainable. Even if lacking statistically significant evidentiary backing, the economic environment for the foreseeable future (i.e., resources and capital are constrained), favors self-sustainable development instruments with measurable outcomes.

While microfinance dates back centuries, its recent use as a component of the global development agenda has pointed to important questions. A particularly heated debate involves the structure and mission of MFIs:

- Are these financial services best provided by nonprofit or for-profit institutions?
- Is profit maximization or social outcomes the best organizational purpose?
- Can a combined goal of improving the lot of the poor and operating sustainability result in sufficient outcomes that warrant a long-term investment?

Consider, India's microfinance sector began as a nonprofit endeavor emphasizing social outcomes but also experienced success commercially. This commercial success has led to a political backlash with potential to have a global impact some contend will be similar to the subprime mortgage meltdown. This empirical paradox illustrates the divergence that occurs in striving to achieve a dual bottom-line mission.

Lending to the poor in Ireland was used to improve both economic and social well-being in the 1800s (i.e., dual bottom-line). Its use today speaks to the persistence of the belief in financial services as central to fighting poverty. Nevertheless, MFIs' centrality in the development paradigm ultimately makes it the focus of critical evaluation. Numerous concerns regarding effectiveness in alleviating poverty and opportunity costs of not funding alternative instruments are often expressed.

The cross-cutting impacts of microfinance on development issues, including gender and education concerns, and its appeal to private and public investors attract researchers spanning organizational, social, political, and economic fields. Researchers have examined MFI governance and financial performance. Studies have considered the impact of subsidies on credit allocation, such as targeting women when providing credit. Scholars have explored questions of microfinance aid allocation around the globe (Armendariz de Aghion & Morduch, 2005; Dichter, 2007; Dunion, 2010; Hulme, 2007; Imboden, Clark, & Herman, 2006). Examining microfinance to understand the relationship between capital volatility and organizational behavior adds to a rich, diverse body of literature.

At present, when income disparities are growing globally, it is important to aim for uncovering instances, descriptions, and explanations of capital flow volatility pursuant to investment deals, especially as they relate to MFIs. Organizational actors in an MFI interacting in foreign aid capital investment need to be understood in terms of lived reality directed at poverty alleviation. It is here that NGOs, international aid agencies, local governments, and nation states can experience organizational learning and organizational intelligence.[5] *Microfinance is an appropriate intervention to study this linkage phenomenon because of its centrality to the global development agenda, the integral role the financial sector has in a nation's administrative institutions, and the apparent interconnectedness of actor behavior and capital flow.* It serves understanding the work of bureaucracy because of its centrality in government institutions and its place in those organizations integral to the global development agenda, as well as influence on actor behavior and capital flow.

Why the First UNCDF Sector Development Programme?

In 2003 the UNCDF created its first Programme as a capital delivery mechanism for Sierra Leone in response to the need for capital and a delivery channel. The project entity was called Microfinance Investment and Technical Assistance Facility (MITAF). From 2003 through 2009 UNCDF formed twenty-two sectors development programs that serve as capital delivery mechanisms.

The MITAF case was the space where one or more donors, a MFI, and the apex (MITAF staffed by a technical service provider) interacted. MITAF was created by a collaborative agreement involving the government of Sierra Leone, Bank of Sierra Leone, UNDP, and UNCDF. Kreditanstalt für Wiederaufbau (KfW), a German development financial institution, and Cordaid, an Amsterdam-based Catholic international NGO (INGO) joined the project's governing Investment Committee (Committee) in August 2004 and December 2004, respectively. The collaboration initially committed $12.5 million USD to assist in developing a pro-poor financial sector in Sierra Leone.

MITAF, functioning as an apex, was administered by a technical service provider (MITAF staff) selected by the Committee in July 2004. Over time, the MITAF staff recommended and the Committee selected, sixteen microfinance institution partners ostensibly according to criteria contained in the UN Programme Support Document (Program Document). Project funding intended to address and underwrite several key sector capital needs, including technical assistance; training fellowships, including institutional development; capitalization; operating losses; fixed assets; and loan funding.

The project approach, as opposed to a corporate entity, was selected as the initiative's vehicle because it was the most expeditious. This decision underscores the importance of rapidly developing an MFI sector as expressed in the Project Document. Time and rapidity were a big deal. This decision created a context that affected organizational behavior and capital volatility. That is, the organizational structure and associated bureaucratic structure had a particular effect on both actors' behavior and capital flow. In the MITAF distinctions of market, government, and civil society were apparent, yet often indistinguishable. Donor diversity, timing, and context relative to the end of armed conflict, in sub-Saharan Africa (SSA), and the interest of international leaders made MITAF a complex and interesting case within which to examine relationships between organizational behavior and capital volatility.

Why Sierra Leone?

Sierra Leone, a postconflict fragile state, has several attributes that made it a valuable setting for this investigation. First, Sierra Leone experienced a brutal civil war that ended in 2002. It was recognized that a vital part of rebuilding the country was the creation of a sound, broad, and far-reaching financial services sector. In Sierra Leone, this need produced significant demands for the diverse set of actors who would develop the financial sector. Second, Sierra Leone developed a national policy to guide postconflict rebuilding, including adopting a National Microfinance Policy. A key component of the policy underscored Count's point regarding the need for capital delivery mechanisms; substantial capital was needed to develop an inclusive financial sector for the country. A vehicle for delivering the capital was just as important due to the fragile state of the postconflict government.

Third, in support of the national policy, diverse donors and leaders in microfinance responded to the need for capital by collaborating with the government of Sierra Leone to develop a pro-poor financial sector. Sierra Leone was the first of twenty-two countries selected for a Programme. This distinguishes the country among developing nations. Leaders in microfinance considered Sierra Leone uniquely situated to serve as a model for West Africa due to its weak framework as a fragile state. It was believed that successful interventions in the country can inform developing effective programs in the region. Particularly important for serving as a model was that the Programme operated exclusively during the critical years following civil war (when conflict is most likely to re-erupt) and the period when postconflict states are most capable of effectively absorbing foreign aid.

The fragile state attribute is inseparable from its prewar colonial history. Sierra Leone's prewar period during the twentieth century was highlighted by independence from British rule in 1961. Sierra Leone is approximately the size of the state of South Carolina in the United States and located on the coast of West Africa (figure 1.1). Pedro da Cintra, a Portuguese explorer, named the country *Serra de Leao* roughly translated as *Lion Mountains* in 1462. The current capital, Freetown, was founded by the Sierra Leone Company in 1787 and

Figure 1.1 Map of Sierra Leone. *Source*: U.S. Central Intelligence Agency, with thanks to the University of Texas Libraries.

has been home to former African slaves from America and the West Indies. After becoming Britain's West African colony in 1792, Sierra Leone served as the residence of the governor for the settlements of Gambia and the Gold Coast.[6] In addition, Sierra Leone was considered to be the educational center of British West Africa. However, the Sierra Leone turned over by the British at independence was extremely poor (e.g., viewed by many as raped of the best diamond reserves), practically illiterate (literacy rate below 10 percent), and possessed frail government institutions.

Following independence, a new prime minister took office pursuant to the 1967 elections. He consolidated power by creating a one-party state and implementing a patrimonial political system. This political situation permitted increased corruption, patrimonialism, and deterioration of government institutions to take place and effectively marginalized Sierra Leone tribes and people. In response, unemployed and excluded young men formed the Revolutionary United Front to overthrow the abusive regime. A civil war ensued that tore the nation once known as the "Athens of West Africa" into ruins and covered it with blood until a peace agreement was finally reached in 2002 (Patton, 1996, pp. 59–60). Rebuilding was essential for national recovery. Part of this recovery was creating a sound, broad-reaching financial system—a hallmark of truly modern societies.

Sierra Leone's poverty and banking-access challenges are reflective of (SSA's distinction in the developing world. According to 2002–2004 data, the proportion of the SSA population with a bank account in prudentially regulated financial institutions[7] was less than 20 percent compared with the West and Asia, with substantially more people holding bank accounts (Karlan & Morduch, 2009). The vast majority of the poorest clients served were in South Asia, which recorded a decrease in the *proportion* of poorest from 1981 to 2005 (from 60 percent to 40 percent) with the *absolute* number remaining constant at approximately 600 million. In SSA, the *proportion* remained virtually unchanged at 50 percent, while almost doubling in *absolute* terms to over 300 million. This comparison illustrates the relationship between access to financial services and reduction in poverty, as well as the disparate experience of SSA.

The connection between microfinance clients, capital flow, and foreign aid in Africa is backed by empirical evidence. A survey recording pricing and other constraints related to financial service access in the top commercial banks (categorized by size) specifically noted the inaccessibility of commercial banks in Sierra Leone. Sierra Leone represents an extreme example where owning a checking account involved fees greater than 25 percent of per capita gross domestic product (Karlan & Morduch, 2009). This illustrates how capital provided to Sierra Leone commercial banks did not translate into improved access to capital for the poor because of factors such as account maintenance costs incurred by customers. In addition, the International Monetary Fund categorized Sierra Leone's financial sector as "underdeveloped" because the nation provided only *one account for every 32 people and private sector credit at 5 percent of gross domestic product.* Data reflect African citizens' capital taking flight off the continent to the tune of 40 percent of portfolio value, with alarming figures in SSA (Cai & Theisman, 2005; Salisu, 2005). Disparate access to financial services and lack of capital employed to address this issue underscore the importance of capital delivery mechanisms with constrained volatility to strengthen aid capital value.

Sierra Leone was a major foreign aid recipient and one of the most challenged nations in human development. Many believe that foreign aid from industrialized nations is a vital capital flow for developing countries. No other part of the world received a greater proportion of aid than Africa. In 2009, aid per capita was $47 USD to Africa, with SSA receiving multiples more than northern Africa. Moreover, aid to Sierra Leone was almost double the amount invested in SSA (Deutscher, 2010; OECD, 2011). SSA had one of the lowest human development measures globally and faced formidable challenges in this area; in 2010, Sierra Leone ranked 158 out of 169 countries on human development progress. Sierra Leone was extremely poor, received substantial amounts of foreign aid, and had a very large segment of the population underserved by the financial sector.

These details point to the urgency and importance of having an effective capital delivery mechanism at the time MITAF was formed. With the end of war, how could poor, untrained people in Sierra Leone make a living while contributing to the rebuilding and restructuring of a devastated country? Sierra Leone's leaders developed a plan that initiated the National Micro-Finance Policy. The policy was developed by a public-private task force and approved by the Sierra Leone Cabinet. The policy acknowledges linkages between reduced poverty and economic growth. The policy also recognizes that microfinance services result in more productive economic activities undertaken by the population. Lack of capital was a major constraint in developing a viable pro-poor microfinance sector.

The validity of this major constraint seems to be reflected in citizen activities and plans. For example, a comparison between 400 Sierra Leone microfinance borrowers and 900 nonborrowers and to national statistics found that activities involving livestock, poultry, and agriculture were more prevalent among microfinance borrowers than both nonborrowers and the national average (BRAC, 2010). In addition, borrowers were found to more often plan starting new enterprises in the near future than nonborrowers (BRAC, 2010; Karlan & Morduch, 2009). The relationship between microfinance clients, higher instances of productive activities, and reports of plans for new enterprises suggested that relief from capital constraints was associated with increased economic activity in Sierra Leone. Investigating capital flow volatility in delivery mechanisms was well served by focusing on a Programme in Sierra Leone.

It is important to understand the perspective of this investigation regarding diverse actors, people interviewed as corporate-actors representing organizations that participated in a Sierra Leone-based capital delivery mechanism. Although the participants in this study consist of three types of corporate actors—or "decision-making entities"—as Ostrom (2005) explains—they are *connected* to other environments or settings. This connection is illustrated by how rules are perceived and understood by different cultures. In other words, people are viewed as organizations, rather than individuals. Many studies examining numerous and different organizations attest to the appropriateness and usefulness of this perspective. As such, the cultural aspect of organizations based in certain countries is not ignored. Accepting that respondents are involved in employment relations (i.e., corporate actors) and utilizing the case study approach are central to avoid problems encountered by linking hierarchical data at different levels. This investigation did not look at the effects of macro or national-level interventions at the level of the MFI. The focus is on interorganizational behaviors related to capital flow, all at the same organizational level.

Though the people I interviewed were corporate actors interacting with other participants in the MITAF project, linkages of actors with other environments/settings were not ignored.

People in MITAF organizations interact with others in settings beyond employment where their individual preferences are shaped and consequently shape deals that result in MITAF organizational action/interaction. For purposes of my investigation, the employment setting was the context for the people interviewed. The neutralizing of private preferences in employment settings is explained by Herbert Simon (1996) as decisions people make as participants in organizations. In other words, he says people set aside private preferences when making decisions in employment settings, in deference to organizational preference, such as policies and procedures.

Simon (1996) identified organizational performance resulting from the self-sacrificing work of people as central to certain business activities being conducted through organizations and not markets. He explains that the views of these people were influenced by the organization's perspective. As such, in my investigation interviewees' perceptions, beliefs, and values were considered to be those of the employer corporate-actor. Equally important, however, is the acknowledgement that there were factors that distinguished the interviewees as shapers of implemented corporate policies, such as culture factors. The apex, MFIs, and donors represent rich, diverse organizational cultures and staffs from different regions of the world.

DONORS: MITAF INVESTMENT COMMITTEE

In my study, donors were the source of capital. Donors comprised the Investment Committee (Committee), which functioned like a nonprofit organization's board of trustees. Donors also operated as corporate investors with their respective organizational interests. The three types of donor institutions are described in this section. Having organizational profiles of the subjects advances the understanding of behaviors that I examined and informs insights on important aspects of bureaucracy in collaborations.

The German development bank (KfW) is considered both a bilateral donor and financial development bank. On the one hand, KfW operates based on many of the same principles as a development, or international, bank (a type of multilateral donor) by investing in nongovernmental entities like MFIs. On the other hand, it is exclusively associated with a particular country, Germany; therefore, it is considered as bilateral. KfW ranked among the top five funders in SSA based on amount of foreign aid. These top five provided 50 percent of the microfinance funding in SSA in 2009. In addition, KfW committed and provided more capital to MITAF than each of the other Committee members.

Two MITAF donors are part of the United Nations (UN) family. The U.N. Development Program (UNDP) and UNCDF are multilateral donors. The UN selected UNCDF as the focal point of its system's activities for the 2005 International Year of Microfinance. MITAF Sierra Leone is part of a UNCDF initiative in Africa, "Building Inclusive Financial Sectors in Africa" (UNCDF, 2004a, 2008). UNDP and UNCDF are financed by numerous nations and UN members.

The final MITAF donor, Cordaid, is an Amsterdam-based INGO with multiple development goals. Cordaid's in-house microfinance expertise is somewhat unique among INGOs (CGAP, 2004; Latortue, Littlefield, Siedek, & McKee, 2007). The relation with its government is a noteworthy attribute as the Dutch were ranked among the top nations investing in microfinance and historically allocated extraordinary amounts of bilateral assistance through NGOs. One survey reports that Cordaid invested in more SSA countries than KfW in 2008 (CGAP, 2004). In addition, Cordaid is a religious, or faith-based, INGO. This faith-based aspect represents a unique and remarkable attribute. A survey at the time of the MITAF project reports that U.S. religious congregations alone contributed an estimated $4.5 billion to U.S. based international relief and development efforts in 2008 (Triplett, 2010). This amount approximates total annual investment in microfinance and may be an indicator of the potential importance of this faith component.

APEX: TECHNICAL SERVICE PROVIDER

There was an intriguing operational link between donors and MFIs: the apex organization. MITAF's purpose was to establish an inclusive financial system to broaden access to financial services to the poor. Important to a financial system are mesolevel organizations, between the macro and micro levels. Mesolevel organizations included customer credit reporting agencies, MFI rating agencies, and other second-tier entities. Apex organizations are one type of second-tier meso mechanism.

Apex organizations serve as channels of funding and/or technical support providers to numerous MFIs in a single nation. The MITAF apex was formed as an administrative mechanism for this UNCDF *project*. The project structure was used rather than a distinct corporate *entity*. This was a conscious decision, in collaboration with the Government of Sierra Leone, to expedite the project's launch (The World Bank, 2004). Creating a corporate entity would have resulted in a distinct ownership structure, accountability lines, and different considerations in designing capital flow. Equally important to note, organizers believed it would have taken at least six months to complete the Sierra Leone bureaucratic process to form a corporate entity, which was deemed an unacceptable delay. An important take away from this is *time was of the essence*.

The apex was charged with both MFI *sector capacity building* (e.g., providing technical assistance to MFIs in business plan preparation for submitting funding proposals to the Committee) and a *financial intermediary* role between donors and MFIs. Regardless of the organizational structure, these are typical roles for apexes. The financial intermediary role can be viewed as the *broker* in investment banking institutions, as discussed earlier. MITAF serves as a market to reduce the transaction costs of connecting capital-providers and capital-seekers. The apex facilitates transactions without taking legal title to the financial *claims*. This role has been emphasized as an important distinction of the MITAF structure. The apex involvement in capital flow varied in important ways as it performed numerous tasks.

The Programme Document provides a detailed and integral role for the apex in MITAF (UNCDF, 2004b). The Committee selected the technical service provider to manage the apex. My reference to the apex is the MITAF staff managing and administering MITAF as a role distinct from the donors, while very much related. The apex was explicitly charged with achieving the projects' outcomes. These included MFIs operating according to minimum financial sustainability standards and achieving considerable customer outreach. To a great extent, the MITAF staff's performance was measured based on these and other project outcome targets specified in the Programme Document. There was a mushrooming of apex organization use in MFI sector initiatives throughout the world during the period of my investigation. The technical service provider role was underscored by numerous experts as being central to the success of apexes. Of all the apex managerial functions, the most important may be the selection of MFIs considered for investment by donors.

MICROFINANCE INSTITUTIONS

In the Preface, I provided a detailed introduction to MFIs as embedded in the broad context of financial intermediaries. MFIs provide the basic services of commercial banks: deposit accounts, loans, transaction services (e.g., ATM cards). Half of the MITAF MFIs offered these basic services. The primary distinction between MFIs participating in MITAF is whether or not they accepted deposits that were not used as collateral for loans.

Sierra Leone MFIs are portrayed as operating in the *informal economy* community. The main function of the financial services sector in Sierra Leone's informal economy is providing deposit and loan products. MITAF MFIs were considered the best prospect for providing leadership to the nation's MFIs. However, many did not easily fit into the commercial bank legal framework that permits institutions to accept customer deposits. Organizing a commercial bank in Sierra Leone is difficult primarily because of high capital requirements. One MFI partner that met these requirements was ProCredit. ProCredit's target market was the same as MITAF's, both of which sought to increase financial service access. Four MITAF members were formed as community banks, which were also technically organized as commercial banks. They resembled community credit unions found in the United States with residents of the chiefdoms as shareholders. ProCredit, in contrast, was substantially owned by an international holding company. MITAF Investment Committee member KfW had a more than 20 percent stake as well. This powerful, resourceful partnership was crucial in ProCredit's satisfaction of commercial bank capital requirement regulations. Community banks were initiated by Sierra Leone's central bank, Bank of Sierra Leone. This included capitalization assistance in the form of loans with very favorable terms and waiver of some capital requirements in the commercial bank legal framework. Many MFIs in MITAF were established without the powerful, resourceful relationships afforded ProCredit and the community banks. Consequently, a large portion of MFI partners were similar to finance companies, providing loan products only (no deposit accounts).

MFIs in MITAF are distinguished by four characteristics: structure, domicile origin, geography, and the year of MITAF capital commitment. Many MFI partners began focusing on lending as one of several programs offered by an NGO. For instance, World Hope International has been registered in Sierra Leone since 1999 and offers education and health programs; microfinance (Hope Micro) was added in 2002. Another example is the American Refugee Committee (ARC). ARC registered in 2000 and sponsors various programs on HIV awareness and skill development. The ARC microfinance initiative began as a program in 2001 and reorganized as a separate institution (Finance Salone) in 2005. Another example, the Grassroots Gender Empowerment Movement (GGEM), is a domestic NGO involved in community development, networking services, and microcredit. In January 2008, its microfinance operation was reorganized to operate in a separate department with separate financial accounting; however, it remains part of the NGO. This structural distinction at GGEM is an important illustration of efforts to satisfy MITAF's emphasis on clarity and transparency in MFI operations, while remaining part of the NGO structure.

The Community Empowerment and Development Agency (CEDA) story gives a sense of the organizational roots shared by many MITAF MFIs. CEDA began as a program, Lunia Agriculture and Rural Development project, focused on agricultural activities and gender empowerment in the southern districts of Bo and Kenema. After restructuring and increasing its institutional capacity to serve more people and communities, the current name was adopted and, in 1994, it was licensed as a national NGO. CEDA developed a program for microcredit with support from the government's Social Action for Poverty Alleviation. As of December 31, 2009, CEDA had more than 6,300 borrowers, ranking among the top five in MITAF MFIs for clients served. It was the expectation and belief that CEDA had capacity to significantly grow the number of clients served.

MFIs in MITAF have diverse backgrounds, structures, and product portfolios to serve those with limited access to financial services. One shared characteristic was the espoused view of MITAF MFIs as partners. This eclectic collection of MITAF MFIs (e.g., NGOs, commercial banks, community banks), selected to be developed as leaders of the MFI sector, often presented challenges to MITAF that could not be effectively addressed with a one-size-fits-all approach.

The diversity and associated challenges were reflected in organizational behaviors and capital flow. My study of this linkage revealed that bureaucracy where it was easy concluded there was only pandemonium.

The new bureaucracy that contextualizes the complexity and interconnectedness impacting the value of capital emerges as the setting and subjects are discretely placed in a framework to serve analysis. In the next chapter, I discuss Institutional Analysis and Development structured environmental factors, which prior research is charged with insufficiently considering.

NOTES

1. "[H]uman mothers, for some reason, churn out an exceptional variety—scientists have identified over 200 human milk oligosaccharides, or HMOs, so far. They are the third-biggest part of human milk, after lactose and fats, and they should be a rich source of energy for growing babies. But babies cannot digest them. . . . Why would a mother spend so much energy manufacturing these complicated chemicals if they were indigestible and therefore useless to her child? In 2006, the team found that the sugars [HMOs] selectively nourish one particular subspecies called . . . *B. infantis* for short. . . . As it digests HMOs, *B. infantis* releases short-chain fatty acids (SCFAs)

that feed an infant's gut cells—so while mothers nourish this microbe, the microbe in turn nourishes the baby" (Yong, 2016, pp. 93–95).

2. This investigation focuses on the period 2006–2009, though not exclusively.

3. Strauss and Corbin draw upon the Glaser and Strauss classification of theories as substantive or formal. Formal theories are useful to broader interests and concerns. They are derived from analysis involving diverse conditions and sampling. Substantive theory applies to the population and context from which it was derived; however, similar conditions and populations can benefit, such as SDPs in conflict, fragile state settings.

4. Bankability is a measure of the poor's insurability, capacity to repay loans, and accumulate savings (Karlan & Morduch, 2009).

5. Organizational learning involves behavior changes as knowledge and awareness are acquired. Organizational intelligence is a sustained improvement in performance as a result of learning (March, 1999).

6. The Gold Coast was the name given by Europeans to the region now known as Ghana. The Portuguese, first to arrive to the region in 1471, found substantial gold deposits in the area. European traders created residences along the coast in the years following the discovery to trade these resources. The British Gold Coast was established in 1821 as the British took control of coastal lands.

7. Prudential regulation pertains to deposit taking institutions (CGAP, 2006, p. 36).

Chapter 2

The Approach to Identifying and Understanding the New Bureaucracy

> Every problem-solving effort must begin with creating a representation for the problem—a problem space in which the search for the solution can take place. . . . Human beings, viewed as behaving systems, are quite simple. The apparent complexity of our behavior over time is largely a reflection of the complexity of the environment in which we find ourselves . . . complexity emerges from the richness of the outer environment, both the world apprehended through the senses and the information about the world stored in long-term memory. (Simon, 1996, pp. 108, 110)

> In the writing, [Elinor Ostrom] provides an example identifying 10 subsystem variables that affect the likelihood of self-organization in efforts to achieve a sustainable social-ecological system. "This is not a KISS (keep it simple, stupid) approach. If we keep it too simple, we lose an understanding of what's going on out there," she says. On the other hand, frameworks and theories always have to focus in on a subset of all of the variables operating in a complex system. (University, 2009)

In this book, I carefully unfold the revealing of the new bureaucracy. The credibility of this effort is in no small measure found in how this work is done. While being careful to not overemphasize research methodology, today's world increasingly values evidence-based practice. This underscores an increased necessity for rigorous, systematic analysis for prescriptions espoused to address our world's most challenging social problems. In this chapter, I describe the process used to identify and understand the new bureaucracy.

Nobel Laureate Elinor Ostrom (2005) explains that a framework is used to identify both the components to be considered in the study of an institution and the questions explored. I use a framework to present patterns of relationships that can be analyzed at any number of points in its structure. In other words, the framework serves narrowing in on the roles and relationships in the collaboration in a manner that gives rise to the properties of the new bureaucracy.

This book employs Ostrom's Institutional Analysis and Development (IAD) framework to accomplish this by providing a number of general variables that can be used to analyze an empirical setting. The general variables, exogenous (environmental) variables, influence the configuration of the action arena where interactions produce outcomes. It is a view of bureaucracy as structure where behavior is observed. These environmental variables represent implicit assumptions. For example, about how relationships are ordered; attributes of the world; and the nature of the setting where MITAF functioned. IAD structured the environmental factors that prior volatility research was charged with insufficiently considering when trying to understand how it occurred.

Research on foreign capital processes cannot draw exclusively on one discipline as this would significantly narrow the influence of other important considerations. Public administration, organizational theory, economics, history, and development studies have vital theoretical constructs pertinent to understand relationships between organizational behavior and donor capital flow characteristics. For example, I employ theories of path dependency, development dependency, and resource dependency to understand how behaviors are linked to capital volatility and to appreciate how activities between organizations (MFIs, donors, apex organizations) are shaped by history, context, and tradition.

This book acknowledges the fundamental, integral role played by three environmental variables: MFI regulation, informal economy, and the Rules. The shaping effect of MFI regulation in Sierra Leone as a public good was understood in terms of its properties as postconflict and fragile state. The community environmental variable, informal economy, was the location of this study. One often used definition views the informal economy as all economic activity not subject to government regulation or taxation. It typically involves self-employed people and households. In this book, the informal economy was a by-product of numerous interrelated events, such as colonialism and the Sierra Leone civil war. The rules involved boundaries and choices. It was assumed that rules were relatively more pliable than the two other environmental variables, in terms of responsiveness to participants' actions/interactions and the resulting outcomes. MFIs, donors, and the apex (MITAF staff) are better positioned to adjust the rules of interaction and the flow of capital than to adjust microfinance regulation or the informal economy. These variables represent implicit assumptions, mainly how relationships are ordered; attributes of the world; and the nature of the setting.

Nobel Laureate Herbert Simon (1996) argues that environmental factors play an important shaping-role in work to reconcile desired and actual states, while being primarily responsible for the complexity observed in participant action/interactions. These three environmental variables have essential, distinctive attributes and properties. Properties are essential, distinctive attributes of concepts and categories. The properties and attributes of environmental variables significantly affected organizations interacting in MITAF.

The properties of bureaucratic systems are shaped by the environment. This is often referred to as the ecology of administration. It is essential to identify the features with the greatest shaping impact, at a minimum. Numerous studies measuring aid effectiveness, many including volatility effects, are sensitive to environmental factors and yet often overlook such exogenous variables in analysis (Oxfam, 2005). The IAD framework aids my including these important considerations.

IAD FRAMEWORK: STUDYING ACTIVITY THAT REVEALS THE NEW BUREAUCRACY

The principal component of the IAD framework is the action arena, which includes two factors (variables): action situation and participants. The action situation is the set of interactions and sphere where the actors of the participants interact. As such, the action situation involves several components, as detailed in figure 2.1. The Action situation includes several variables, such as set of actors (participants), positions (occupied by actors), and actions and linkages to outcomes. "Situations are structured interactions among participants where individuals must make decisions about actions that affect them and others" (Ostrom et al., 2002, p. 23).

The IAD action arena is the equivalent of the case study, the space where one or more donors, a MFI, and the MITAF staff interacted. The action situation was represented by the capital investment agreement between a donor(s) and a MFI, negotiated by MITAF staff. It prescribed certain conditions and terms of payment for capital disbursements. This agreement will be referred to as a *deal*. The deal is the center of my analysis to understand the relationship between capital flow and organizational behavior, which resulted in the new bureaucracy emerging. The deal is the structured interaction of the participants. The components of the action situations, such as actors, positions, and outcomes were stipulated in a capital investment agreement (deal), the Program Document, and other official documents. Participants were MITAF actors involved in the deal and each had particular attributes:

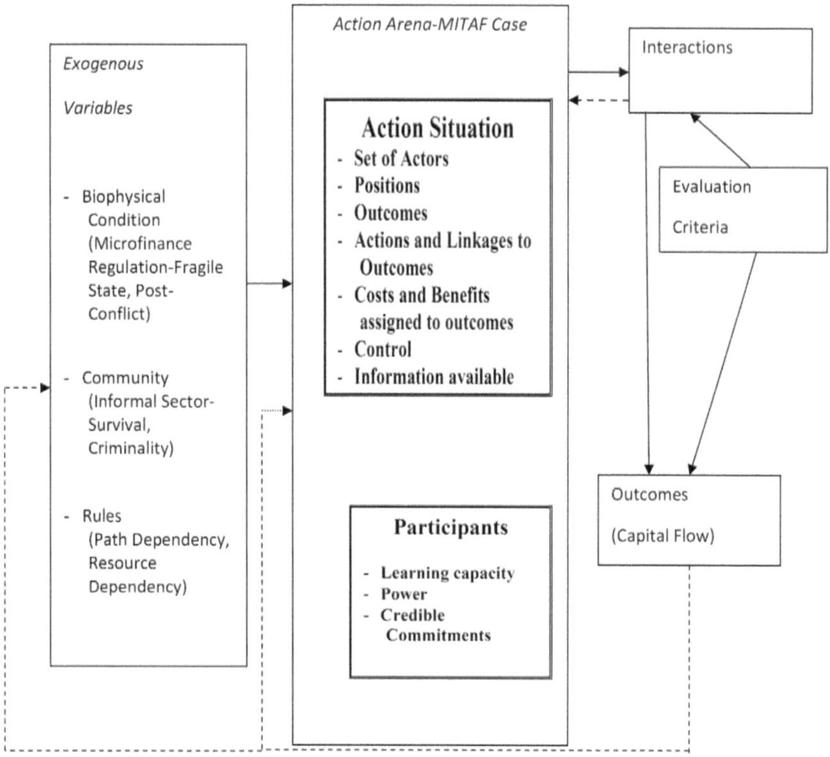

Figure 2.1 Institutional Analysis and Development (IAD) Framework.

learning capacity, power, and credible commitments. Interactions in the IAD framework are actions/interactions of the participants that explicate the working rules, or theories-in-use. That is, interactions are what really happened regardless to agreements or rules. As an environmental variable, working rules govern behavior in an action arena. Capital flow was the outcome of behavior, which was valued by volatility measures and MFI condition at disbursement.

ENVIRONMENTAL VARIABLES: OFTEN IGNORED, VERY IMPORTANT TO BUREAUCRATIC ORGANIZATIONS

Feedback from outcomes has the potential, over time, to change both the action arena and environmental variables. My goal was to identify and examine linkages between interactions and outcome characteristics. In other words, I sought out the connections between organizational behavior and capital flow volatility. Accomplishing this goal resulted in a new lens for viewing bureaucracy. Following is a discussion of the specific environmental variables that shaped outcome-producing interactions in MITAF.

MFI Regulatory Environment

The shaping effect of MFI regulation in Sierra Leone as a public good was understood in terms of its properties: postconflict and fragile state.

The MITAF project intended to create a pro-poor financial sector. By its very nature, the financial sector is a legal and regulatory framework infused by capital in order to create robust institutions and reliably provide the public financial services. This book views the state as using microfinance regulation to influence and shape the interactions between microfinance institutions, donors, and the apex organization (MITAF).

Microfinance regulation can be viewed as a Rule in the framework. On the other hand, when considering the characteristics of the good influencing the MITAF case, my focus on the public good attributes of microfinance regulation allowed for it to be considered as an IAD Biophysical Condition (Ostrom, 2005; Ostrom, Gibson, Shivakumar, & Andersson, 2002; Joseph Stiglitz, 1993). In other words, the first matter to be addressed is accessibility to the benefit of MITAF invested capital: a propoor, inclusive financial sector. A key function included in the role of a regulatory institution is monitoring risk and management. The monitoring attribute provides the MFI regulator access to potentially valuable and damaging information about MFIs. This threat of disclosure, backed by its legitimacy as a public organization, is used by governments regulating MFIs to provide identity to the sector in terms of social acceptance and expected behaviors. As a farmer plants in soil with certain climatic conditions, an MFI operates in a specific publicly created financial sector framework. The institutional strength and specifics can vary greatly, yet the regulatory framework's centrality is particularly true in a nation's financial sector.

How the importance of regulation is reflected in MFI outcomes has mixed results. In an effort to inform India's microfinance regulatory design, the IRIS Center analyzed key characteristics of MFI financial sector regulatory frameworks in seven nations (Meagher et al., 2006). The research found that MFI regulation takes the form represented by a place on a spectrum. On one end of the spectrum is state ownership of MFIs and at the other end unlimited market entry with monitoring provided by market forces. These researchers and others reported that outreach, sustainable growth, and financial constraints are impacted by the location of MFI regulation on that spectrum. Limited data availability has constrained analysis on the impact of regulation on MFI performance, or interaction with capital markets in my study. Other research assembled data on 108 MFIs serving thirty nations to analyze the impact of various governance mechanisms, including regulation, on MFI outreach (i.e., number of active borrowers) and return on assets (Hartarska, 2009). Although the model excluded findings on the effect of regulation on financial performance, the analysis found there is no relationship between regulation and outreach. This shows the mixed results of limited research to-date and speaks to the need for more studies of these important linkages.

I observed that linkages between regulation in Sierra Leone and MFIs required special consideration of both the postconflict context and fragile state infrastructure. The postconflict context required examining MFI regulation with questions of imperatives and preferences for providing a propoor financial sector. The fragile-state infrastructure considered measures of governance, political will and commitment, as well as propensity to resume conflict. The regulatory function, operating as a public good, provided definition and identity to MFIs because of its legitimacy in monitoring MFI solvency and management.

Insight into the postconflict property is provided by Karen Doyle's work (1998), considered by many as the foremost research on practitioner experience in postconflict nations. Perhaps the most important aspect of her study for my work is the exploration of practitioners' considerations of linkages between the postconflict setting and services provided by MFIs. The study primarily drew on sixteen MFI initiatives operating in the SSA nations of Rwanda and Mozambique, plus Cambodia and Bosnia-Herzegovina. Also, additional data collected to ensure the quality of the findings was obtained from the SSA nations of Angola, Uganda, and Sierra Leone, in addition to Tajikistan and Albania. The programs in the study, all implemented in the aftermath of war, demonstrated that MFIs have few environmental imperatives. She asserts donors are coming to understand how imperative it is for them to be intimately involved in postconflict settings. Her assertion underscores the importance and value of my focus on years when conflict frequently reignites and foreign aid is wasted or maximized. Doyle's work and that of others point to the unique properties of postconflict microfinance sectors and attributes of available capital during the crucial decade after peace is achieved (Bigombe et al., 2000; Clarke, 2006; Collier & Hoeffler, 2002; Smillie, 2009).

Donors and regulators of Sierra Leone MFIs came together to create the MITAF project approximately two years after reaching a peace agreement. MITAF was a key policy intervention to restore the economy. The document that created the project (Development of a Sustainable Pro-Poor Financial Sector in Sierra Leone (2004–2009)) describes the MFI operating environment as "comparable to other post conflict situations" (UNCDF, 2004b, p. 2). One key "policy-dependent" conflict risk factor is the absence of economic opportunities.

Although minimal political and financial infrastructure was required for operations, it is important to that other conditions must be considered to ensure MFIs operate beyond the immediate emergency and rebuilding stage to the stage of operating sustainable solutions (Doyle, 1998; Manalo, 2003). Microfinance regulation in the form of laws and institutions is the preferred method of this institutionalization.

Laws and institutions struggle in fragile state nations. The term *fragile* state does not have a universal definition, nor is the status generally seen as a dichotomy. In the parlance of donor-participants in MITAF, it seems that *fragile state* and *poor performer* were synonymous for a time leading up to 2001. The absence of ownership and credible commitment to effective policies, including implementation, are key characteristics of nations characterized as difficult partners. For a country to be considered among the difficult partnerships two criteria must be satisfied: low-income in accordance to per capital GNP classifications of the World Bank, and ranking in the lower two quintiles of the Country Policy and Institutional Assessment (CPIA). Regardless of the prevailing definition or scale of measurement, Sierra Leone was generally considered a *fragile state.*

Community: Informal Economy

MITAF as a space of negotiating deals was also shaped by the informal economy. A very large segment of Sierra Leone's economy is considered informal. The informal economy was understood in this investigation by its properties of *survival* and *criminality.* The people participating in the informal economy are seeking not only to survive physically but also to cope with the many social factors affecting their livelihoods. These factors include norms of behavior and equality of assets, income, and opportunity. The criminality property considers the tenuous nature of the informal economy and the potential for illicit activities to reach very destructive levels with international implications. Sierra Leone's leaders are focused on the informal economy to provide licit, viable employment in the fight against poverty and the propensities toward criminality.

Given that microfinance is integral to the poor experiencing improved outcomes from economic exchanges, such as through personal enterprises, MFIs are embedded in the informal sector. John Rapley refers to Africa's empirical data and draws on thinking that emerged in the 1990s, questioning both the development agenda and the idea of development itself. Rapley (2007) describes how postdevelopment thinkers assert development is never about improving the lives of citizens; rather development is intended to surface people from the informal sector to be taxed. It is argued the result is consolidation of government control over people. The informal sector is a substantial economic and social space in developing countries like Sierra Leone.

The persistence of the informal sector is in part due to weak incentives provided by a formal economy. In numerous African countries, the ability of the state to govern beyond the borders of the capital city is critically weak. This includes the ability to provide basic services to the rural areas that provide the most resources to the state. This is seen in bureaucratic structures where authority and power are centralized in the urban center rather than decentralized or devolved to local communities. The informal economy serves the formal economy at below value wages and prices. Informal economy participants also generally perceive government services to be insufficient or inequitably provided in favor of higher income earners. As a result, scores of citizens in numerous fragile African states avoid the government as much as possible through tax evasion, illegal trade, and a general disregard of the formal law—operating outside the formal economy.

Another approach to understanding the informal sector builds on the above views of labor markets and small firms in a functioning local economy. Bottom of the pyramid (BOP), or lower-income market, is labels used by some researchers of multinational corporations in developing nations. There are market approaches to development where people are characterized as producers or consumers rather than by level of daily income. Beyond corporate social responsibility, multinational corporations are considering lower-income markets due to slowing growth and increased competition in industrialized nations. The Africa BOP market has been estimated to be approximately $429 billion USD and includes over 485 million people. Multinational corporations can transfer capital and technology to these vast markets with the potential for great productivity at lower cost.

Austrian economist Friedrich Schneider used a definition involving economic activities that are unregistered, yet contribute to determining official GNP (Schneider, 2002). Looking at economic activity in African countries, including Sierra Leone's West African neighbors of Cote D'Ivoire, Ghana, Benin, and Burkina Faso, it was found that the average size of the informal sector was 42 percent of GNP from 1999 to 2000, shortly before MITAF started. This is considered to be a quite large informal economy. The International Monetary Fund's labeled Sierra Leone's informal economy as "a large volume of activity" (IMF, 2009a). Economic exchange in Sierra Leone to a great extent occurred in the informal sector. From a global cross-country perspective, the most salient distinction between developed and developing nations involves the theory of "survival." In other words, survival is central in decisions to participate in the informal sector of developing nations. This sociological aspect of explaining the informal sector understandably has economic implications.

The "social relations of household production" may not serve to incentivize markets to produce at a level beyond consumption needs. It is, however, a vital mechanism for survival in many SSA societies, where agriculture is particularly important. Survival explanations, often referred to as peasant rationality, underscore the consumption aspect of households more than the production aspect. The value in the survival rationale can be found by observing agricultural arrangements, such as sharecropping. The value of survival behavior in these arrangements is a favorable combination of the landowner bears all the risk, rather than where risk is assumed by the worker. Poor people avoid risk since they vacillate between survival and catastrophe (Allen, 2007). The place of microfinance in the informal sector is one of assisting people in managing risk concerns through savings and credit products.

Developed and developing nations converge on most of the explanations of the presence and increased activity in the informal sector, including criminality. Aristotle said, "Poverty is the parent of revolution and crime." Aristotle's poverty-crime propensity is found in the belief that community attributes found in the informal sectors of most African postconflict fragile states represent a nearly indistinguishable interconnection between legal and illegal activities involving government, business, perpetrators, and violence triggers. Identifying and responding to capital flow volatility effects in funding MFIs can assist efforts to advance licit, labor-intensive employment and enterprise activities that can thwart propensities to resume conflict or engage in illegal activity in order to survive.

The potentially destructive impact, both nationally and internationally, of this theoretical convergent point of criminality theory is implicated in a multiyear research project conducted by Pierre Arnaud Chouvy and Laurent R. Laniel (2007). This study sheds light on the darker aspects of the informal sector. Part of the analysis examines the complex linkages between illicit agricultural production and armed conflict within underdeveloped states. West Africa, where Sierra Leone is located, is considered one of the main narcotic-producing areas on the globe. An important take away from this work is the complex and extensive consequences associated with this illicit activity, including environment and human health degradation, as well as socioeconomic issues of maintaining peace and perpetuation of the elitist status quo. In addition, in 2005 "an alarming trend" was reported as cocaine smuggling was becoming big business is West Africa with connections to Europe, the Middle East, and United States (Bhattacharjee, 2015).

Columbian drug cartels had established safe passage in several West African countries, including Sierra Leone.

Probably, the most notorious connection between Sierra Leone's informal economy and illicit trade is the diamond industry. Officially, the diamond trade makes up 50 percent of exports from the country. Informally, according to the IMF, "External transactions are characterized by a large volume of activity in the informal sector, principally diamond smuggling. . . . Estimates of smuggled imports and exports, in particular diamonds, are also not available" (IMF, 2009, Informational Annex, p. 11). Global Witness and others report substantial illegal diamond trading. Substantial income is apparently inequitably distributed in illicit informal activities.

This inequality aspect is an element of measuring the progress of development efforts and provides insight into human behavior and potential. Dudly Seers in his seminal 1972 article, "What Are We Trying to Measure?," formed three basic questions that have been used repeatedly in the debate about measuring development: "What has been happening to poverty? What has been happening to unemployment? What has been happening to inequality?" (Seers, 1972). He contends that equality is valuable both as an end and a means of economic development.

Interactions in MITAF that produced capital flow to MFIs were shaped by an environment where people worked to improve their lifestyle by leveraging their potential. Capital provided by MITAF to MFIs was a strategy of legal activities that had positive wealth distribution effects.

Rules

Rules frame interactions of actors, such as rights and responsibilities of participating in a capital investment deal. It often helps to understand the classic view of bureaucracy as a rule-based approach to organizing relationships and functions to produce results. MITAF was shaped by rules that linked with participant perceptions and responses relative to both espoused theories and working theories (theories-in-use). What actors believed, valued, and perceived, along with their historical experiences, were central to rules in effect (working theories). The centrality of participant perceptions of and responses to espoused theories and working theories is embedded in a particular public policy perspective. I embrace the view that public policy administration is the actual expression of policy and speaks to espoused theories' relevance in attacking societal problems. In other words, people do not care what is stated as policy, they care about what is implemented as policy. Moreover, rules are viewed in terms of characteristics that form boundaries and explain choice. Research consistently finds that the absence of these two organizational rule categories—boundaries and choice—contribute to poor performance. This finding provides insight into the enduring popularity of bureaucratic organizational structures.

Capital volatility in this book was determined by participant interactions. Path dependency theorists teach that the outcome of interactions within an environment is a by-product of both the present environment and the previous environment (history). This historical path shapes possible outcomes, and path dependence is not an inevitability. It explains action-choice linkages over history. Path dependency theorists posit that past constraints, such as colonialism, narrow subsequent choice options and reflect the reinforcing attribute of IAD framework environment variables, including rules.

Research describes a colonial past connected to modern foreign aid. Economist Alberto Alesina and former World Bank economist David Dollar, explain the aid allocation behavior bilateral donors (Alesina & Dollar, 2000). Many believe that donor nations tend to provide more aid to former colonies than to other countries. Moreover, the colonial relationship is strong and contributes more robust explanations than variables such as quality of institutions, economic policies of the recipient, and whether the nation is a democracy.

I was interested in power relative to rules involving the organizational control over aid provision (i.e., capital flow). The degree of one organization's dependence on another is related to the extent to which resource control is concentrated. Of critical importance to the degree of control are alternatives available to the organization. In this investigation, the organization can be the MFI, MITAF staff, or the donor depending on interaction particulars. This understanding of power in dependency theory, including exchange relationships, is founded in the work of many researchers who portray dependence as the basis of power.

The seminal work of Emeritus Professor J. Kenneth Benson (1975), University of Missouri-Columbia, frames the resource dependency theory discussion,

> [I]nteractions must be explained ultimately at the level of resource acquisition . . . a system resource view of organizations. . . . Such an orientation becomes, for decision makers, an operational definition of the purposes of the organization . . . responsible largely for maintaining or expanding this established organizational machine." (p. 231)

Benson's theoretical framework of interorganizational interaction was created from empirical research of exchanges between human service nonprofit organizations. He contended that missions and visions take a subordinate position as an understood assumption that can be retrieved as a legitimization mechanism for continued operations. Benson and others suggest that the acquisition and maintenance of reliable and sufficient sources of capital and authority are the primary orientation of organizational decision-makers.

According to Benson, the basis for between-organization power differences is partially accounted for by the linkage of organizations to society-at-large. Many societies in Africa are characterized by households with husbands working in the nation's center region and wives raising children in the periphery with inadequate resources. At times wives have provided sex to the landlord in lieu of paying rent, a brutal reality of survival in a vicious market. Understanding resource dependency between organizations requires both the powerful societal factors, such as dependency theory at the national level, and the linkage with path dependency.

Nancy Jurik and Julie Cowgill (2005) conducted a case study of a training and microlending program offered by a nonprofit community organization struggling with resource dependency. The researchers recorded struggles of daily providing client services while also trying to secure capital for operations and lending. Competition for limited capital investment was the most pressing challenge, according to organization staff. It was felt that the pressing challenge compelled them to trade quality for rapidly achievable outcome measures, which would help to impression-manage investors. The espoused focus on poor and very low-income people by government investors, combined with accountability measures of client success and high repayment rates, created an environment where organizational beliefs acquiesced to the capital infusion imperative.

When one or more actors are resource-dependent on another actor, there is pressure to conform to the powerful actor's wishes. This renders irrelevant the rich, unique, organizational characteristics of dependent actors. That is, the insights gain from organizational differences tends to be lost when a resource-dependent organization is pressured to conform with the view of the donor. Regardless of using rules as institutions or an informal framing of human interactions, Deng's renowned statement on the use of power to achieve economic development illustrates the linkage and persistence of imperialism, "It does not matter if the cat is black or white, as long as it catches the mice" (Collier, Dollar, & Stern, 2000, p. 6, n. 4). As long as more powerful actors are able to exploit resources of others, the exact mechanism—colonialism or neocolonialism—is irrelevant.

MITAF participants engaged in deals where action decisions were controlled by diverse and sometimes conflicting agendas. Power in MITAF was more complex than donor decisions regarding capital and disbursement conditions. For example, power involved both political interests related to resource distribution and MFI social mission imperatives. Another complicating factor was disbursement pressure involving foreign aid machinery. My examining capital investment deals was aided by viewing rules from the perspective of foreign aid as investment capital, and also recognizing organizational behavior shaped by resource dependency theory. Analyzing years of investment commitment data, including focused interviews, provided important insights to the power relationship between actors and control over capital flows to MFIs. This analysis involved identifying important characteristics of various capital disbursements. It also necessitated connecting these disbursements with certain organizational behaviors, such as institutional strengthening, outreach, sustainable operations, and investment accountability. All of these were instrumental in revealing and describing bureaucracy as it existed in the donor collaboration.

Actor interactions occurred in a context shaped by environmental variables. Developing a propoor financial sector as a capital delivery mechanism to low-income people is, in essence, a public good defined by MFI regulation. MFIs provided services to people primarily operating in the informal economy, which affected participant interactions. Central to shaping interactions were rules defining behavior that was required, forbidden, and permitted. Examining behavior-volatility linkages requires the consideration of interaction shaping variables, such as IAD environmental variables.

Chapter 3

The Espoused Process (or the Planned Collaborative Bureaucratic Structure and Process)

Organization behavior in this chapter is viewed by examining formal processes as recorded in archival documents and expressed in participants' own words. Another way to look at is it to ask what does the formal structure of bureaucracy look like in a collaboration? I focus on actions intended to consummate and implement MFI capital investment deals. The portrayal of how the agreement, expressed in a capital investment contract, can be viewed from different perspectives is described. Also depicted is the constraining-empowering tension of organizational imperatives and collaborative commitments. The tension is observed in original processes (MITAF espoused theory) experiencing numerous changes, primarily due to conflict with individual donor organization imperatives. That is, the planned process was changed, when there was a substantial conflict with a donor's rules.

The formalized changes, developed in response to working theories or implemented processes, demonstrated MITAF's learning capacity and limitations. The importance of MITAF's learning capacity and limitations is embedded in the view that public policy *administration* is the actual *expression* of policy and speaks to espoused theories' relevance in attacking societal problems. On some occasions, MITAF limitations were seen in formalized changes that complicated consummation and the deal implementation process. As such, MITAF's adapted behavior (i.e., bureaucratic organizational learning) is best observed by focusing on the process to formalize commitments of capital investment in MFIs. Moreover, behavior and participants' expressions regarding the implementation of performance-based agreements (commitment formalization) revealed perceptions and beliefs important to understanding interpretations of mutually agreed stipulations. The description of the MITAF capital investment process, including adaptations over time, from Investment Committee approval through disbursements, depicts complexity in developing MFIs in the post-conflict fragile state Sierra Leone.

Here I lay the foundation for analysis of behavior and volatility. The chapter aims to vividly, richly portray and provide comprehensive insight on MITAF capital flow processes as part of its bureaucracy. It is quintessential data-driven exploration. James Ferguson (1994), in his seminal work on development politics and bureaucracy, demonstrates with care the differences between development and academic discourses, as well as employed detailed descriptions to translate "certain unmanageable sorts of facts" (p. 28). In a similar fashion, I first exhibit the espoused theory of MITAF capital flow. Though there were some changes to the formal processes, understanding the established formal processes is important because these express an agreed to theory of change to achieve the project's outcomes and organizational values. Examination of official documents, and interview data triangulation constructed the evolving espoused capital flow process.

The descriptions of espoused processes are rich. The MITAF project was created to do much more than provide capital to relieve a "major constraint" in developing the microfinance sector. Prescribed project outcomes included assisting the Bank of Sierra Leone to establish a microfinance unit and disseminate sound microfinance principles to be widely accepted and practiced throughout the sector in Sierra Leone. The linkages between organizational behavior and capital flow volatility are connected to activities involving numerous related initiatives.

Central to understanding linkages is understanding the capital flow process as designed to function, while MITAF also worked to advance-related initiatives. Examination of the MITAF project capital disbursement process is important, and "failing to deal with process will lead to incomplete and misleading understandings" (Nutt, 2010, p. 600). Perceived values—what should be—were reflected in the design, while effect was reflected in practice.

MITAF BIG PICTURE VIEW OF AIM AND PROCESS

Microfinance as a mechanism to deliver capital to the poor was one of four key initiatives stressed by Sierra Leone to restore the economy during post-conflict reconstruction. As such, MITAF was designed and implemented pursuant to the government's microfinance initiative (RSL, 2002). Investigation of capital investment deals involved activity intertwined with many actions/interactions beyond capital investment, such as government initiatives and related MITAF activities. These actions/interactions were intended to be "mutually enforcing" (UNCDF, 2004b, p. 7).

Investors engaged in actions/interactions were ostensibly guided by the project's "overarching goal" to achieve the poverty reduction objective in the Millennium Development Goals (UNCDF, 2004b, p. 6). MITAF intended to assist in guaranteeing a "rapid development of the microfinance sector" by developing "professional microfinance institutions . . . leaders." These leaders were to drive sector development by demonstrating to other MFIs and the public that investments in the "lower end of the market are bankable" (p. 6). The Sierra Leone government, U.N. Development Program (UNDP), and U.N. Capital Development Fund (UNCDF) all agreed,[1] as evidenced by signing the UN Programme Support Document, that rapid sector expansion was important and the absence of MFI leadership was a "principal constraint" to expansion (pp. 4, 6). Also, one of the four output concentrations was to support the Bank of Sierra Leone in establishing "an optimal enabling environment for development of the microfinance industry" (p. 7). MITAF support was to include providing staff training, developing studies on sector constraints and opportunities, distributing information, and developing the nation's capacity support services (mesolevel institutions), such as information technology, legal services, and accounting. MITAF aims included creating an enabling regulatory microfinance environment (not constraining), removing MFI leadership-void constraints, and propelling MFI sector development.

Utilizing the MITAF project for sector development utilizing the MITAF project, rather than directing aid to the Sierra Leone government, is a fundamental distinction of this investigation to other capital volatility literature. Many capital volatility researchers analyzed sector aid administered through government recipients. This investigation focused on the provision of sector aid to service delivery organizations (MFIs) through a project mechanism (MITAF). Macro studies do not delve as deeply into volatility and organizational behavior data as compared to this investigation. Macrolevel studies used statistical techniques to analyze measurements aggregated at the nation state level. The role of the state, and analytical depth and detail, are fundamental, substantial distinctions of this investigation.

Designed Bureaucracy: Espoused Theory of MITAF Capital Flow

The process designed for donors to provide capital to MFIs reflects situational expediency, innovativeness, and commitment to collaboration and bureaucratic organizational learning. It focused on accountability, concessions, participatory engagement, and sound financial principles. It has the aroma of Weber's (1937) rational bureaucratic administration. Individual institutional imperatives quickly surfaced to mandate adjustments from the

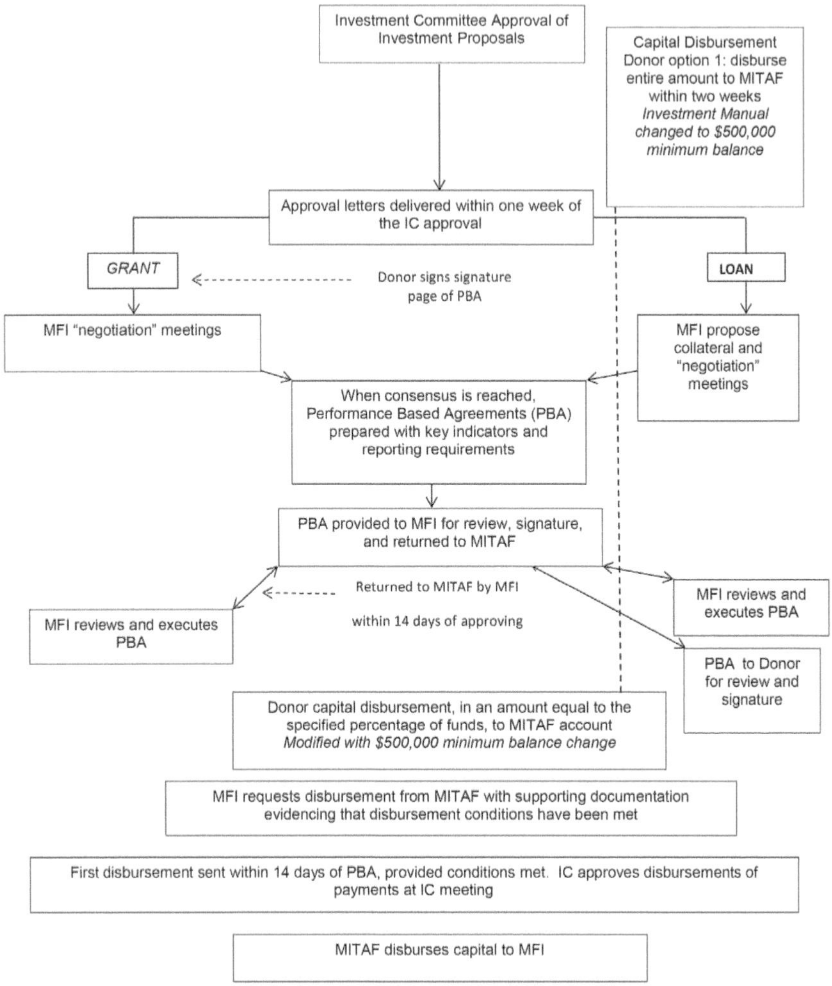

Figure 3.1 Process of Capital Flow as Designed (Espoused Theory).

design. These adjustments involved greater accommodations of individual organizational interests and prevented the essential central function—the flow of capital—from encountering project-halting process problems. To be clear, of all the designed outcomes of MITAF capital investment to MFIs for capacity building and growth of loan portfolios was central: it was about the money.

The design for capital disbursement capital from donors to MFIs served to implement MITAF Investment Committee (Committee) decisions aimed at building MFI capacity and investment in MFI market leaders

(UNCDF, 2004b). This disbursement process was intended to, "function as an effective and conducive mechanism for donors to channel their investments to MFIs" (p. 7). It was designed with the explicit intent of mobilizing additional donors or "strategic partnerships that enable MFIs access to capital (grants, loans [hard and soft] and commercial equity)" while maintaining the focus of providing financial service access to the poor (p. 12). The essential components of the process are depicted in figure 3.1. The illustration reflects a process that continually engaged the various participants.

UN PROGRAM SUPPORT DOCUMENT AND MITAF MANUAL

I focused on organizational behavior and capital flow from the time a deal was approved at a Committee meeting until the last tranche of capital was disbursed and available to the MFI. The MITAF process for disbursing investment capital involved actions that various participants were empowered to take. In the UN Programme Support Document (Program Document), for example, the rules for investing capital in MFIs were intended to clearly present required, permitted, and forbidden actions. MFIs were required to meet agreed conditions to receive capital; donors were required to maintain certain funds with the apex (MITAF project bank account); and the apex was required to meet with MFIs after approval to negotiate terms. The objective is order and reliability in behavior and the flow (disbursement) of capital. It is the expression of credible commitments.

The capital flow design and the empowered actions are generally set forth in the Program Document and the MITAF *Investment Committee Policy and Procedures Manual* (Manual). For example, the tranche design, which involves disbursing loans using installments, is an example provided in the Base Loan Product available from MITAF. The specific design and actions are contained in a performance-based agreement (Agreement). The Agreement served as the investment contract between donors and MFIs. Figure 3.2 contains an excerpt from the Program Document setting forth the process.

The process of capital disbursement begins with Committee approval. Then, the process is understood by going through first the Program Document, then the Manual, and finally the Agreement. Donors agreed to the choice rules (rules governing choice) of utilizing the same key performance indicators and required MFI reporting to donors. For instance, key indicators

8. Execution/Implementation Arrangements:

UNCDF/SUM will serve as executing agent for its own funds, and implementing agent for some UNDP budget lines. Other donors are encouraged to cost-share through UNCDF/SUM in order to 1) minimize disbursement pressure; 2) harmonize reporting; 3) reduce administrative costs; and 4) expedite payments and implementation.

The project will establish a forex, interest-bearing main account with sub-accounts for each MFI or programme component. The Technical Service Provider and CEO of each MFI supported will serve as co-signatories of the respective sub-accounts. Donor/Investors will ensure that either: 1] investments approved by the Investment Committee can be paid within two (2) weeks of approval; or 2] that a certain percentage of committed funds (i.e. concretely committed via contracts for specific projects) is kept in the main account. It will be replenished upon proof that the previous tranche has been adequately used. Donor funds will be expended on a pro-rata basis (calculated according to the percentage of funds accepted under management) based on the payments approved at each meeting. Arrangements will be made for external auditing of the use of funds on a yearly basis by an independent auditing firm who will report to the Investment Committee.

Donors will have the right to cease support to an MFI, programme component or the programme if deemed necessary (non-fulfillment of performance criteria, misappropriation of funds). The decision should be discussed in the Investment Committee, or between the relevant donors in the case of support to a specific MFI.

If needed, the Investment Committee will review these Terms of Reference to adjust them to changing realities and to ensure smooth implementation arrangements (2004b, pp. 8, 9).

Figure 3.2 UN Programme Support Document.

used to determine minimum performance standards for MFI capital disbursements are as follows:

- outreach understood as the number of MFI active clients;
- loan portfolio quality measured by portfolio-at-risk (PaR) of those loans thirty days or more past-due on payments;
- profitability/sustainability measure utilizing the computation of Adjusted Rate Return on Assets (AROA).[2]

After performance indicators are stipulated for donor use, the Program Document focuses on donor activities involving capital disbursements. The Manual, however, discusses the process between donors' agreement to key indicators and actual disbursement of capital to MFIs. In addition, the Manual details the process through Agreement completion.

Additional detail on the design of the capital flow process is found in the Investment Cycle section of the Investment Committee Policy and Procedures Manual. The Manual provides additional insight on the choices, actions, and general involvement of the MFIs and apex (TSP) in the capital investment process. The Manual is dated approximately three years after the Program Document that created MITAF. The Manual reflects participant effort to enhance the espoused, formalized capital investment process.

After Committee approval of the deal, the apex (MITAF staff) is required to act, and interact, with the MFIs. MITAF staff prepares a letter announcing the Committee's decision and it is "delivered to the local office" of the MFI (2006, p. 20). In practice, this involved sending an e-mail with the notification and proposed conditions as attachments. At times, the MFI was called and requested to pick-up the letter from the MITAF office. The letter is followed by interaction of the apex with the MFI in a personal way. A meeting between the MITAF staff and the MFI is explicitly required to negotiate the rules of the particular deal. These rules (Agreement terms) specifically included duration of the deal, performance targets, specific conditions (other than performance targets), fund transfer specifics (e.g., foreign currency issues[3]) and, in the case of a subsidized loan, loan terms. Upon reaching consensus, the MITAF staff drafts the Agreement for MFI review. When consensus is reached on a final document the espoused process calls for the MFI to execute it. Action and interaction of all participants in the deal is expected to occur, according to the espoused rules, once an agreement is reached.

The formal design implies that donors will sign the document first, especially for grant deals, and that MFIs will not secure any substantive changes in negotiations that necessitate execution of new documents. The Manual provides that MFIs return the Agreement within fourteen days of approving it followed by fund disbursement. The donor signing is described in the prior section of the Manual (4.5 Approval) and occurs before discussing approval letters or MFI performance-based agreement negotiations. Discussing Agreement signatures before negotiations to produce Agreements may seem out of sequence. Closer examination, however, combined with interview data, provided insight on efforts aimed at developing an expeditious process. The design reflects that time was important. The signing discussion in the Manual specifically references the grant agreement page. The conclusion that donors were intended to sign first was supported by a donor's recount of how the process operated in the early years,

> Now, in some of the early investment committee meetings, we had literally the grant agreements printed and ready to be signed once we knew at the end of the meeting what had been approved. And so, we literally would, KFW, UNDP, and UNCDF would just pass the papers back and forth and say ok, we approved six, let's sign them, let's go. And we each left with our own copies that we could take and put into our financial process and start the approvals.

> That worked fairly well in some of the early meetings. When it didn't work well it was because the technical secretariat wouldn't follow our requests and get the MFI to sign their grant agreement in advance. They sort of argued well, we don't want to raise expectations. And we said, well, you know, look, you can just tell, we're approving 90 % of what you propose anyway. (Donor 07 "personal communication," September 23, 2010)

Special provisions were made for loan deal complexity. Although the Program Document is silent on the distinction, the Manual implies that donor signatures come after the apex negotiates within donor-stipulated parameters. Committee approval is explicitly described as a decision to support, with loan conditions and performance indicators subsequently negotiated. Furthermore, signed loan documents are described as "approval" forms, not "agreements" (2006, p. 20). As a result, Section 4.6.3 of the Manual requires that each donor in a loan deal signs individually and subsequent to the MFI (figure 3.3).

The Manual is dated July 2006. The date in the file name, as provided to this researcher, was October 7, 2006. The dates corresponded with the MITAF mid-term evaluation, which commenced September 6, 2006, and included an on-site examination September 18–30 (Duval & Bendu, 2006). One of the findings of the mid-term evaluation was that "[t]he procedures still in place for disbursing donor funds to partner lending institutions are unwieldy and contribute to unnecessary and disruptive delays in financing" (p. 33). Findings and recommendations were presented to MITAF and other stakeholders in a meeting to review an Aide Memoire after the mission ended September 30, 2006. The Manual's detail espoused tighter procedures and more explicit donor funding requirements.

This investigation found that some donor behavior deemed objectionable during mid-term evaluation was still occurring through the end of MITAF. However, focusing on administrative incidents and brief explanations of the mid-term evaluation obfuscate more substantive behaviors by MITAF participants that are linked to capital flow volatility. The behavior and process described, combined with the Agreement, reflected the struggles of establishing rules involving choice (e.g., duties, rights, and resource allocation) and boundaries (entry and exit).

The Execution/Implementation Arrangements section in the Program Document focuses on donor actions (figure 3.3). This reflects the orientation of MITAF's beginning, the interests, rights, and responsibilities of the donors. The capital disbursement process was provided for in substantial detail, while allowing flexibility.

Capital investment disbursement stipulations in the Program Document provided donors two options. After a MFI proposal was approved by the Committee, donors that were party to the deal were to either: (1) pay to

4.6 Closing

4.6.1 Letters of approval or rejection

After the IC meeting, approval and rejection letters are delivered to the local office of all applicant MFIs within one week of the decision. All letters will follow the standard format (see MFI Grant Approval Letter.doc and MFI Grant Rejection Letter.doc). When MFIs are approved for a loan, they are to propose collateral. Further, a meeting is scheduled to finalize the negotiations.

4.6.2 Negotiations/Closing with approved MFIs

MITAF meets with the selected MFIs to discuss the duration of the contract, performance targets, specific conditions, fund transfers and where applicable loan terms and collateral. Once a consensus is reached, grant or loan agreements are drafted. The agreements are provided to the MFIs for review and signature.

4.6.3 Contracts with approved MFIs

The MFI returns a copy of the signed contract to MITAF within 14 days of approval. Funds placed by donors under MITAF management are signed by UNDP, UNCDF and KfW on behalf of MITAF. Signatories for the MFI are the Executive Director or other high level senior manager.

Performance based financing agreements are negotiated and signed with the approved applicants. Consensus is reached on the financing to be made available (loans or grants for the loan fund or operational cost support) and the performance targets to be reached during the funding period in all areas of the Performance Standards (see the monitoring section 4.8).

The Investment Committee uses separate agreements for grants and loans (see Grant Agreement.doc and Loan Agreement.doc). Agreements include responsibilities of the MFI, contract duration, MFI bank account information, records, information and reports and general provisions. The loan contracts include also MITAF bank information and repayment schedules

4.7 Disbursement

MITAF maintains an MFI Investment account in Freetown (grants and loans) to facilitate initial and subsequent tranche payments. Donor/investors will transfer the approved/foreseen funding amounts into the account, upon which MITAF will domestically transfer funds to the MFIs' dollar accounts. All MFIs are required to exchange dollars for leones through a legally registered exchange bureau or commercial bank.

Initial funds are disbursed within 14 days of the signing of contracts. Subsequent tranches will be disbursed as per contract. The funds will be transferred by MITAF from the MITAF MFI Investment account to the MFI account.

MFIs are obliged to maintain certain performance standards to remain eligible for ongoing and future financing. In the case of non-performance, funds may be recalled and reallocated to a better performing institution.

Donors have the right to cease support to an MFI, to a programme component or to a programme, if performance criteria have not been met or if there has been a misappropriation of funds. The decision should be discussed in the Investment Committee or between the relevant donors in the case of support to a specific MFI.

To ensure that investments approved by the Investment Committee can be paid within two weeks of approval, at least $500,000 is maintained in the MITAF Investment account. It will be replenished upon request from MITAF and proof that the previous tranches have been adequately used. The KfW, UNCDF, UNDP funds are expended on a pro-rata basis (calculated according to the percentage of funds accepted under management)

Figure 3.3 MITAF Manual.

MITAF their portion of the deal within two weeks of Committee approval, or (2) maintain in the MITAF main account a percentage (unspecified) of the amount provided for in the executed Agreement (percentage approach). Presumably, the initial payment was due when the donor returned the executed the Agreement. The percentage was maintained by replenishing payments once proof was received that the prior tranche was used appropriately.

DESIGN ADJUSTMENTS: A LEARNING ORGANIZATION

Organizational learning recorded in the Manual is visible when it is juxtaposed with the Program Document on matters of capital disbursement. MITAF demonstrated the attributes of an adapting, learning organization on the matter of donors making capital available for disbursement to MFIs by MITAF. For instance, the percentage approach was modified from the Program Document to a fixed, specified amount in the Manual. The two options were replaced in the espoused process with a flat $500,000 minimum balance in each donor's account, all maintained in the MITAF main bank account. Although this practically addressed most disbursement needs, the Manual also stipulates the donor was required to transfer to MITAF the amount of approved capital for MITAF to disburse to the MFI. This change, combined with limited donor behavior, was arguably evidence that organizational learning occurred pursuant to experience and the formative mid-term evaluation.

The espoused process provided that capital disbursements to MFIs were accounted for on a pro rata basis between the donors in the deal, in accordance to disbursement decisions made at each Committee meeting. In addition, disbursements were subject to specific conditions as expressed in the consummated Agreement. In other words, at each of the two annual Committee meetings, disbursement decisions were expected on prior deals and the payment of those disbursements from the MITAF main account were charged on a pro rata basis to each donor's account.

A hypothetical deal depicts the process. Assume the donors' portion of the total capital commitment to the MITAF project is as follows: KfW 50 percent, UNCDF 20 percent, UNDP 20 percent, and Cordaid 10 percent (table 3.1). Committee approves a deal for investment capital totaling $300,000 to an MFI for staff capacity building and office equipment. The capital commitment allocation of the deal is: KfW 50 percent ($150,000),

Table 3.1 Example of Capital Pro-Rata Commitment for $300,000 MFI Deal

(Not actual percentages or amounts)

Donor	*Percentage of Total Capital Committed to MITAF (%)*	*MFI Capital Commitment Allocation-Total $300,000*	*First Tranche Allocation-Total $60,000*
KfW	50	$150,000	$30,000
UNCDF	20	$60,000	$12,000
UNDP	20	$60,000	$12,000
Cordaid	10	$30,000	$6,000

UNCDF 20 percent ($60,000), UNDP 20 percent ($60,000), and Cordaid 10 percent ($30,000). In this example, the Agreement calls for the initial payment to the MFI to be $60,000 after resumes and applications for three prospective operations officers are submitted to MITAF.

When the MFI provided a request for disbursement, accompanied by the resumes and applications, the MITAF staff presented the disbursement request for approval at the next Committee meeting. Upon receiving Committee approval, the capital is disbursed by MITAF staff from each donor's balance in the MITAF's main account charging the investors accordingly: KfW, $30,000; UNCDF, $12,000; UNDP, $12,000; and Cordaid, $6,000.

Subsequently, MITAF provides donors a request for replenishment in the event their balance goes below $500,000. The Manual provides that MITAF disburses the initial payment to the MFI within fourteen days of receiving a completely executed Agreement.

The Agreement consummated the capital investment deal and, in harmony with the Program Document and Manual, set forth choice options and boundaries to the parties of the deal. For example, the "Payment/Date" by the donor ("Grantor") to the MFI ("Recipient Institution") was contained in the Agreement along with "disbursement conditions," "key/results milestones" ("Expected Results"), and reporting requirements. The espoused rules provided in the first section of the Agreement were as follows:

> The Recipient Institution agrees to: complete the key results/milestones specified in the Section III below, including providing reports and statements to the grantor in accordance with the Monitoring Schedule. The Recipient Institution shall be responsible for verifying the accuracy of all reports. Funds provided pursuant to this Agreement shall be used to achieve these results/milestones. The Recipient Institution shall be free to reallocate resources as needed in order to produce the expected results.

The initial payment, or tranche payment, date stipulated in the agreement was mandated to occur within fourteen days of agreement execution. This suggested that initial payment requirements stipulated in the "Disbursement Conditions" portion of the Agreement were fully achievable within fourteen days, if not immediately, in order to for these various documents to work in harmony (e.g., Agreement and Manual not in conflict). In addition, it suggested that funding requirements in the Manual, as amended June 19, 2007, are satisfied (e.g., PaR maximum of 5 percent for loan-funding grants). Noteworthy was the explicit choice rule that the MFI had sole discretion in resource use to achieve "expected results."

One of the most insightful provisions regarding organizational learning is Section 3.4 of the 2009 version of the Agreement template:

> 3.4 The Recipient Institution shall request disbursements with the supporting information to show that disbursement conditions have been met. All payments shall be deposited into the Recipient Institution's bank account of which the details are as follows:
>
> Name of the Bank:
> Bank Routing Number:
> SWIFT Code:
> Beneficiary Account Name:
> Beneficiary Account Number:
> Address of Bank:

The agreement provided that capital disbursed by a donor pursuant to the deal was not to MITAF, but directly to the MFI's bank account.

The espoused capital flow theory in MITAF provided several valuable insights. The design consolidates capital from donors, as a collaborative mechanism, for disbursement by MITAF to MFIs. Donors were obligated to proactively make the capital available. The initial disbursement of capital was required to occur quickly after approval of the Agreement. MFIs bought-in to expected results and conditions as the process explicitly called for "negotiations," as opposed to presentation of terms. Furthermore, it was reasonable to conclude the Agreement signatory process for grants, plus the "negotiation" approach for Agreement development, resulted in terms reasonable and achievable for the MFI. However, the working rules, as expressed by MITAF participants, differed in substantial ways from what was espoused.

NOTES

1. KfW (German Development Bank) is prominently noted as a founding member of MITAF both in the UN Programme Support Document (2004b, pp. signature cover page, 26) and the Investment Committee Manual (2006, pp. 4, 7). MITAF was a UN project with the government of Sierra Leone and KfW was not a signatory.

2. AROA is computed in the conventional method for return-on-assets (profit/assets) with total consolidated profit reduced for an inflation computation using a rate provided by the Bank of Sierra Leone and applied against a change in the MFIs equity/net assets; subsidized cost-of-funding computed using a market rate for loans provided by the Bank of Sierra Leone applied against compulsory savings balances and subsidized loans to the MFI; and in-kind subsidies (nonmonetary) computed

using data from the Bank of Sierra Leone and applied against a particular MFI's activity.

3. Capital comes in the form of foreign currency and needs to be converted to leones. This can be especially sensitive on loan deals where, over the period of the loan, the relative currency value can change dramatically.

Chapter 4

The Actual Process (or the Collaborative Bureaucracy at Work)

> [I]t is unsafe to rely wholly on official codes and a sense of inner responsibility; but, on the other hand, a formal system in itself is inadequate. (White, 1942, p. 215)

In this chapter, I lay the foundation for analysis of behavior and volatility by describing specific MITAF participant actions related to capital investment that emerged above other actions. This is not a discussion of how the system *might work*, but how it actually worked. Goodnow (1900) explains, "A rule of conduct, *i.e.* an expression of the state will, practically amounts to nothing if it is not executed" (p. 23). Riggs (2006) undergirds this point by distinguishing between actual implementation of bureaucratic systems from conceptualizing them and considers behavior to be dangers that fails to make the distinction. Understanding bureaucracy necessitates understanding how it works. Central to understanding behavior-volatility linkages is understanding the capital flow process as actually implemented. Perceived values—what should be—were reflected in the design, while effect was reflected in practice. This chapter vividly, richly portrays and provides comprehensive insight on MITAF capital flow processes as actually implemented.

The actual process used for capital disbursement in MITAF is described to understand both what was done and how adapted behavior came into being. The descriptions of actual processes portray flexibility and vibrancy. Individual organizational imperatives, collaborative commitments, and administrative expediencies created dynamic tensions that affected capital flow. Finally, capital disbursement action was focused. The constraining-empowering tensions of organizational imperatives and collaborative commitments affected bureaucratic organizational learning. Also, capital flow was affected by struggles of dual bottom-line objectives (financial performance and outreach to people) and operations administered with ambiguous identity. The new bureaucracy begins to emerge and take shape with distinctive properties expressed in a model: Collaboration Bureaucratic Triad.

Remember, the MITAF project was created to do much more than provide capital to relieve a "major constraint" in developing the microfinance sector. *The linkages between organizational behavior and capital flow volatility are connected to activities involving numerous related initiatives.* Here I advance understanding these linkages by first explaining the capital flow process as actually implemented. The effect of process was reflected in practice.

In this chapter, I present the MITAF working theories, or process as practiced, to provide capital to microfinance institutions. Peter Blau (1963) considered it very important to understand that certain behavior and linkages in bureaucracies are more than discrete deviations from espoused (formal) processes and resulted in organizational change and learning.

THE PROCESS AS IMPLEMENTED: THEORY-IN-USE

The key components of consummating and implementing a capital investment deal are related and intertwined. The Agreement is required to officially and legally do the deal, especially for loan capital. Certain provisions of the Agreement are central and located in section III: Key Results/Milestones and Payments. These provisions included conditions for disbursement and reporting. The official definition of these terms versus participants' view of their operationalization reflected beliefs and perceptions that surpassed framing of document provisions. In practice, deals proved to be imperfect, loosely structured understandings deeply embedded in complex historical and human factors. Data providing insight into practice is provided in the following sections.

PERFORMANCE-BASED AGREEMENTS

The immediate focus after Committee approval was consummating the capital investment deal through a completed performance based agreement (Agreement). MFIs in the field described the beginning of the process with approval letter receipt. They then spoke of a process to agree on loan terms that created the Agreement,

> And then we agreed on loan terms and conditions, you know, and once we agreed on loan terms and conditions, the formal document was sent to us for

the review details and send it back and we agreed on the final loan terms and conditions. (M0202, "personal communication," July 14, 2010)

The MFIs recounted a process very much in line with espoused procedures for executing the Agreement up to completion. However, some explanations suggested that organizational behavior was not consistent with espoused theory on matters pertaining to donor execution of the Agreements. *Bureaucracy was a concept that emerged in MFI interviews to explain delays in donor Agreement completion; they seemed to view the process as a black box.*

MFI interviewees had some specific insights on donor and apex processes, but their view was substantially limited to information entering the process and decisions emerging. For the most part, they were unsure how disbursement processing occurred. Suggestions regarding donor Agreement execution embedded in MFI interview data were empirically supported in an official May 2009 MITAF archival document, "Investments approved in mid-February 2009. . . . The donors had not even signed the grant and loan agreements" (MITAF Narrative Report-3rd Quarter 2009).

The Agreement was the essence of the capital investment deal. This perception was especially so for complex donor institutions. As emphasized in the banking discussion in the Preface, the fractional reserve banking system functioned on the ability to trust and act on promises as integral to economic systems. Capital investment in a financial institution (i.e., MFIs) was a foundational component of the financial trust apparatus. One donor explained the centrality of mutual commitments in the deal involving donor-MFI relationships,

Person: Basically, this performance-based agreement stated the target to be achieved and the way that the resources will be disbursed, as well as the purpose of the resources and as well as the monitoring aspect.

Investigator: So this performance-based agreement makes out the stipulation of the approval for the grant or the loan?

Person: More than the approval, it's as a name is performance-based agreement, agreed performance between the microfinance institution and [donor], which are the conditions to release the funds.

Investigator: Ok. There it is.

Person: So, it's very important, it's the commitment that is made in both times. Microfinance institution saying that look, if I receive this amount of resources, I will use all the resources to do this and that, and this is what I want to achieve as far as outreach is concerned, portfolio quality is concerned, financial sustainability is concerned, and impact on the population is concerned. So, this is the binding and legal agreement between the microfinance institution and the [donor]. And it also includes the reporting, including a template of quarterly

> reporting on the achievement of the set targets as well as reporting on audited statements and so on and so forth. So, this is really a discussion between the microfinance institution and [donor]. (M0305, "personal communication," July 16, 2010)

The tenor of the response suggested that a donor-MFI deal is a particularly intimate relationship that strains the limits of donor collaboration in packaging deals. The respondent characterized the commitments as "very important," underscoring intimacy. Collaboration limits were vivid in the characterization of the deal as a "discussion" between the MFI and a donor. In practice, investment packages most often included more than one donor and many deals had cross-connecting properties.

One MITAF participant shared particularly interesting insights on how collaborating donors came to participate in a deal. Neither MFI notification letters nor the MFI negotiation meetings were mentioned by this respondent. Rather, the actual process of multiple donors participating in a deal was emphasized, as were apex efforts to prepare an agreement and secure participating donor signatures. Contrary to the espoused allocation technique for determining a given donor's investment in a deal, the actual process was much more fragmented. Also, the evolution of the last few years of the donor Agreement execution process was excruciating. Understanding actual capital disbursement necessitates looking beyond the point of approval because the amount to be disbursed does not follow the allocation scheme outlined by MITAF's espoused rules. Donald Kettl (2007) explains, "Bureaucracies are the result of rules" (p. 107) and "Eventually, the demand for rules of the game become inescapable" (p. 27).

Actual donor collaboration in a deal was driven much more by individual organizational preferences and goals than espoused collaborative processes. A simple, two-donor illustration was provided during an interview,

> One donor giving a grant, and one donor giving a loan and because of their own whatever, one donor says no, I have no more money for grants. And the other one says, okay, I have money for grant. For example . . . UNDP is not allowed to do loans. So, UNDP will say, okay, I will give them a grant, you give them a loan. They do that kind of, but the loan will not be shared between donors. One donor will give a loan, the other one will give a grant. (M-0303, "personal communication," July 20, 2010)

The Committee would agree to invest capital in an MFI and individual donor organizations discussed what specific deal (aspect) their organization would participate in (grant, loan, or both). An investment package for an MFI was considered by the Committee. Then particular donors would participate in portions of a package. These portions could stand alone or be cross- connected. For example, one portion of the package could be a deal for capacity building and the other portion could be for loan capital once capacity building occurs. In this instance, the deals were cross-connected as the loan capital was intended to be available after capacity building occurred.

Decision-making on deals not only considered the investment tool (grant or loan), but also the type of MFI. Although my research focus is after the decision was made to invest capital, investment decision actions impacted the actual disbursement conditions of the deal. A MITAF participant provided an illustration of this oft repeated message. "In many cases you find out Cordaid normally goes for the local, small MFIs. And, KFW tends to be more commercial oriented and they prefer big players like BRAC, LAPO" (M-0303, "personal communication," July 20, 2010). Empirically, in November 2009 Committee meeting, the TSP recommended a grant deal of less than $20,000 for an MFI. The apex was directed to fund such requests from a MITAF budget line item; however, on this occasion Cordaid provided the capital. This behavior is consistent with the Cordaid Agreement to participate in MITAF.

These types of organizational attributes directly relate to conditions of capital volatility. Deals made one-on-one between MFIs and donors, though in a collaborative fashion, allowed for individually designed Agreements without technically impacting other parties. For instance, a participant provided an example of a deal with a 7 percent loan default[1] for the first disbursement, rather than the collaboration espoused requirement of 5 percent. The condition for the second tranche was in-line with the 5 percent requirement. This reflected a more lenient, less commercially rigid philosophy.

Organizational learning reflected in MITAF's adaptation underscored their commitment to collaboration and benefiting from each donor's unique contribution. Beyond the simple two donor illustration provided earlier, one participant shared the complexity and finesse involved in the MITAF donor collaborative,

> So because we were 3 or 4 donors through MITAF, we should evenly decide, it goes each donor has to say for example, ok through the investment committee, I can fund this or that. So let's say UNCDF would come and say ok, I'm willing to, to give a loan to let's say ARD, or I'm willing to give a grant for capacity building to finance the loan for such amount...KFW would say we are funding, we are giving a loan to Hope Microfinance, for example. UNDP would say ok, we are not allowed to give loan, but we can give grant for capacity building for example. And CORDAID would say ok, we can give some funds, you know, for capacity building and loans as well. So, it depends on what we agreed upon. (D0306, "personal communication," July 22, 2010)

Investment opportunities included collaboration within a given MFI investment package and among different MFI investment packages presented at the same Committee meeting. The strength of the collaboration was felt in the commitment of each donor to work cooperatively, when considering numerous investment opportunities, through the expression of individual organizational imperatives. Similarly, the complexity and finesse involved in the collaboration was felt in not only consensus building work among investors, but the shaping effect of environmental factors, such as an MFI regulator (a signatory to the Program Document).

> One of the key challenges was that, you know, decisions were taken by consensus with the investment committee. And you have a range of interests present. Now, I think one of the key challenges is national ownership. The nominal chair, non-voting chair of the investment committee was the governor or deputy governor of the Central Bank. That really wasn't always a problem per se. You know, it is the Central Bank. They were related to one specific group of institutions, the community banks. (D0508, "personal communication," September 23, 2010)

One response to the complexity and finesse associated with the MFI regulatory presence was to change the rules. MITAF voted to adjust the structure to include the Central Bank representative on the advisory board and removed that role from the Investment Committee.

This structural adaptation also illustrated MITAF's organizational learning.

The actual process for completing the Agreement reflected MITAF learned the limits of collaboration contained in the same attributes providing strength. Individual organizational objectives were difficult for a donor to abandon when the collaborative operational directive required each donor to work out the deal (i.e., complete the Agreement) directly with the MFI. One donor recounted that,

> Actually, even the investment committee decisions were made for approval of applications, but in practice, afterwards, the individual donors were requested to take up responsibility for contracting and disbursement. So, during MITAF period, that's what we did. After investment committee decisions, we took up well, the obligation and contact individuals. (D0407, "personal communication," September 16, 2010)

The implicit message in such an action/interaction strategy was one of customization that stretched the limits of order and reliability among participants. That is, the collaborative commitment was strained. If there is not a master Agreement with multiple signatories, to accommodate the practicalities of execution across nations, then the expediency of individuality was at the expense of commonality. Below is one donor's explanation,

> Because, exactly having those double procedures, because everybody, if you're making a contract, you will have to follow your own procedures as well. There's no organization that says ok, you've approved it somewhere outside. Let's make a contract right away.
>
> No. Everybody still has his or her own procedures. (D0407, "personal communication," September 10, 2010)

Reaching agreement on terms and preparing Agreement documents, and especially securing signatures from donors, on occasion involved a considerable amount of time. This was particularly so in multiparty deals. Two deals for one MFI, valued at over $500,000, from the November 2009 Committee meeting, still had undrafted Agreements at year-end. Once prepared, the agreements were unsigned by the donor as of March 2010 in part due to a deteriorating outreach problem at the MFI. Could this deterioration have been related to the delay of over $500,000 in capital the MFI ostensibly expected within weeks after negotiating conditions? Getting agreements written and signed was not as swift as provided for in the espoused disbursement process.

This donor described efforts to complete a grant deal, which espoused procedures depicted as simpler than loan deals,

> No, let's assume that we're talking about a grant contract. That was more frequent under MITAF. So, the next step will be preparation of the grant contract, taking a template as the underlying format, and the template had been agreed upon in advance, and so, we as donors ok, receive the template with the terms and conditions. Ideally the terms and conditions had been agreed upon in the Committee. The donor reviews the grant contract and it has been always the case that there have been changes in terms of conditions or the contract was not properly made, so formal mistakes. So, it's known that you have let's say one round of review. Some cases you have two or one or three, so the donor reviews the contract, sends it back to the TSP and the TSP gets in touch with the respective MFI to discuss the changes if relevant and if of importance . . . and sends it back to the donor, in this case, (donor) and if we agree to the version, we sign. (D0609, "personal communication," October 13, 2010)

In this instance, term changes and preparation mistakes were donor explanations for delayed Agreement completion. Also, this donor expressed the feeling that there had always been multiple drafts involving at least one round of views and redraft.

As suggested by the espoused process, loan deals were more specifically structured by intimate donor involvement in Agreement preparation. "[T]he loan terms are whatever the donor says, but normally each donor will approve funding for each particular investment. They will lend, they have their own conditions or whatever. So, they will draw up the loan agreement" (M-0303, "personal communication," July 20, 2010). Another participant referenced the cross-national challenges and connected them, in part, to the institutional structure of MITAF,

> when they didn't get all the agreements signed at the investment committee meeting pdf files were flying around the internet like can you sign mine and send it back to me and people were traveling all over the world, that dragged out the process, the process of payments very long. And I think that became a big problem. I think, you know, from one of the design issues you face at the beginning of these funds. And I call them, I put them in the category of funds for inclusive finance, and one of the decisions you face early on is what's the legal identity of this. (D0508, "personal communication," September 23, 2010)

The cross-national challenges of consummating Agreements further exemplified MITAF as a learning organization. There was continual change and adaptation to find processes that served both collaboration and individual organizational imperatives. One participant summarized the learning process as demonstrating extensive effort to operate collaboratively,

> And that impacts their [MFIs] performance. If you have a business plan and their projections are saying one year, these are my targets and the money comes 2 years after it then you're business plan is derailed. And actually, that's how we operated in the initial three years or so. And they now decided and said no, this is causing more problems. Now, one investment, one donor. (M-0303, "personal communication," July 20, 2010)

Rather than attempt to pro rate a deal among two or more donors, as originally espoused in the formal process, it was decided each investment deal had only one donor; however, an MFI investment package often involved more than one deal.

The Agreement was a complex document and process. This was not only because it is a legal document, but because of its meaning in relationships and differences in agreements were reflected in different actions regarding the same MFI investment package. Individual donor imperatives were balanced with collaborative commitment. The apex administered the Agreement preparation process to the extent that agent relationships were not complicated (e.g., some loan deals). MFIs sought the most favorable terms possible, while seeking clarity on how boundary constraints applied to aid evaluation of the opportunity; a deal or no deal dilemma.

Central to the Agreement were disbursement conditions. In the end, the complexity of relationships and guiding processes were expressed in capital disbursements; it was about the money!

MFI ACTIONS: CONDITIONS AND REPORTING

Here I describe MFI actions that pertain to conditions and reporting. Upon looking at the types of conditions through the lens of working-rules, the linkages and correlations begin to erupt. Obvious linkages are addressed in a surface manner, as was in the Agreement discussion. I present here how conditions and reporting operated in practice. Linkages are discussed in the next chapter. It is important to realize the ethical commitment the parties to Agreements attached to conditions, as well as organizational ontological struggles involved in action/interaction strategies. When viewed through the partnership language of MITAF, actions related to reporting can be understood as part of Gulick's (1937) bureaucratic executive function.

Conditions in Investment Deals

Observed MFI behavior reveals a lot, especially with respect to the conditions (rules) in investment deals. Conditions also tell much about the agreement process. Boundary rules gave potential parties to a deal the power of choice: deal or no deal. Also, there can be agreement, but implementation can be viewed from meaningfully different perspectives. For instances, conditions set forth in the Agreement as rigid expressions of commitments gave place in practice to understandings best described as an evolving set of disbursement conditions with exceptions. Though not unheard of, MITAF agreements to invest given certain disbursement conditions rarely received the *no deal* response from MFIs. MFIs generally viewed the condition-disbursement connection as a key factor in their decisions.

There is evidence that condition setting was a negotiation process. Agreeing to conditions empirically involved some give and take. On the one hand, conditions emerged from the Committee and were generally believed to reflect interests and agenda of capital providers.

These conditions prevailed in limited instances of divergence. On the other hand, one MFI explained there was negotiation on currency denomination for the loan. The MFI seemed adamant about the loan being in domestic currency (Leones) and apparently won a concession from the donor.[2] In the mind of this MFI, the foreign currency issue was a condition, but the context of deals normally considered that conditions pertain to requirements for capital disbursement to MFIs. This is one example of how properties of a particular stipulation in deals were perceived differently. At times terms (conditions) involving repayment of capital were as important to an MFI as conditions for disbursement; capital flows both ways. The following interview excerpt presents the example:

Person: Once the loan was approved, we had a series of meetings, a couple, I think one meeting with the representatives of those who came here, the representatives of the donors who were here and we agreed on a loan terms and conditions.

Investigator: So, after the loan had been approved, there was a meeting, the donors came and had a meeting with you?

Person: Yes, yes. The next investment committee meeting, they didn't come closer to approval or anything . . . there was a meeting, it was with them. And then we agreed on loan terms and conditions, you know, and once we agreed on loan terms and conditions, the formal document was sent to us for the review details and send it back and we agreed on the final loan terms and conditions. There were targets, benchmarks set, you know, so they advance the first loan . . .

Investigator: We talked about sitting down with the donors and working out the specifics of the conditions . . .

Person: Right

Investigator: And as a result, an agreement coming out of that. How does (interrupted)

Person: Let me give you an instance. One of the issues that we are very concerned with a government loan is foreign exchange risk, Ok. We operate in Leones [domestic currency] and we just can't see ourselves paying who knows, in Euro, to our donor. (M0202, "personal community." July 14, 2010)

Negotiation and flexibility were constrained and framed by the espoused intent of the MITAF project to develop a sustainable pro-poor financial sector. The sustainable property, reflected in the performance indicator dimensions, depicts the preponderance toward financial performance. For example, the one social indicator provided for in official documents is, *outreach understood as the number of active clients*. MFIs were required to report numerous statistics about the poverty and gender of their clients; however, these indicators were not used for performance measurement. Outreach measurements are diverse and complex in the literature. For NGO MFIs, the mere number of clients does not adequately account for the challenge of sustainably providing financial services to the poor.

Conditions for disbursement perceived to be excessively and inflexibly focused on financial performance indicators may result in an MFI making action-decisions that caused ethical struggles. One MFI explains the struggle in embracing performance indicators perceived as moving the MFI from its mission:

> Does it have an OSS that is 100% plausible? Does it have an FSS that is 100% plausible?[3] Does it have a yield productivity of its portfolio? Hmm. Ah ah. Why are these people looking at those numbers? We are looking at the survival of people. So, I will go these MITAF meetings and argue that look, if a woman is late for one day, we should show understanding. These people are struggling. If they don't pay the loan today, they pay it tomorrow or they pay it next week. Let us be magnanimous to accommodate them. And [MITAF staff] would say "oh, the chief executive of [MFI] is not prepared. He himself is not prepared to be a microfinance person because we need to change him. He has not shifted from the mindset, you know. Par-time repayment, full-time repayment, he doesn't pay, he doesn't pay." Ouch! Come on [MITAF staff]. Why are they thinking this way? Well later, we started calculating what it means to the quality of our portfolio . . . if somebody is to pay us today and failed to pay.
>
> But, today we carry two missions. We have a social mission, we have a commercial mission. How do you blend all of these? And in the process, we cannot reach many of the rural population because of permanently watching OSS, permanently watching productivity, permanently watching FSS, permanently watching our targets. The [MFI] set up, it should have been moving to support more people. It's so focused on sustainability issues that we are missing out on many deserving people. (M0101, "personal communication," July 14, 2010)

Is this financial-social dichotomy represented by MFI-MITAF relations reminiscent of work produced by Amin (1972) and Reed (2009), which found the African trade system replaced with colonial-type trade? Central to the dual bottom-line dilemma, as expressed by the MFI above, were diverse beliefs regarding the characteristics of "deserving people" in the sense of people qualifying for loans.

Complexity and nuanced word use are important in discussing Agreement conditions.

Donor agreement to use common performance indicators indicated the scale; however, the measure of achievement on that scale could vary. MITAF's aim was to develop the sector as a place where industry practice standards were the norm. Nevertheless, the actual indicators used to establish standard Agreement conditions varied. Perhaps more important were perceptions that achievement was inconsistently determined by a fixed scale. For example, there was a perception that Agreement conditions placed existing domestic MFIs in a conditional and contextual disadvantage:

> Procredit at that time was not yet fully established in Sierra Leone. They were just playing with the idea of setting up Procredits. Of course, they had their international donor. And when they came, we understood that a tranche of one million dollars was provided to Procredit to commence their business. And because we already had systems, we already had PaR [loan defaults], we already had clients on the ground, we already had challenges on the ground, I mean we are not just conceptualizing an idea. We are already, so we raised the point, can somebody be really punished simply because he has put an idea into practice? If I already doing business, definitely, I will have the defaulters, I will have PaRs, that's the nature of our business. So, the tranches were in that direction one would see, they may not be purely on conditionalities. (M0101, "personal communications," July 14, 2010)

A perception existed that applying the same conditions to both a domestic MFI and an international MFI, without an established business in Sierra Leone, may not give adequate consideration to the particular challenges of the nation. For example, Sierra Leone has for years been ranked among the lowest in the Human Development Index. In 2005, ProCredit received $1 million, making it the highest single capital investment made to an MFI and the fourth highest total capital investment made to an MFI during the life of MITAF. Investment and timely grant disbursement may have been, in part, due to existing donor relationships as much as commercially based criteria.[4] In early 2010, ProCredit was sold to Ecobank Sierra Leone due to high customer defaults (PaR) and fraud. Official MITAF records suggested that Sierra Leone's fragile state, postconflict setting may have been central to ProCredit's performance problems. "Considering the ample financing and high level of management capacity and governance, the situation of ProCredit Sierra Leone is concerning and possibly illustrative of the challenging environment for microfinance in Sierra Leone" (MITAF Narrative Report-4th Quarter 2009).

MFI Reporting Requirements in Deals

The reporting requirement for MFIs involved substantial work. It was understood and accepted by MFIs as integral to the decision to be a MITAF partner. For many, it was also seen as a necessary action to operate a sustainable, relevant MFI. Donors valued the apex role of collecting MFI reports and providing quarterly reports, as well as specific information with requests for disbursement pursuant to satisfying conditions in a deal. There was some concern that ongoing MFI reporting requirements were potentially difficult to enforce after capital was invested (disbursed); however, no specific instances were reported.

Reports required in the Agreement were varied and took different forms in practice. The *quarterly reports* contained numerous statistics beyond specific performance indicators in the Agreement. In practice, MFIs submitted similarly detailed monthly reports to MITAF. *Audited financial statements* were at times challenging to provide. Some external auditors produced suspect reports and MITAF provided training to assist the auditor most used by MFIs. For example, official documents report that normal examination procedures such as loan balance verification, loan classification review, and loan loss verification and examination were not performed. Such expertise and resources are not plentifully available in postconflict fragile state settings. *Mix Market*[5] was contained in the Agreement as part of a broader goal to ensure an environment conducive to industry development. This effort included an industry database, such as Mix Market, that developed from monthly reporting. This reflects the intertwined nature of actions/interactions in MITAF. Most MITAF MFIs did not report to Mix Market and some of those that did were not consistent reporters.

Two other reporting requirements involved evaluations. MITAF underwent mid-term and final evaluation and the Agreement required MFIs to cooperate with both. The mid-term evaluation included data from visits to eight MFIs, and the final evaluation visited five MFIs with survey questionnaires sent to thirteen MFIs. This reporting approach kept MFI management very close to the operating and market indices of their organization, as well as enhanced transparency with other stakeholders (Duval & Bendu, 2006, 2009; Interview 2).

The connection between reporting and capital disbursement is vivid and important. One MFI spoke candidly about reporting information that constrains capital disbursement, mostly because some conditions were considered unfair:

> Person: Here, a bit of culture here. Our customer here, about 80% of them, are farmers. Normally we give to them such, I'm a business man. In the end you see they only do business in the off-season, but after which they go back to the farms. . . . The conditions that because of the time. For the past three years, or two years we have not accessed loan funds. Any grants from MITAF . . . who are all fighting for a 5% PaR, I don't think it's fair.
>
> Like these past two years is a universal disease, and business fall [worldwide recession]. So even now, even right now, most of our traders, they are termed traders. If that occurred, goods like rice, then that's it. But the price has not

> moved far, it has been since they bought it, so now what can they do? So, they have to default, some of them their final payment has passed. We're not getting money from it. And as soon as his family thinks he owes more than they think he should be, then your PaR starts to increase. . . . This is the thing . . . We are honest with ourselves. We can say our PaR is 1. But they should not beat us with it. It's just to access the form. We tell the truth, and they refuse to give us the funds. One day, we're going to tell lies, which is not good for business. (M0410, "personal communication," July 20, 2010)

This MFI had a loan approved four years earlier yet had not received a single disbursement. However, it received grant capital totaling over $200,000. A powerful point regarding conditions and reporting was found in perceptions that conditions were unfair, given that a "universal disease" of economic collapse had gripped both Sierra Leone and the world. MITAF official documents also referred to economic conditions in explaining deteriorating loan portfolios across the sector. "The situation [deteriorating loan portfolios] has been exacerbated by the economic downturn" (MITAF Narrative Report-1st Quarter 2010). Consequently, if the desired reasonableness did not prevail, the MFI above suggested that reports could be falsified in the future (i.e., "we're going to tell lies").

SHOW ME THE MONEY: DISBURSEMENT OF CAPITAL

Disbursement commitment and performance of conditions were central to capital flow. MFIs developed action/interaction strategies based on them. Apex performance indices were impacted by them. Donor accountability and public scrutiny focused on them. Nevertheless, investigation empirically found capital volatility with properties and dimensions involving all three institutions: MFIs, apex, and donors. These properties and dimensions express the essence of the new bureaucracy excavated in the MITAF collaboration. I now move from the condition and reporting aspect of deals to disbursement of capital. Essentially, it was about the money!

The empirical capital disbursement process illustrates the struggle of organizational learning in a context of constraining-empowering tensions, organizational imperatives, and collaborative commitments. The classical view of bureaucracy begins to breakdown when applied to MITAF as a collaborative entity where work is performed by different and numerous organizational actors. The capital disbursement process also illustrates struggles of dual bottom-line objectives and administration with ambiguous identity. Using MFI day-to-day business as the point of departure, I expand the analysis of capital disbursement to the apex efforts to achieve numerous outcomes designed to be mutually enforcing. Apex actions resulted in MFIs experiencing various degrees and types of scrutiny. In turn, at times MFIs did not distinguish between a disbursement request verification visit, donor field visit, and a rating institution assessment. The apex "drowning in data" (Snibbe, 2006), worked to synthesize and summarize to prepare stakeholder communications, while also being prepared for a plethora of detailed questions regarding the impact and strength of the nascent MFI sector. Finally, donors experienced calls for accountability from above and beneath, working in a complex collaborative that frequently changed cash disbursement processes and, thereby impacted their respective organization's performance.

THE ACT OF DISBURSING CAPITAL

The scale expressing the distinctiveness and variableness of the disbursement process was vast, ranging from before an official request for disbursement, to considerably after disbursement approval. One account records how donor behavior seemed inconsistent with supporting the collaborative process,

> And in some cases, the donors even send the money to the MFI before they can meet the conditions . . . ok, now the MFI has met the condition, all the conditions in the loan agreement, in the grant agreement . . . go ahead and disburse the money. But there are cases where the donors will just send. (M-0303, "personal communication," July 20, 2010)

Similarly, the final evaluation reports Investment Committee members doing deals directly with MFIs, utilizing the apex to varying degrees, and investing capital without prior IC approval (Duval & Bendu, 2009). The record reflects an occasion when the IC officially directed the TSP to negotiate more flexible conditions on existing deals; however, the final evaluation accounts seem to be outside that collaborative process.

In another account, an MFI had two different loan capital disbursement experiences. In this interview, an example was given about an account very close to the espoused process, absent the procedural details.

> And then we agreed on loan terms and conditions, you know, and once we agreed on loan terms and conditions, the formal document was sent to review details and send it back and we agreed on the final loan terms and conditions. There were targets, benchmarks set, you know, so they advance the first loan. Then, they said the second loan, the second tranche, second disbursement would be as soon as you meet performance targets A, B, C, as we agreed upon. So that's one aspect. Once the institution meets that target, and usually within a

week or two, the payment is made. So that is in the case of a loan. (M0202, "personal communication," July 14, 2010)

This MFI also had a prior loan that was disbursed approximately two years after committee approval. In one official document, the delay was connected to a two-year delay in consummating the loan agreement. Another official document stated concerns about this particular deal, "The loan approved by MITAF Investment Committee for [MFI] was released in 2008 after [MFI] met the disbursement conditions" (MITAF Annual Narrative Report 2008).

Similar to earlier examples of Agreement signature delays, capital volatility in this deal was not reflected in certain records used to calculate volatility by most volatility studies. Technically, the agreement was not completed until conditions were satisfied. Such organizational behavior conceals a volatility property from traditional capital flow statistical calculations.

Once the Agreement was executed, disbursing the investment capital became the focus. The disbursement process, in practice, changed significantly from the design as individual donor imperatives were accommodated to achieve the collaborative goal of providing capital to the nascent Sierra Leone MFI sector. KfW employed an imprest account, which is an account providing MITAF authority to release funds deposited by the donor. This operated much like MITAF's original design, with adaptations illustrative of experiential learning. For example, KfW disbursed all capital for the deal to MITAF upon the MFI satisfying conditions for release of the first tranche. Cordaid, on the other hand, disbursed directly to the MFI. UNDP activity reflects both disbursements to MITAF and to MFIs directly. UNCDF, after crafting the Program Document to use an imprest account, encountered organizational concerns involving accountability and the potential for fraud. The collaboration to invest capital in the MFI sector responded to individual organizational accountability imperatives with behaviors affecting capital flow effectiveness, efficiency, and impact. The between-donor aspect and behaviors affecting capital flow value (i.e., effectiveness, efficiency, and impact) will be discussed further in the next two chapters.

CAPITAL DISBURSEMENT: PERCEPTIONS, STRATEGIES, AND IMPACTS

MFIs worked to expand service and operate sustainably, and they were challenged by capital volatility regardless of cause. This was especially the case for NGO MFIs that embraced the social mandate of serving those on the fringe of credit quality, as much as commercially driven MFIs embraced the financial performance mandate. As the MITAF Program Document explained, Sierra Leone MFIs operated in a capital-constrained environment, and this capital was vital to achieving their dual bottom-line objective.

An analysis of capital disbursements provided a statistical profile of MFIs with the most deals, thus the greatest opportunity to observe variance in behavior and capital flow. A Univariate ANOVA was conducted to investigate *percent* of total number deals differences in capital investments by year (Yes, MFI received a capital investment commitment; No, MFI did not receive a commitment). The years selected had the highest number of capital investment deals for the MITAF project. The results showed a significant main effect for 2006 capital investment deals, ($F(1, 8) = 9.876$, $p = .014$, partial $\eta 2 = .552$), and 2008 capital investment deals ($F(1, 8) = 11.878$, $p = .009$, partial $\eta 2 = .598$). The effect size indicated that a large proportion of percent variance was accounted for by 2006 and 2008 when looking at the three years with the most capital investment deals. On the other hand, MFIs that received the most capital did not provide more opportunities to observe frequent *interactions* (deals). For example, the four MFIs that received over 49 percent of the capital invested represented less than 30 percent of capital investment deals.[6]

MFIs drew upon numerous MITAF capital investment deals to express views of MITAF staff and donors when considering a mission mandate to serve communities. This MFI shared, with conviction, the challenge of serving people living in areas where more profit-oriented MFIs would not go. They spoke of the belief that their vital, urgent need for capital would be addressed as donors saw the tremendous need and worthiness of their mission:

> So, in our cases we are purely relying on MITAF to actually push our business plan forward to ensure that we are taking into our consideration, our own mission, we are there to target the vulnerable, actual poor. So, if we don't get into these areas where we cannot get so much, other NGOs that will eventually go there. . . . But we are there with a social mission to target these people, to make sure that we develop them to live above the poverty line. So, if we are meeting these constraints in terms of accessing funds to meet these people [it] is actually a big problem for us. So, if only MITAF can ensure that we have a direct sort of a direct contact with the donors instead of having this intermediary as MITAF is playing now, but if we have a direct contact with the donors, wherein they can see exactly where we are operating and the constraints we are going through, I believe things can move more faster. (M0305, "personal communication," July 16, 2010)

Another view speaks of the impact capital delays can have on MFI integrity and reliability,

> So for now we are really ready. But the only thing is that we are the fast track the disbursement. Because, like for instance, if you've already talk to a client that I will disbursed to you, and blah, blah and you failed to do that. They'll start calling you, that person's lying. They don't even have the capacity. Already you've talk to them. You have done your document, and you have the go ahead from MITAF.(M0305, "personal communication," July 16, 2010)

Official MITAF documents from November 2009 recorded one property of capital disbursement practice that could apply to the view shared above. This property is also found in MITAF official documents reporting on the quarter ending December 31, 2009, and addressed a grant deal where disbursement conditions have been satisfied,

> The grant approved in mid-February 2009 for (MFI) by [donor] has not been disbursed by end of this quarter despite several reminders by the TSP. These delays have impacted negatively on meeting outreach targets as MFIs have not received the needed funds to expand outreach. (MITAF Narrative Report-4th Quarter 2009)

Interview data from the donor in this grant deal, combined with disbursement empirical records, were examined and interpreted this excerpt as pertaining to the accountability property of the bureaucracy category. Accountability processes at the donor both contributed to disbursement delays and MFI accountability activity involving its community stakeholders.

Many capital disbursement experiences fit closely to the illustration below. All participants acknowledged that unsatisfied disbursement conditions were factors in the capital disbursement process:

> Secondly, most of the institutions will not meet the criteria at once, it's difficult for one institution to meet all the criteria, but if you have 75% of the criteria met, the institution will say ok, we will provisionally approve of this funding until you can go and meet these 20% or 25% once you meet the 25% then we'll release the money. That's where some kind of delay comes in. The institution takes looooooong sometime to meet these criteria and so by the time they meet the criteria and they send it back to the institution, and then because it's been a period of time before, so the institution takes time to respond. You have to wait sometimes a looooong time before it comes because things are moving. So if the institution acts very fast to meet the 25% criteria and send it back within that timeframe, then the institution, the organization can respond quickly, but when you take so much time there are things, higher priorities emerge and then that particular need gets, subsumed, you know submerged. (D0104, "personal communication," July 15, 2010)

Both prior research and the MITAF experience supported the importance of institutional strength to the value of aid and aid absorption. The net value of capital flow in MITAF was shaped not only by volatility, but MFI condition at capital disbursement time. The interview excerpt below illustrates one approach used to support MFI development when MITAF faced weak MFI institutional strength:

> Because they are weak. We have to buy and we have to give them the equipment, the motorbikes whatever. But for some mature institutions, we give them the money, but we make sure they give us a budget. They give us a budget, put down whatever it is they're going to buy and then we give them the money and they move the money to the operation officer and they have to follow-up and then they buy the equipment that they promised to buy. (M-0303, "personal communication," July 20, 2010)

Disbursement conditions are a mechanism designed in part to ensure MFIs are prepared to effectively and efficiently employ capital investments to impact target populations.

It seems disbursement conditions could have been more effectively employed with a focus on MFI condition over MFI performance:

Investigator: Institutional conditionalities for disbursement. Whether it be a loan or a grant. And you gave me an example where we might call it capacity building.

Respondent: Yeah

Investigator: Can you talk a little bit about the use of that indicator in making a disbursement decision?

Respondent: I must say that these type of indicators were not very often proposed by the TSP. These were the type of things that we came up later with, making really the contract. Because when making the contract then . . . you want to put incentives and specifically, when you make a combination . . . of a grant and a loan, also you want to know that what happens with . . . the loan is also reliant on making good use of the grant. (D0407, "personal communication," September 16, 2010)

> I mean one point that is quite striking is for example, the very heavy caseload of loan officers. And sometimes a loan officer has to serve up to six, seven, or even eight hundred clients, which could not be deemed as effective and productive anymore because these amounts are simply not manageable by loan officers. But MFIs abstain from hiring and recruiting new staff because their operational costs would have increased, and they would have not have met certain objectives. So, institutional development was kind of hindered at the expense of, fulfilling the MITAF criteria. (D0609, "personal communication," October 13, 2010)

The dual bottom-line objective of social targets (e.g., outreach) and financial targets (e.g., PaR, OSS, and FSS) were important measures in MITAF. Nevertheless, critical to developing a sustainable pro-poor financial sector were strong MFIs, as measured by institutional factors.

Low volatility capital, disbursed judiciously and expeditiously by MITAF, was observed to improve MFI institutional strength. Unfortunately, investments did not often appear to focus on institutional weaknesses in substantial amounts.

Of the various targeted outcomes, organizational behavior clearly indicated it was about the money not only effectiveness and efficiency but also flow. Capital investment and disbursement (i.e., capital flow) was always pursuant to deal formalization in a performance-based agreement. Also, capital investment deal provisions were viewed and implemented differently by participants in the deal. One participant recounted a conversation involving an MFI that disagreed with MITAF's philosophy, "I'm disappointed in people like [MFI], He's the guy that is so adamant. The [MFI] guy . . . Your [MITAF] recommendations are brilliant, but we [MFI] don't share [the views]" (M-0303, "personal communication," July 20, 2010). Certain MITAF policy standards did not seem appropriate to some participants for various reasons. On the other hand, none of the standards were more demanding than those provided by industry good practice recommendations. Were there instances when the Program Document provision for revising and resubmitting a proposal should have been invoked rather than approving a proposal with conditions that could have been extremely demanding?

In the next chapter, I explore *linkages* by presenting concepts excavated from data. With the prior descriptive illustrations as a foundation, I present explanations for capital volatility and related organizational behavior that provide the foundation of the Collaboration Bureaucratic Triad substantive theory that emerged.

NOTES

1. Portfolio-at-Risk (PaR) is a loan portfolio default measurement of "the outstanding principal amount of all loans that have one or more installments of principal past due by a certain number of days (often 30, 60, or 90 days), divided by the total outstanding principal amount" (Rosenberg, 2006, pp. questionnaire, 9).

2. The UN Programme Support Document urges donors to be considerate of certain MFIs in this regard, "Care should be taken to avoid burdening young institutions with foreign exchange risk in loans denominated in foreign currency, unless adequate precautions are taken" (2004b, p. 15 note 17).

3. Operational Self-Sustainability (OSS) and Financial Self-Sustainable (FSS) are organizational performance measurements. They are computed by dividing total

revenue by total cost, and total revenue divided by total adjusted cost (inflation + subsidized cost of funding + in-kind subsidies) respectively. See note 2 for more information on total adjusted cost.

4. See chapter three's discussion of ProCredit in the microfinance institutions portion of the case study explanation.

5. The Microfinance Information eXchange (MIX), a nonprofit organization, develops the MFI market infrastructure. This is accomplished by, among other activities, providing data sourcing and monitoring tools (2006).

6. Two of these four MFIs are included in this study's interview sample.

Chapter 5

Context of Behavior-Volatility Linkages

The New Bureaucracy's Emerging

MITAF participant's actions/interactions affected capital value by increasing or decreasing volatility and strengthening or weakening MFIs. That is to say, certain actions added to or subtracted from capital value. In this chapter I argue that, in addition to routine responses to everyday events, it was strategic, intentional, premeditated actions that illuminated and redefined the classic capital flow equation. In so doing, a different conception of bureaucracy was formed.

My investigation analyzed complexity and interconnectedness that resulted in decision-making dilemmas (actions) and volatility in capital flow. The focus was not on categorizing empirical activity codes (e.g., open, axial, and selective). Instead, it focused on certain structures (conditions) and the way they interconnected to elicit participant action (Strauss & Corbin, 1998). Toward this end, the chapter presents a context to analyze action (Simon, 1996). I present the context as consummation of capital investment deals in an executed performance-based agreement (Agreement). The next chapter presents an intervening condition, the MITAF mid-term evaluation. Of several contexts and conditions in this investigation these two not only accounted for substantial variability, but possessed interesting properties not explored extensively by others. Also, this chapter examines a MITAF staff leadership change. The MITAF staff perspective and practice moved from a dimension of a northern hemisphere attributes to southern attributes. This 2007 leadership change had capital volatility effects.

Linkages between organizational behavior and capital flow volatility involved complexity and interconnectedness. This complexity and interconnectedness were best viewed by analyzing progression as a process with a specified starting point. I must note that behavior-volatility linkages did not function as simply and neatly as this heuristic portrayal suggests. The particular parties involved, past experience of each party, shared experiences, and factors within the MITAF case (but outside of the deal) were just a few of the contributing dynamics to complexity and interconnectedness. Similar to the work of Rosalind Eyben and her colleagues (2012), I found this complexity and interconnectedness is integral to organizational learning. That is, it is not divorced from bureaucracy but embedded within. This chapter's simplified illustrations are not intended to depict the deep, vast complexity and interconnectedness that impacted capital flow value, but rather to provide a logical illustration of the complexity and interconnectedness of bureaucratic organizational behavior and capital volatility. In other words, it serves the new bureaucracy emerging from the data.

Fundamental to seeing linkages between an action and capital volatility is the working definition of volatility. The actions, from commitment to complete disbursement, formed a structured process. More precisely, from the time MITAF was to have delivered the approval letter to an MFI until the last tranche was placed in an unrestricted account or the resource benefits were accessible by the MFI, mutual understandings formed a structure. *Volatility is variability in disbursement timing of each tranche from the time a capital investment deal was approved and as measured against the structure of the deal (e.g., length of time to satisfy conditions, and length of time between satisfying conditions, TSP/MITAF staff requesting donor disbursement/processing disbursement, MITAF process/procedure).*

I believe it is important to view dimensions of volatility in the data as more nuanced than a dichotomy (i.e., capital commitment point, and point of last disbursement). The first tranche disbursement was intended to be universally expedient, but not prior to the prescribed point. Not only was volatility understood through the last tranche's disbursement, but also through the timing of each tranche. *Structuring a capital investment deal* to provide money or other resources, single or multitranche, are examples of actions (behavior) linked to volatility. In this chapter I present the analysis of this linkage.

Researchers are often forced, by method and data constraints, to attack complexity and interconnectedness in a manner that produces narrow explanations. At times rigid investigative processes overemphasize technical correctness at the price of not capturing the dynamic flow and quintessence of data. Understanding linkages between behavior and capital flow volatility involves examining interconnections and complexity, rather than assuming them out of the analysis and focusing on a few variables. The new bureaucracy is observed in examining behavior-volatility linkages. Fundamental to this examination are the relationships in the MITAF collaborative bureaucracy.

RELATIONSHIP FORMATION: POSTDECISION, PRE-MONEY, AND DISBURSEMENTS

Bureaucracy is about the organization of relationships involving defined roles with the aim of producing results. The first action after approval of a deal was the MITAF staff communicating approval to the MFI. MITAF staff actions are integral to capital flow and include Agreement preparation, implementation support to MFIs and donors, and disbursement completion. Table 5.1 contains several key apex actions in the *apex-MFI* exchange, constructed by MFIs, donors, and apex actors (MITAF staff). It illustrates how MITAF participant interactions were viewed in this investigation. Approval notification letter delivery and ensuing MFI Agreement condition negotiations were closely related, but remained separate and distinct actions. In this section, 2008 and 2009 deals are used to view complexity, interconnectedness, and variability between participants and between years. For example, there was no empirical evidence the MITAF staff did not generally administer approval letter delivery and MFI condition negotiations effectively and efficiently. Approval letter delivery and MFI condition negotiations are linked to capital volatility because donors did not disburse capital until the Agreement was complete.

PERFORMANCE-BASED AGREEMENT INTERACTIONS

In practice, apex-MFI interactions were not the sole purview of investment deal condition negotiations. Evidence reveals donors were actively involved with MFIs, especially in loan deals. This illustrates that MITAF

Table 5.1 Apex-MFI Interaction

Organizations Interacting	*Action/Interaction*
Apex-MFI Interaction	Notification letter
	Agreement-negotiate conditions
	Monitoring satisfaction of conditions
	Trainings
	Technical Assistance
	Advocating for capital disbursements
	Flexibly/Rigidly administering condition satisfaction assessments
	Communicating program emphasis (e.g., sustainability, outreach, dual objective)
	Notification of condition satisfaction and request for disbursement
	Reporting MFI performance

became a learning organization, adapting to operational realities as they appeared. The evidence supports that *donor-MFI* interactions produce different conditions, at times, from those agreed to in Committee meetings. On occasion direct donor involvement created greater leniency in disbursement conditions, which could result in lower capital volatility. Direct donor involvement in Agreement condition negotiations was linked to capital volatility because information asymmetries (e.g., unequal access to certain information by the parties due to limited access to each other) were reduced and donors better addressed their interests in concert with MITAF goals. Also, direct donor involvement added another step to the Agreement completion effort. Donor-MFI interactions increased or decreased capital volatility.

Figure 5.1 depicts complexity in the Agreement context. Two or more organizations interacted directly with a MFI at different stages to varying degrees, depending on the deal. All parties and interactions worked to implement Committee approvals: apex-MFI, donor-MFI, and *apex-donor*. Direct donor-MFI contact did not necessarily reduce time or add time to the Agreement completion process. Nor did it necessarily result in conditions different from those reached by apex-MFI condition negotiations. Effectiveness and efficiency in certain organizational settings were served by greater intimacy between parties to a deal.

Donor-MFI interaction dimensions extended from better quality, less-filtered information shared between parties to delays in receiving information needed for compliance monitoring. There was evidence that donor-MFI interaction placed a greater focus on strengthening institutional capacity over financial performance than by apex-MFI condition negotiations (Duval & Bendu, 2009). On the other hand, donor-MFI direct contact did add complexity. This complexity accounted, in part, for Agreements not being executed in

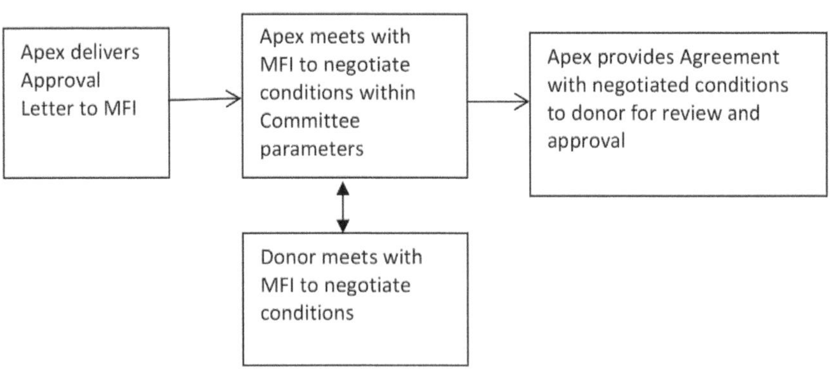

Figure 5.1 Performance Based Agreement Context.

a timely fashion. For example, official records suggest that a loan Agreement was not executed for two years after the terms were negotiated by the donor (MITAF Narrative Report-Annual 2008; MITAF Narrative Report-4th Quarter, Annex R). In another instance, the apex responsible for monitoring and reporting on MFI Agreement compliance had not received the donor-MFI negotiated grant Agreement approximately three months after it was completed, nor had the grant been disbursed. In contrast, donor-MFI interaction could reduce the number of apex-donor Agreement draft exchanges and allow for finely tuned Agreements as donors and MFIs had increased access to unfiltered information.

Beyond approval notification and negotiating disbursement conditions, additional action/interaction linkages were observed in the Agreement context. *MITAF staff/Apex-donor* interactions throughout Agreement production were central to agreement completion and necessary for capital disbursement. There was considerable variability based on deal particulars and donor imperatives. Interview data reported Agreements always had at least one exchange of Agreement modifications between the apex and donor. This required another review by the MFI. Again, direct donor-MFI interactions were linked to apex-donor interactions because of the Agreement context (e.g., apex was responsible to notify MFI of approval and is accountable to the Committee for the deal). There were instances when the Agreement had several bureaucratic levels to supersede before execution. For example, in 2005, UNCDF instituted centralized processing of Agreements that required all documents be sent to New York City from around the world. In contrast, another donor provided for Agreement signatures and disbursements to be decentralized and processed in Sierra Leone. Loan deals were considered more complex than grant deals. One donor discussed the practical and theoretical aspects of Agreement completion,

> The only thing is signing the agreement between the institution and (donor). Back and forth, you know, between MITAF. So, you know, sometimes, you missed this. Oh, you forgot this. Oh, you sent it to me I forgot, please send it back to me again. You know, these kind of things. That's a lot of bureaucracy. But in, really, it's not a big deal. I mean it could take a very short period of time to report this. Once we agree in the investment committee. (D0306, "personal communication," July 22, 2010)

Agreement completion was theoretically simple and direct; however, as an empirical context, Agreements involved complexity affecting capital flow.

Agreements became more complex in deals that were cross-connected, implicitly if not explicitly, especially when different types of deals (grants and loans) were involved. One donor underscored the importance and complexity of cross-connected deals (i.e., linkages between objectives of different deals in the same MFI capital investment package),

> That's a good issue. Sometimes that happened. That the loan and the grant were contracted by different donors and then if you need to check before disbursement whether they have committed, whether the other, for example, if disbursement was related then to also having disbursement of the grant. So you need to double check. (D0407, "personal communication," September 16, 2010)

Another participant provided a scenario illustrating the challenge of linkages between actions/interactions of donor-MFIs in separate deals, but part of the same MFI capital investment package,

> Let's say UNCDF will say ok, we can fund capacity building grant. . . . And KFW will say ok, we have money for loan. We don't have money for capacity building, we have money for loans, because institutions request both. . . . But then, if the institution gets the loan before it gets the capacity building money, because, for example, KFW might be faster than UNCDF in terms of processing, then, perhaps . . . the loan is given because the grant has to be made so that they can improve the capacity building. But if they get the money for the loan, and they don't have the money for capacity building, then, you know. (D0306, "personal communication," July 22, 2010)

Greater complexity and linkage connections were observed in cross-connected deals.

The Agreement context is used in figure 5.2 to set forth the complexity of cross-connected deals. Donor collaboration and coordination are considered a key output in the MITAF Program Document. "Strategic partnerships are built with other donors and private sector in joint support of a sustainable pro-poor financial sector" (UNCDF, 2004b, p. 12). The more partners in a collaborative, the more opportunity existed for complexity, including cross-connection deals.

This complexity affected capital volatility.

Close examination of Agreement consummation revealed there were important actions linked to capital disbursement timing and the context of cross-connected linkages. One criticism of the apex in midterm, and final evaluations was the cumbersome financial tracking system. This was related in some measure to the MITAF structure as an entity. Nevertheless, it complicated and constrained detailed analysis of capital flow in deals. Combining analysis of financial records of deals with archival and interview data provided an important perspective on Agreement linkages,

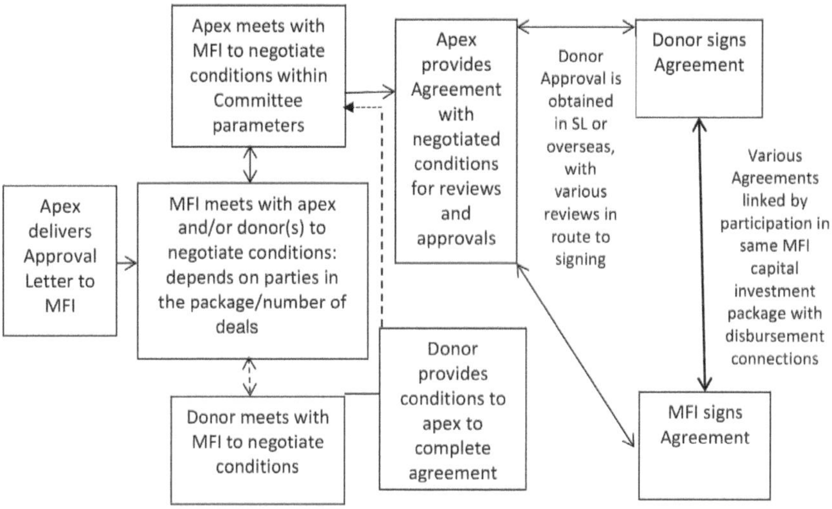

Figure 5.2 Performance Based Agreement Context—Complexity of Multiple Linkages.

a prerequisite for capital disbursements. A substantial number of deals revealed cross-connected linkages with complex actions/interactions (apex-MFI, donor-MFI, apex-donor).

2009 AGREEMENT CONTEXT: DELAYED DEALS AND CROSS-CONNECTIONS

A good example of cross-connected linkages, and delayed deals was exemplified in the last year of MITAF. There were seventeen deals in 2009, totaling approximately $2.77 million USD, the largest dollar amount committed to MFIs for a single year and the third largest year for number of deals. Five MFIs representing twelve deals (over two-third of 2009 deals) approved in February and November 2009 experienced Agreement delays. The deals involved three of the four Committee members. All twelve deals primarily involved donor delays. The length of time these Agreements were delayed was the minimum time capital flow was delayed; capital disbursements delays could have been extended for other reasons. Delays due to Agreement matters did not consider action/interactions after Agreement completion that added additional delays, such as the MFI not satisfying conditions for disbursement. Moreover, cross-connectivity was observed among deals in 2009.

Table 5.2 Deals, MFIs, and Donors 2009

MFIs	*Donor 09a*	*Donor 09b*	*Donor 09c*
MFI 09a		November 09, Grant and Loan	
MFI 09b		November 09, Grant and Loan	
MFI 09c	February 09, Grant*		February 09, Loan*

*Cross-connected deals.

February 2009: Several Deals with Several Donors

Agreement delays from February 2009 Committee approvals involved six deals. Table 5.2 frames the deals, MFIs, and donors involved. Three deals involved one donor (Donor 09a), and the agreements were completed in the fourth quarter of the calendar year (over six months later). The other three deals involved two donors (Donor 09b, Donor 09c). Two of these deals were with one donor (Donor 09b), involving one MFI (MFI 09b), and the agreements were completed by June 30. Completion occurred after the third day window within which Agreements were expected to be completed. Following is a discussion of the last of these three deals with Donor 09a and Donor 09c, which illustrates cross-connected linkages and complexities.

Donor 09a was party to a February 2009 deal cross-connected with another deal capitalized by Donor 09c (figure 5.3). In this instance, the loan capital donor completed the Agreement and disbursed capital before the grant Agreement was completed. The loan deal was implicitly cross-connected to the grant deal. The grant was for technical assistance by Planet Rating, which conducted an institutional appraisal and loan portfolio due diligence study

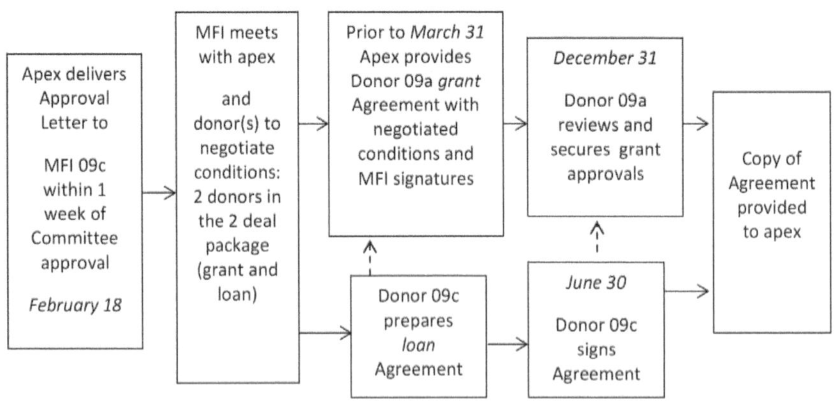

Figure 5.3 February 2009 Deals with Cross-Connected Linkages and Delayed Agreement.

that provided recommendations. Ostensibly, this study provided by the grant deal would inform the apex administering the loan deal's conditions with greater specificity, based on the belief that technical assistance would build MFI 09c's institutional capacity to better employ loan capital.

As depicted in figure 5.3, the loan Agreement was completed by June 30, as was the disbursement. The grant Agreement was completed in the fourth quarter (October–December), much later than expected and after loan capital was disbursed. This illustrates potential spillover effects of one donor adhering to time constraints when another donor, whose deal is connected, engages in actions prohibited by the rules (e.g., delayed Agreement completion). Not only was the MFI impacted, but a donor collaborative partner could have been potentially affected.

Although 2009 only had one cross-connected deal, 2008 had eight such deals (20 percent of the 2008 deals), adding a different dimension of complexity.

Using the timeframes discussed earlier, the MFI approval letter is delivered within one week of Committee approval with the MFI returning the Agreement within two weeks of approval. A close approximation of the minimum capital delay can be computed based on a close examination of this process. The loan deal in figure 5.3 involved a delay of up to three months due to Agreement consummation alone. The grant deal was possibly extended up to an additional six months beyond the loan deal. If the two deals were implemented to complement each other, then loan capital would have been disbursed after grant capital and, given the grant's delay, the loan deal could have been a year or more delayed.

November 2009: A Focus on Deals with One Donor

An examination of Agreement consummation of deals approved in November 2009 provided additional insights on actions linked to capital volatility. Four of the six deals experiencing Agreement delays had only one donor (Donor 09b), representing approximately 25 percent of the total dollar investment for the year. This dollar investment proportion for 2009, the largest of all MITAF years, is a substantial concentration. Drafting of the agreements did not begin until after the New Year. Important and interesting behavior was observed when carefully considering the data on these deals.

Review of official documents indicated two of the four deals with Donor 09b involved one MFI (MFI 09a) where Agreement consummation was constrained by the Committee, "subject to conditions being met" (MITAF Narrative Report-4th Quarter 2009). More specifically, as another official document put it, "the grant and loan agreements will be processed once PaR30 is 5% or below" (MITAF Narrative Report-1st Quarter 2010). This same donor made a loan investment in MFI 09a in 2006 with the same PaR restriction of 5 percent as a condition. After over three years of the MFI not meeting the condition, in November 2009, the apex recommended a wavier in recognition of progress made so that the load could be disbursed. A new November 2009 deal was committed to with the same conditions that were waived in November 2009 for a deal approved three years earlier.

MFI 09a events made two other November deals with Donor 09b more interesting. Two November deals did not have a Committee constraint on Agreement consummation. This was particularly relevant as the record reflected extensive Committee discussion about these two deals,[1] both comprising an investment package for one MFI (MFI 09b). Nevertheless, the record shows that Agreement work began considerably late on the MFI 09b deals, and then the MITAF staff took action to withhold recommending Donor 09b sign the Agreements due to observing a substantial drop (approximately 20 percent) in MFI 09b's outreach in the quarter following Committee approval. It was reported that the reduction was due to suspended loan activity after detecting fraud in one of its nine branches and wanting to monitor the situation (MITAF Narrative Report—1st Quarter 2010). Eventually, two 2009 loans were approved totaling $650,000 (MITAF Minutes November 2009; MITAF Narrative Report-4th Quarter 2009) for MFI 09b from donor 09b and were adjusted in the records to reflect one loan of $300,000 approved November 2009 (MITAF Narrative Report-4th Quarter, Annex R). This formalization suggested that resulting disbursement activity had minimal volatilities and delays; close examination of the detail supported disbursements were made that pertained to the deal consummated months earlier, the *February 2009* loan deal (MITAF Minutes November 2009).

The point was not that an unauthorized transaction may have occurred, which involved placing conditions on a Committee directive without authorization. Rather, the point was that strategies were employed using noteworthy techniques. Also, the strategies were based on data not normally available if behavior complied with Agreement completion policy.

Conditions based on information about MFI performance, such as PaR deterioration, were provisions in the Agreement. The Committee was also permitted to decide whether a proposal must be revised and resubmitted to allow the MFI to address its weaknesses. Committee policies and procedures governed approval criteria, such as having a "good credit history" (2006, p. 5). It was interesting that the Committee constrained the donor (Donor 09b) by placing a condition on consummating two deals (MFI 09a). Collaboration could obfuscate one organization as the *bad guy* in such constraining situations. Also, the apex-donor decision to delay Agreement consummation in two deals involving one MFI (MFI 09b) was based on MFI outreach data that may not have been available if Agreements were timely processed. In addition, evidence suggested the disbursement delay actually contributed to the outreach reduction, beyond the fraud.[2] For example, MFI 09b opened three new branches sixty days before the November Committee meeting. The branches reduced not only the MFI's financial performance ratios, but likely reduced available cash for loans important to increase and maintain outreach as higher expenses demanded cash. Volatility in the Agreement context was particularly clear when apex-donor restrictive action was compared to donor action to timely complete a 2008 Agreement for a MFI that also experienced outreach challenges. Such a comparison is provided in the next section.

There are various explanations of Agreement delays, and how they impacted capital volatility. Delay in Agreement commencement and completion was at times related to Committee imposed constraints. Consummation delays were also due to strategic, intentional, premeditated actions responding to perceived problems, such as MFI outreach contraction. At times, efficient document processing was a contributory factor. In 2008, MITAF had fewer Agreement consummation constraints and Agreement disbursement conditions were relaxed from industry standards. Agreement delays were important action-links to capital volatility because capital commitment notifications after a Committee meeting, though perhaps real to the MFIs, were not formalized outside the Agreement. They were, therefore, not tracked transparently and capital volatility was not constrained.

2008 AGREEMENT CONDITION DIFFERENCES: UNDP AND YES

Examination of 2008 capital commitment formalization identified actions linked to capital volatility. In 2008, there were twenty-one deals totaling \$1.67 million USD. A UNDP program new to MITAF, Youth Employment Secretariat (YES), completed paper-work in early 2008 to pave the way for participation in MITAF and was a capital source for UNDP to invest in five of ten MFIs approved by the Committee for capital investment. UNDP/YES provided approximately half of the amount approved for capital investment in 2008. Moreover, each MFI selected for UNDP/YES capital investment received both grant and loan capital investment types. The significance of types was investigated utilizing a Univariate ANOVA. The *percent* of total number deals differences in capital investments by year, by type of deal (grants, loans, grants, and loans) was examined. Except for 2008, all main effects and interaction effects were not significant. Results revealed that the deal type *grants and loans* (M = 10.30 percent, $\mu 1/2$ = 9.2 percent) in 2008 significantly differed in percent of deals from all other types ($p < 0.005$).

The 2008 main effects represent the amount of variance in the percent of deals accounted for by types of deals ($F(2, 4)=7.0$, $p = .049$, partial $\eta 2=.778$).

UNDP/YES is noteworthy because each of its recipients was provided grants and loans, and it represents a substantial proportion of 2008 investment. Also, there was no evidence of Agreement delay, dispute on conditions, post-Agreement consummation disbursement delay, or premature disbursement criticism. The noteworthiness primarily resides in the profile of the MFIs receiving capital; which, as a group, are leaders in the number of capital investment deals in MITAF.

UNDP capital disbursement to MFIs unfolded efficiently and effectively. A memorandum of understanding was executed between MITAF and YES early in the second quarter of 2008 and the Committee met in March, May, and July (UNDP was the agent for YES). Expected timeframes for key tasks were reported or were inferred from observed events. The records reflect the investments were approved at May, and July meetings; therefore, Agreement completion was expected to be the end of June and August, respectively. There were no official records reporting this occurred; however, nothing refuted it. For example, Agreements outstanding from the March 2008 Committee meeting and afterward were specifically disclosed in the 2009 first quarter narrative report; UNDP/YES deals were not reflected as delinquent. These 2008 Agreement completions demonstrated volatility was constrained on numerous occasions.

A closer look at a few MFIs was warranted because between-donor variability in actions occurred in capital investments. Three MFIs were approved for capital investments in both 2008 and 2009. Looking at the loan portfolios of these three MFIs provides some insight on conditions that may have been included in the Agreements, or at least insight on how disbursement decisions were made. As pointed out earlier, donor-apex-MFI negotiation of Agreement conditions is central to timely Agreement completion and condition specifics central to capital disbursement timing. Two of three MFIs (MFI 08c, MFI 08d) maintained loan defaults (portfolio-at-risk, PaR) at an acceptable level in 2008 and 2009. The other MFI (MFI 08e), approved for both grant and loan capital at July 2008 Committee meeting, had chronic challenges.

In 2008, the loan portfolio of MFI 08e did not meet industry standards (e.g., PaR and write-off levels). During each quarter of 2009, PaR and the amount written off as uncollectable (WO) struggled to improve. This information is provided in table 5.3, which compares MFI 08e with MFI 09b. Strengthening the MFI 08e portfolio was very slow, with a bumpy improving trend. Especially encouraging progress was achieved after short-term technical assistance focusing on PaR reduction was provided during the first quarter of 2009. In November 2009, the Committee approved another grant and loan

Table 5.3 MFI 08e and MFI 09b Comparison

Indicator and Event	*MFI 08e*	*MFI 09b*	*Comment*
PaR/WO information at time Agreement to be completed	• 9.34%/1.99% 4th quarter 2008; • 8.73/2.78% 3rd quarter 2009	<5%/0% 3rd quarter 2009	MFI 08e 2008 best information available; November 09 decision based on 3rd quarter information
Outreach at time of Agreement • July 08 • November 09	• 2008 30% decrease from 2007; • 2009 increase 8.6% (MITAF increase 20+%)	• 12% increase from 2nd quarter to 3rd quarter 2009 • 1% decrease from 3rd quarter to 4th quarter 2009 • 19% decrease from 4th quarter 2009 to 1st quarter 2010	• MFI 08e received capital investment during year of 30% decrease in outreach, the following year reflected outreach growth • MFI 09b did not receive capital investment when experienced small decrease in outreach, downward trend continued.
Timing of Agreement	• July 08 Committee grant and loan deals, Agreement completed by January 1, 2009; • November 09 loan deal, Agreement completed by December 31, 2009	Two November 09 deals: drafting started after December 31, 2009	MFI 08e grant deal total and loan deal first tranche disbursed by December 31, 2008, so Agreements were likely completed close to expected timeframe
PaR/WO information at disbursement time	• 9.34%/1.99% 4th quarter 2008; • 6.82%/2.02% 4th quarter 2009	• 5.11%/0% 1st quarter 2010	MFI 08e was basically stable from 4th quarter 2009 to 1st quarter 2010: 8.94%/0%
Timing of disbursement	• First tranche by 1st quarter 2009 (2008 total grant); • Second tranche (2008 loan final) 2nd quarter 2009; • 2009 deals not disbursed by March 31, 2010	2009 deals not disbursed by March 31, 2010	

investment package for MFI 08e. The loan amount was almost twice the UNDP/YES loan, with the explicit stipulation that disbursements were conditioned on a PaR below 5 percent. The loan Agreement was completed before year's end.[3] As of March 31, 2010, MFI 08e's PaR was almost 9 percent (0 percent WO), a 40 percent decrease in PaR and WO from a year earlier. The reduction from June 2009 to March 31, 2010 was over 20 percent. Yet, it needed to decrease another 40 percent in the following two quarters for MFI 08e to receive a disbursement within a year of the November Committee approval. That was a very tall order. In contrast, all indications were the 2008 UNDP/YES grant was totally disbursed by December 31, 2008, and the loan was disbursed in two tranches by June 30, 2009. As of June 30, 2009, MFI 08e's combined PaR and WO was over 11 percent (7 percent, 4.11 percent), considerably above industry standards. Perhaps more important was MFI 08e's combined PaR/WO decreasing approximately 2 percent during the disbursement period of the July 2008 deals.

Compare this MFI 08e experience in 2008 and 2009 to MFI 09b in 2009, where the apex withheld a recommendation for the donor to sign the MFI 09b Agreement because of a reduction in outreach. The dimensions of actions linked to capital volatility are vivid. As reflected in table 5.3, two 2008 deals for MFI 08e experienced timely Agreement consummation. In addition, MFI 08e was approved for additional capital investment in 2009 (grant and loan), even while performing below industry standards and with outreach challenges. The 2009 Agreements were competed timely. In contrast, MFI 09b experienced a reduction in outreach that resulted in a several week postponement of Agreement drafting. Official documents available at the time of the investment decision characterized the 2009 outreach reduction as "slight" and forecasted increased outreach (MITAF Narrative Report-4th Quarter 2009). Furthermore, there were additional delays due to strategic, intentional actions utilizing information on events that would not have been available (and may not have occurred) with the timely processing of Agreements. The scope of organizational response dimensions related to outreach reductions reflected variations in behavior.

The three MFIs involved in 2008 and 2009 deals (MFI 08 c, d, and e) illustrated how Agreement completion occurred with substantially equal dispatch in 2008, apparently with conditions more lenient than industry standards, where disparate MFI performance existed. The result was minimal capital volatility, with portfolio quality improving into 2010. Also, an underperforming MFI (MFI 08e) received desperately needed liquidity to respond to outreach demands after seeing an outreach reduction of approximately 30 percent from 2007 to 2008 (MFI 08e experienced 8.6v percent growth 2008 to 2009, compared to MITAF MFIs overall growth above 20 percent).

2007 APEX LEADERSHIP CHANGE: PERSPECTIVE AND PRACTICE

This is a noteworthy year in several respects. First, there were no deals approved, not one (only an addendum to a 2006 deal). Second, at least $1.2 million USD was distributed to MFIs during 2007. This is particularly important because it was the year that a cash flow crunch was experienced around the world as the Great Recession began to emerge (Brunnermeier, 2009; Isidore, 2008). Third, it was the year after the MITAF midterm evaluation. The midterm evaluation occurred in 2006 and, as explained later, experienced substantial activity impacting volatility that affected 2007 operations. Fourth, and perhaps most important for understanding 2007's effect on capital volatility, the apex experienced a leadership change at the Sierra Leone office in October 2007. This leadership change was perceived to move the *perspective and practice* dimension from more of a northern perspective to more of a southern perspective. Although more precise data from various sources is needed to isolate this change variable from the UNDP/YES funding source and MFI profile variables, evidence is too strong to deny an affect.

Empirically, a nuanced, careful view of data adds credibility to perceptions the *perspective and practice property* measured differently with the leadership change. This perception was expressed during interviews,

> And again, I don't know when one is African and one is over on the other side, if that difference. But we also saw as an MFI, some dramatic changes of the way MITAF conducted in terms of accessing resources [after chief of party change] . . . The north-south divide . . . So south, somebody from the south is not white, he is European . . . I don't want to sound racist. It's just people coming from the north in development paradigms. When we engage them, the way southern NGOs sometime articulate development ideas and the way our northern colleagues, by no fault of theirs, based on their own background exposure, when you engage in the debate, you see them sometimes taking sides, which, with respect, sometimes you feel I wish they will have shifted. But of course, shifting people is not easy. Shifting south people to north, north people south is quite a challenge, eh? In development eh? So, you see we are both on these sides and sometimes some people will hold firmly, eh? (M0101, "personal communication," July 14, 2010)

The following interview excerpt provides an example of divergent perspectives spanning the scale from commercial MFI paradigm (northern) to accommodative developing MFI paradigm (southern):

> And yeah, I was present at the investment committee meeting when the technical advisor [former MITAF chief of party] went on for about 15 minutes talking

> about the weaknesses of the community banks. And the governor of the Central or the deputy governor of the Central Bank said yes, I hear you, but you know, you think you can try and make them work? (D0508, "personal communication," September 23, 2010)

The following respondents to the north-south hypothesis discussed policies and mutually agreed Agreement terms (scope) as experiencing culturally shaped applications,

Person 2: While you are within a certain scope, but there are things you need to understand for this to carry. At the outset, they are so many other thinkings. Whatever they [Sierra Leone MFIs] do it's about is he Mende, is he Temne [two different Sierra Leone tribes]. Everything you do, it sounded like that. Researcher: So, the outside of the scope, there's this thinking of these cultural factors that might be, these people they are serving.

Person: Definitely.

Person 2: Even when they are in the same office that is the dividing line. (M-0304, "personal communication," July 20, 2010)

Interviews and empirical capital flow records shaped understanding of the midterm evaluation's criticism of investor risk approaches. "While there were justifiable reasons for this, the Committee has erred on the side of caution in supporting the larger MFIs, not taking enough risk on the smaller organizations that may well have the potential to become sustainable" (Duval & Bendu, 2006, p. 33). On the one hand, the criticism acknowledges the validity of commercial MFI criteria in selecting capital investment deals; on the other hand, the assessment questions the sufficiency of risk taking in selecting deals. This view of criticisms related to capital flow is supported by an earlier criticism in the evaluation:

> [D]isbursement of all types of funding approved by the Investment Committee is tied to the tailored performance criteria . . . As a result, the little grant funding that has been approved for operating costs and/or the acquisition of fixed assets has been withheld along with approved loan funds. This is counterproductive in that some MFIs—particularly the smaller indigenous institutions that are still experiencing serious difficulties with portfolio quality—are not receiving the very funding that could help increase the institutional capacity necessary to meet the performance criteria. (Duval & Bendu, 2006, p. 27)

MITAF disbursement processes were not only observed in different MFI profiles for 2008 investment deals, but in movement along the perspective and practice property of MITAF staff. How Agreement terms were interpreted and implemented by MITAF staff were perceived to be different after the north-to-south leadership change. The implication is that MITAF adapted by changing its cultural application of the MITAF model. Agreement cultural application differences were also detected in expressions by southern staffs of northern MITAF donor institutions and in the faith-shaped operations of Cordaid. The interview expressions, archival documents, and disbursement record of 2008 supported the claim that the change in apex leadership, north to south, was a factor in reducing volatility experienced pre-2008.

Next, I will explain how linkages between capital volatility and organizational behavior reflected new properties when viewed through the lens of 2006 deals. In the next chapter, I will add an *intervening condition* to this examination of the Agreement as a *context*. The 2006 deals demonstrate the importance of intervening conditions on efficiency, effectiveness, and reduced volatility. A key property in the new bureaucracy is complicated attributes of accountability.

The intervening condition drives this point home.

NOTES

1. A key Committee concern regarding MFI 09b, an international MFI forming a Sierra Leone MFI, involved capital structure. It was important that international debt capital be reclassified as equity. This was likely to improve the priority of any donor loans relative to the international MFI's capital (MITAF Minutes November 2009).

2. Although it is not suggested that fraud and malfeasance is an everyday occurrence, fraud in branches and various departments in financial institutions around the world is not infrequent and is a matter requiring constant vigilance. In this instance, the officer involved at the branch was dismissed and by March 31, 2010, OSS increased over 10 percent to approximately 100 percent while the increase in PaR afterward was less than 100 basis points.

3. This was based on the deal not being listed among Agreements incomplete as of December 31, 2009.

Chapter 6

Perennials of the New Bureaucracy

Evaluation, Time, and Diverse Partners

As Charles Goodsell points out "bureaucracy is neither a generalized failure nor sinkhole of waste as mythologized by anti-government ideologues." It is indispensable for the effective implementation of the social contract citizens have with their government. Moreover, it is the most reliable and dependable mechanism for providing the goods and services citizens deserve (Harvey White, Foreword).

This chapter examines the behavior-volatility linkages in a manner that illuminates the new bureaucracy. An intervening condition, the midterm evaluation, focuses on important linkages. I explain time, in numerous respects, was an important and very serious matter in the MITAF project. Not just urgency but strategically and as a credible commitment time was a ubiquitous consideration. In addition, participant perceptions concerning others' positions and responsibilities were often fundamental in linking the variation in behavior and capital flow.

One year that is unique in the pre-2008 experience of disbursement delays is 2006. Capital investment and capital volatility had particular attributes in response to the 2006 mid-term evaluation as an *intervening condition.* The actions/interactions in 2007 were largely related to the massive activity in 2006.

I detailed several insightful actions/interactions in the earlier examination of linkages in the Agreement consummation *context.* The MITAF staff and a donor postponed document preparation over a month after a November Committee approval, with no explicit reason other than perhaps holiday (festive) season and procrastination. Similarly, MFI outreach decline was explicitly attributed to the holiday (festive) season in official documents. The Committee actually constrained the preparation of an Agreement based on achieving a specified level of past-due loans (PaR), rather than making it a condition for disbursement or deciding a specific proposal be revised and resubmitted. Similarly, the MITAF staff and a donor agreed not to move forward with deal consummation after Committee approval upon learning the MFI experienced a large reduction in outreach, which was plausibly related to the delayed action on the approved deal. Participant actions/interactions in the context of Agreement consummation affected capital volatility.

Linkages between capital volatility and organizational behavior reflected new properties when viewed through the lens of 2006 deals. Examining deals from 2006 demonstrated the importance of intervening conditions, such as program evaluation. Understanding the new bureaucracy is improved when observing the linkage of program evaluation as an intervening condition with efficiency, effectiveness, and reduced volatility.

MIDTERM EVALUATION: AN EMPIRICAL PERFORMANCE RECORD

Whereas 2008 and 2009 primarily served observing linkages and interactions in the context of Agreement consummation, 2006 was to observe process differences when a program evaluation was introduced into operations. The evaluation was designed to be formative, rather than summative. Its focus as a performance enhancement tool notwithstanding, it was a record of performance and an accountability mechanism.

DEALS, DISBURSEMENTS, AND DEVELOPMENT OF BUREAUCRATIC CAPACITY

When I viewed the work surrounding and during the midterm evaluation important linkages emerged. The draft Terms of Reference were likely circulated to stakeholders in approximately March 2006, the time of the first IC meeting. An official document records the evaluation began with phone calls to stakeholders on September 6 and on-site examination was conducted September 18–30. Evaluation results were provided in an Aide Memoire to MITAF and other stakeholders in a meeting after the mission ended September 30, 2006. Activity leading up to March 2006 through and shortly after September 30, 2006, demonstrate the midterm evaluation as an intervening condition the affected capital volatility.

Investment Committee behavior demonstrated a keen awareness of the imminence of the midterm evaluation. Table 6.1 provides details on deals and disbursements. The twenty deals approved in 2006 were more than in 2004, 2005, and any other year, except for 2008 (21). It tied with 2005 as the year with those most MFIs approved for deals (9, 2008 had ten deals).

Table 6.1 Deals Receiving Disbursements by Timing of Disbursement (Months): Amount and Percent of Total Amount

Year of Deals	*Total Number: -Deals -MFIs*	*Total Amount*	*< 6*	*7–12*	*13–24*	*> 24*
2004	6	979,850	614,850	139,500	37,000	188,500
	5		62.7%	14.2%	3.8%	19.2%
2005	11	2,264,000	256,170	225,830	1,432,000	350,000
	9[1 2]		11.3%	10.0%	63.3%	15.5%
2006	20	1,750,133	669,038	363,635	317,460	400,000
	9[2]		38.2%	20.8%	18.1%	22.9%
2007	0	0	0	0	0	0
	0		0	0	0	0
2008	21	1,668,063	106,499	1,151,181	217,447	192,936
	10		6.4%	69.0%	13.0%	11.6%
2009	17[3]	2,773,811	879,557	307,900	1,436,354	150,000
	8		31.7%	11.1%	51.8%	5.4%

[1]One MFI received 64 percent of the total amount in one payment, 13 to 24 months from approving the deal.
[2]One MFI in this year did not receive U.S.$50,000 as of records prepared through April 2010.
[3]Two MFIs in this year received 53.5 percent of approved investments, 19.8 percent of the year's total approved investments were disbursed to these institutions within six months of approval, 9.3 percent was disbursed within 7 to 12 months.
From Bell, D. (2017). Evaluation Influence: The evaluation event and capital flow in international development. *Evaluation Review*, 41(6), p. 579.

Committee meetings and action of donors resulted a substantial number of deals for a substantial number of MFIs. The year of 2006 stands out from the other years:

- When a year had more deals, the total dollar amount of approved investments was less.
- When a year had a higher dollar amount of approved investments, the number of deals and/or number of MFIs was lower.
- When a year had a higher number of MFIs receiving approved investments, the number the total dollar amount of approved investments was less.

More importantly for this investigation, disbursements during the year for all deals to that point were almost 300 percent of that disbursed the prior year. Why? Where Agreement conditions satisfied?

Investments and disbursements are reported in table 6.1 (Bell, 2017). For instance, deals made in 2006 experience 38.2 percent ($669,038) of the approved amount ($1,750,133) paid-out within six months of approval and another 20.8 percent disbursed within a year of approval. In addition, as much as $1,432,000 of deals approved in 2005 (63.3 percent of $2,264,000) was disbursed in 2006. There is a clear connection between the mid-term evaluation and constrained capital volatility.

Data indicated that four of twelve deals received disbursement in 2006, including two being completely disbursed (invested). The data also show the remainder of the deals were completely disbursed by the end of 2007, with the exception of three large, rather complicated deals.[1] Of all years, the disbursements for 2006 and 2008 investment deals experienced the lowest capital volatility. Table 6.1 shows how a greater proportion of deals experienced quicker capital disbursements (within twelve months) in 2006 and 2008 compared to both 2005 and 2009.[2] In 2008 capital volatility was primarily related to fewer Agreement consummation constraints and disbursement conditions relaxed from industry standards, including the key role of one funding source (YES/UNDP). I attribute the 2006 experience primarily to self-interest associated with accountability in the MITAF mid-term evaluation.

The structure and processes of MITAF also reflect the effect of the evaluation. An early version of the *Investment Committee Policy and Procedures Manual* was dated July 2006. Not only did the Manual espouse tighter procedures and more explicit donor funding requirements, but empirical evidence of 2006 seemed intent on proving it. Early disbursements for the March deals began in August and September. The development of capacity through in improved processes and structure (Wignaraja, 2009) is linked to the evaluation, as reflected in the report issued months later. One of the findings of the mid-term evaluation was that "The procedures still in place for disbursing donor funds to partner lending institutions are unwieldy and contribute to unnecessary and disruptive delays in financing" (Duval & Bendu, 2006, p. 33).

The capital investment machine worked to demonstrate and create an empirical record that MITAF, as of 2006, was an improved, learning organization. October produced further refinements to the *Investment Committee Policy and Procedures Manual*, demonstrating official action taken to improve operations in a transparent, accountable manner. Also, investment disbursements continued in November and December for March deals. Unlike 2009, 2006 did not experience increased capital volatility due to the holiday (festive) season. The 2007 New Year continued this cycle with investment disbursements beginning for the November deals: February, March, May, and July. The midterm evaluation intervening condition accounted for substantial variation in the linkages between behavior and capital volatility.

OTHER EXPLANATIONS FOR THESE OBSERVATIONS?

Were the deals in 2006 more simply structured than in later years? If so, this could account for part of the observed activity (i.e., deals, disbursements, and development of bureaucratic capacity). This seems to not be the case as eight cross-connected deals were involved in the observed activity.[3] The three loan deals involved made 2006 less complicated; however, cross-connected grant deals, even the type in 2006 (i.e., pro-rata commitments, not linked by conditions), were still fraught with challenges of reaching agreement on conditions and obtaining all the signatures. The deals of 2006 were not substantially simpler than later years.

Were the MFIs performing better, such as in accordance with industry standards, in 2006 as compared to other years? Leading up to, and including 2006, economies around the world were still growing. This environment could have contributed to the MFIs satisfying disbursement conditions in the Agreements (i.e., performing according to industry standards) and account for the observed activity. Relatedly, it was plausible the MFIs' financial performance may have declined substantially beginning in 2007 due to the Great Recession. The midterm evaluation included a close examination of data. The resulting report (Duval & Bendu, 2006) includes important insights on the MFIs financial condition and performance,

> Rapid assessments carried out in 2004, immediately after project inception, showed that all of the NGO microcredit programs that were initially financed (ARC/Finance Salone, World Hope/Hope Micro, CEDA, ARD and CCF) had significant institutional weaknesses. In most cases, the programs themselves could not accurately measure basic performance ratios like operational self-sufficiency and PaR [past due loans] due to the lack of adequate systems and financial management capacity. (p. 25)

> MFI performance targets related to PaR have been included in the project grant agreements, and it is clear that most institutions have made considerable progress on improving the quality of their portfolios. Nevertheless, the current PaR within a number of the partner lending institutions is well above internationally recognized good practice, and jeopardizes their potential sustainability. Another indicator of portfolio quality is the loan loss ratio, which is also extremely high in several of the MFIs. In many cases, a significant portion of the PaR and loan losses can probably be traced to serious incidents of fraud within the institutions. (p. 15)

Data for June 30, 2009, reported MFIs approved for capital investments in 2006 had the highest possible ranking on financial condition and performance ratings (operating self-sustainability ratios above 100 percent indicating self-sustainability), except three. This indicates improvement, not deterioration, from 2006. Furthermore, all initially financed MFIs referred to in the evaluation had ratios over 100 percent. MFIs were not performing comparatively better in 2006.

Other possible explanations include the familiarity of donors with MFIs and constrained transaction costs from few donors involved. Familiarity is generally observed in MITAF when large investments are made in a few MFIs accompanied by timely disbursements. For example, familiarity likely explains part of the observed activity for 2004 and 2005 investments. The data on the number of MFIs, deals, and amount invested distinguishes 2006. Furthermore, constrained transaction cost in MITAF is likely experience when conditions for disbursements are easier to administer, such as experience in 2008 with the substantial involvement of YES/UNDP program. Transaction costs were not relatively lower in 2006 as evidenced in data such as the number of cross-connected deals, which involves increased transaction costs. The midterm evaluation is the most distinctive difference between 2006 and other years (Bell, 2017).

TIME IN MITAF

Fundamental to understanding different perspectives of volatility was MITAF's expressed intent about timeframes in both original design and formalized adaptations. Also, very important were words or deeds that were not official or formalized. These reflected organizational imperatives that strained collaboration and yet-to-be formalized commitments.

A brief review serves underscoring the importance and ubiquity of time considerations. It was explicitly clear as late as 2007, more than halfway through MITAF, that payment of the first capital disbursement (first tranche) was to occur one month after providing the MFI an approval letter. The MFI approval letter was to go out within one week of Committee. The donor capital was to be on-hand for MITAF within two weeks of Committee approval. Conditions were negotiated with the MFI and, when approved by the MFI, the Agreement incorporated these conditions were returned to MITAF within two weeks of approval. Implicitly, the donor signed the Agreement within two weeks of the MFI returning the Agreement. The implication was found in the fact that MITAF was the donor's designated agent in negotiations and donor capital was expected to be on-hand for disbursement within two weeks of Committee approval. The first tranche of capital was to be disbursed to the MFI within two weeks of Agreement consummation. To be clear, both premature and delayed disbursements could detract from capital value. However, in a country with a nascent MFI sector that is resource constrained, a program intent on "rapid development of the microfinance sector" strove to minimize extraneous delays in capital flow (UNCDF, 2004b, p. 6). Disbursements occurred differently than the formalized plan and official procedures constituted capital volatility.

John Tucker, a MITAF architect and coauthor of, *Microfinance Sector in Sierra Leone: An Assessment*, explained the big-picture connectivity of capital commitments, timing expectations, executive focus, and strategic action:

> During the Sierra Leone sector diagnostic, one of the issues we heard from the CEOs of the microfinance institutions, was that the CEOs were spending 50, 60% of their time going door to door to prospective funders to raise funds. They all liked the idea of an investment committee [IC] where they could make one application, and if their business plan was accepted, they would not have to reapply in future years, but rather, only focus on meeting their performance targets in their business plan that were mirrored in the agreement with the IC. If they met minimum performance standards, their annual tranche of funding would be released. So, this helped streamline a lot of the transaction costs of mobilizing funding for them. It was one stop funding for them. (Tucker, 2011)

Time in MITAF was not viewed as a flexible framework to guide action. Time allocation was important and a very serious matter. Streamlining and reliability of commitments were important. Remember, MITAF was developed with a sense of urgency and a driving imperative for immediate change.

A COLLABORATIVE OF DIVERSE ORGANIZATIONS: APEX, MFIS, DONORS

As reflected in Tucker's remarks, from the time of Agreement consummation all participants were in their positions ostensibly avoiding the forbidden yet doing what was required or permitted by their MITAF participation. MFIs were serving their clients, working strategically to accomplish goals to further their mission, while simultaneously abiding by their Agreement commitments. Tucker speaks of MFI CEOs focusing on business plans rather than raising funds. The Agreement sets forth a teleological ethical framework for MFIs to decide on resource deployment. "Funds provided pursuant to this Agreement shall be used to achieve these results/milestones. The Recipient Institution shall be free to reallocate resources as needed in order to produce the expected results" (Agreement Template). In other words, the MFI was permitted to employ MITAF invested resources as deemed appropriate to achieve agreed to results.

The MITAF staff worked to realize the same results. Different techniques and technologies were employed to build MFI capacity, provide capital in accordance with deals' conditions, and monitor the MFIs for achievement and targeted assistance. Donors, as Investment Committee members, met at least twice a year to oversee the project, including related between meeting duties typical of such governance responsibilities. Also, as capital investors, they monitored MFI reports in their investment portfolios. How each participant perceived the other's position, and the responsibilities of others in light of respective responsibilities, was often fundamental to the variableness of behavior and capital flow.

Environment affects participant perception. The 2009 annual report of the UK Department for International Development (2009) called to mind that Sierra Leone was in the ten-year period in a postconflict state when a peaceful environment is fragile and conflict could reignite,

> Future conflict remains a real risk unless economic growth continues and people's quality of life improves. Poverty remains wide-spread and health indicators are very poor.
>
> Amongst the factors causing persistent fragility are: the inability by the Government of Sierra Leone to deliver basic health and education services in rural areas; the threat to economic stability caused by diminishing revenues due to the global downturn; weak accountability to citizens by government and public institutions and lack of employment opportunities for the youth. (p. 156)

Behavior and capital flows were affected by achieving results/milestones, such as outreach in rural areas, and MITAF participants' perceptions of actions/interactions in the MITAF case. Capital flow to MFIs was considered vital to support economic growth, improve living standards, and provide economic stability by accountably collaborating to produce effective, efficient, poverty-reducing outcomes in a sustainable fashion.

MFI perceptions of MITAF staff and donors were different and complex. Perceptions were more than an individual opinion, but a strategic assessment of a business association shaped and evolved by factors such as history, information access, representations, and experience.

MFIs worked to advance their mission while striving simultaneously to satisfy conditions for the release of capital. This capital was needed to secure technical assistance, equipment, operating capital, and loan capital. While advancing their mission, MFIs continually assessed the apex and donor in this new partnership. Below are expressions from four MFIs. These different perspectives, provided in their own words, were important to sensing how MFIs viewed their partners in serving the people of their nation:

> You see that the processes of transmitting grants to these MFIs through MITAF is very slow. Ok? So, our institution here as a case study is very slow. Because MITAF do peg their grant on the portfolio performance. That is the PaR [past-due loans]. That you can only have access to this grant if your PaR is below 5%.

O.k. And most of these MFIs operate, cannot meet that target because we have the behavior of our people here towards loans is not good so we cannot get that 5% PaR as MITAF required. (M0410, "personal communication," July 20, 2010)

So in our cases we are purely relying on MITAF to actually push our business plan forward, to ensure that we are, because taking into our consideration our own mission, we are there to target the vulnerable, actual poor. (M0305, "personal communication," July 16, 2010)

On the one hand, MFIs believed the MITAF project did not fully appreciate the borrower's credit culture, the need to "reshift people's perception from charity to self-reliance" (UNCDF, 2004b, p. 4). On the other hand, MFIs viewed MITAF as a vital partner in implementing the business plan.

They look at your board, they look at your governance. They look at your operations, they look at management. So, basically you have to have a board, you have to have this, you have to have this. You know, most things which come over time. I mean for men like you, I always tell people, the high mortality rates of institutions in the south, we have the high mortality of NGOs and MFIs, they are here today, and gone tomorrow. And to sustain them and make them not to die, sometimes requires not doing certain things. Let me emphasize. It requires delaying on certain actions and sometimes it requires fast-tracking on certain items to protect it because they are very vulnerable. . . . Everyday people start new ones, new ones, new ones. . . . There is always some confusion, people destroying each other, there's envy, jealousy, and all that. It creates so much bad blood that these institutions will die. So, managing them is not as straightforward as where you have all the parameters of legality and all that. [MITAF leadership] wanted everything to be put in place or not to be put in place all in a very simple logical framework. That was where I personally had difficulties in appreciating the MITAF approach. (M0101, "personal communication," July 14, 2010)

The only unfortunate thing is since my being here and three years as manager I have not, not received a cent from MITAF but the accountant and some ministry officials were here during at the time . . . So, I don't know, they can help. (M0410, "personal communication," July 20, 2010)

The two MFIs above discussed timing as applied to different concerns: governance as it relates to capital disbursement conditions, and delays in capital disbursements.

But believe me, when we went through it [adding a branch office], and I said this was what [MITAF] deprived us of, the ability to learn, to know. You know.

> When people are given the opportunity to learn, to know, to test, the learning is stronger. Hmm? For example, they say your portfolio risk should not be x, you know . . . They say, you know, your loan has been approved but disbursements are delayed until you meet the targets. So they are targets that MITAF sets and usually PaR, portfolio risk is one of them, is one of the core targets . . . Now, so delays can come from the institution not meetings the targets that MITAF thinks the institution should meet, and delays can also come from the donor actually moving . . . the forms. The challenges, I would say is one, the donor's reluctance to put the money in one basket . . . it was also not totally under the control of MITAF if a donor has not sent money. I mean what can MITAF do? The money was not in pool of basket. A second challenge of course was the fact that MITAF itself, coming new to the country, did not understand the dynamics of how we, coming from an NGO background, transforming into a microfinance institution, so we are trapped in the transformation process. People measure us as if we are already high class MFIs and not transforming into MFIs. So that was also a challenge. (M0101, "personal communication," July 14, 2010)

> But if we have a direct contact with the donors, wherein they can see exactly where we are operating and the constraints we are going through, I believe things can move more faster. (M0305, "personal communication," July 16, 2010)

> My thinking is that the donors really don't spend much time looking at it. They depend a lot, rely heavily on MITAF and MITAF prepare like a summary, you know, they send it out and usually . . . and they make some recommendations. I believe that the donors take the recommendations from MITAF fairly seriously and, and they use those recommendations to base their decisions. (M0202, "personal communication," July 16, 2010).

The above responses indicate that MFIs believed MITAF participants viewed development differently. Information asymmetries existed, in the minds of MFIs, involving a powerful intermediary (apex) and impacted capital disbursement delays. MITAF using measurements more reflective of the sectors nascent stage, and donors more directly involved with MFIs were believed to result in decreased capital volatility.

> In terms of releasing monies, I think once the investment committee has approved there was a commitment by these donors to transfer the tranches approved. What was not forthcoming was the MITAF green light [staff]. Because even if they have approved, the green light to transfer has to come from MITAF [staff]. And that's where the leadership of MITAF, if the leadership is not, for lack of a word, sympathetic to the aspirations to this particular MFI, it can hold on to these or raise the issue that the conditions have not yet been met.

> The third challenge of course, was the fact that the very investment committee made of donors, central bank, MITAF [staff]. I mean all the bureaucracy of the investment committee itself was also a challenge. (M0101, "personal communication," July 14, 2011)

Above, MFI perceptions regarding the power of MITAF staff and subjectivity in disbursement decisions and collaborative bureaucracy were believed to be related to capital volatility.

These four institutions present a cross-section of different MFI views of MITAF staff and donors when discussing challenges and capital flow. Interviews are not intended to suggest or imply a lack of value or appreciation for MITAF staff and the donors. Rather, it presents, in their words, important perceptions involving action/interaction. The views range from advocate, disinterested party, and partner to gatekeeper and insensitive keeper of the purse.

These perceptions were important for a host of reasons, but in this study, chief among them was the type of cooperation and flexibility required to operate in high levels of complexity and interconnectivity. That is, the type of bureaucratic relationships and processes required in successful collaborative human development work. There are difficult challenges in maintaining a positive atmosphere important to living and working in a postconflict setting, especially when the "going door to door" process for accessing capital was substantially changed, maybe to an MFI's disadvantage. For instance, the main options for domestic MFI capital were now collaborating, ostensibly no longer directly accessible, and they agreed to invest capital in new international MFIs. New international MFI investment could have been part of strategy to bolster MFI sector leadership with successful MFIs based in African countries, such as Life above Poverty Organization of Nigeria. The internationally sponsored Sierra Leone MFIs had no experience, or baggage, from the Sierra Leone market. At the same time, a domestic MFI operating in Sierra Leone for years was required to wait because of having baggage from serving the local market. Maintaining a positive atmosphere could be difficult and complicated. There was little consolation later when one international MFI experienced back-breaking financial losses. Once the poster child for policies, procedures, and capacity building training, the international MFI ended up on the auction block. Nevertheless, it received the money and the domestic MFI was still waiting.

A positive atmosphere, including specific cooperation attributes and flexibility, was important to living and working with high levels of complexity and interconnectivity and was shaped in large part by trust. Trust, as in donors' trust of MFIs, and its importance to future capital investments, has been studied and supported empirically (Gutierrez-Nieto & Serrano-Cinca, 2010). What about MFIs trust of donors? Community stakeholder data was used to explicate linkages of capital volatility and MFI integrity and reliability. Above, data was used to illustrate an MFI's perception that donors encapsulate their interests. Karen Cook, Russell Hardin, and Margaret Levi (2005) discuss asymmetrical power by underscoring trust's value and suggesting methods to gain trust from less powerful participants. Their work draws on theoretical and empirical research that examined trust in creating and sustaining cooperation in numerous contexts. One of their key perspectives of trust is "one party to the relation believes the other party has incentive to act in his or her interest or to take his or her interest to heart" (p. 2). They explain it as believing the other party "encapsulates our interest" (p. 5). *This encapsulation of another's interest precisely responds to the question of characterizing power concentration as power asymmetry in the theory of resource dependency.* Actors who would mutually benefit from exchange and cooperation are often constrained by asymmetrical power. Structuring interactions to increase the cooperation level can improve performance indicator outcomes.

Records show many MFIs over the years did not consistently produce outcomes according to industry standards. Only a few reached the point of consistently achieving the PaR standard. Although several attained OSS and FSS toward MITAF's end, it was a constant battle for most MFIs. Outreach attained levels beyond expectations; meanwhile, the stress of competition was evident. Capital volatility was an ever-present nemesis. As reflected in one official document reporting on the first quarter of 2009, "outreach is at 87,417, 93% and the June 2009 target is 93,000. Meeting the target is contingent on prompt disbursement of approved funds by the donors to the MFIs, which has been delayed in the past and . . . this quarter" (MITAF Narrative Report-1st Quarter 2009). In the same document an insightful communication to the Committee from the Advisory Committee was included, chaired by the Bank of Sierra Leone. "The TSP will initiate renegotiation and release of approved funds to MFIs if conditions have not been fulfilled 100 percent" (MITAF Narrative Report-1st Quarter 2009). Capital volatility is connected to the value of outcomes. And the value of outcomes *is* the ultimate value of capital.

The views of the MITAF staff and donors are also important. To protect interviewee confidentially, the apex comments are not specifically identified. The comments and views of MITAF staff are sprinkled throughout. Also, MITAF staff interview data was analyzed by fragmentation and reassembling in the concept indicator model of grounded theory. With respect to their views, the best response was to provide an excerpt from the final evaluation about how the apex and its predicament was viewed, a reflection of its perception-guided behavior in a precarious position:

> While donors and MFIs alike appreciate the services that the TSP [MITAF staff] has provided in preparing investments (working with PLIs to develop

> reasonable requests, assessing the PLI capacity to use the funding effectively and presenting requests to the IC [Investment Committee]), there has always been a conflict of interest for the TSP on the ground. . . . Further, the TSP becomes both "judge and jury" in the untenable position of advising the institutions on their capacity-building strategies on the one hand while assessing their performance on the other. (Duval & Bendu, 2009, p. 9)

Donor views of MFIs, MITAF staff, each other, and Sierra Leone illustrated their operational philosophies and their approaches to development. For this investigation, philosophies and approaches translate to varying degrees into organizational behavior on matters relating to capital investment:

> Because at the same time we are having pressure on the other end, an MFI wants to know they are getting the money. They are waiting for it. And they've been waiting for some time now. And because it's based on the opportunities so if the funds do not come as fast as they expected then maybe they can just miss the opportunities. (M0306, "personal communication," July 22, 2010)

> You see the donors are there to support the MFI. The donors are there to ensure the MFI grows, they mature, they become sustainable. And if you deny a support, you're killing it. But again, you want to see a vibrant, institution that's going to grow wisely, you know efficiently if the funder provided to them. So all these things are taken into consideration so when the presentations are made like, you know, for funding by the TSP you look at some, they're weak, but you say look, they're, weak, ok, but what do we do? If we deny them they die. Sometime they operate in certain areas where other institutions are not.
>
> And you want to make sure they are in as much as possible, you cover a lot of areas. Especially inaccessible areas like rural areas where you don't have access to critical funds for small businesses to fight over it. So, you want to ensure that each institution survive and can provide its services. So, you say ok, it's not too strong, but if it can meet part of the criteria we will do this, you know. Ok, we will not outright deny them. So this is donors, they don't want to deny an institution unless it becomes extremely necessary. (D0104, "personal communication," July 15, 2010)

The above donors were cognizant of pressures MFIs experienced from community stakeholders and were pressured themselves by awareness that MFIs were capacity challenged and committed to reaching people in difficult to service parts of the country. The excerpts below reflect donors differed in their MFI focus, which expressed their development philosophies and strategies.

> And ok, in addition to that, yes, there is sometimes, we're facing conflict of personalities because it depends on who you represent. . . . The mitigating thing

> is that we actually don't necessarily fund the same thing. And we don't also necessarily fund the same institution. So, perhaps we can just sit there and see, as some people say, I can fund this. And you say ok, then go ahead. I am not funding that. So, but there will be an institution that you will be interested in and nobody's going to fund it. So, you say ok, I will take this one. That's how it goes. (D0306, "personal communication," July 22, 2010)

> If you represent [donor] that funds, let's say [amount] or [amount] of the total program, then of course, you might be in an uncomfortable position towards this [person] because, you know, he can talk louder than you if he wants. Yeah, that's what happens actually. It has happened. (D0306, "personal communication," July 14, 2010)

> That they wanted, this was their idea how to get their rural access going, community banks . . . And, you know, it was an agreement, that as a package what we had, we thought, you know, was a good group of institutions to help build a sector in Sierra Leone. Now, some of those community banks are still having trouble. A few of them may be viable, but we haven't gone beyond those four. (D0306, "personal communication," September 23, 2010)

> I would say yes, it's quite a favorable environment, that's why international [MFIs] like LAPO and BRAC entered the market. I think MITAF was instrumental and also contributed to the entry of these two big players . . . But of course there is still room for improvement. And my major concern is the absence of second tier regulations. That means that transforming into a deposit taking MFI is not that easy . . . and that, yes, for a country like Sierra Leone, being at the bottom of the human development index and having experienced an eleven year civil war, the microfinance sector is doing pretty well. (D0609, "personal communication," October 13, 2010)

Donor, MITAF staff, and government interactions involved strategies that, at times, were difficult to reconcile with industry standards.

> But, you know, a year from the initial approval, the investment committee would meet, the technical secretariat would say here's the progress. These are the institutions that have met their performance criteria, they're ready for the next tranche. These are the institutions that have not met them, but I think, you know, they understand the problem, they've got a good plan to fix it, by giving them funding, it will help them actually fix the problem. So we might do a waiver and even though they're missing some of their performance targets, do one more tranche of funding, and then keep a close eye on them. If they don't improve, it becomes more difficult. There may be some that are just suspended,

> that, in effect, they've missed their performance targets, the technical advisor think they understand the problem, they don't think they're taking it seriously, funding is not going to solve the problem. And actually what you need to do is just intensify technical assistance or write it off. You know. It's venture capital. You invest in seven institutions, two of them you're going to have to write off. (D0508, "personal communication," September 23, 2010)

> Not really [do donors visit MFIs for due diligence and monitoring]. Really, to be honest, actually, when they go for the investment committee, just get to town the day before and leave the day after. For the advisory committee, and the next day we meet, the investment committee, and ok, if you want to stay, if you are planning to stay then you can perhaps visit some, like we do usually. We can visit some MFIs. (D0306, "personal communication," July 22, 2010)

On the one hand, the MITAF collaboration was a powerful participant in affecting donor capital flow behavior, as indicated in excerpts above. On the other hand, donors utilized information sources other than MITAF to assess MFI performance.

> But in the, if [donor] takes up the contracting of one of the applicants, then we start also a direct dialogue with the, with the applicant so that is our direct source of information.
>
> And then, beyond that, we also have, well we have other programs in Sierra Leone as well. And my colleagues also work on other programs in Sierra Leone. So it's, the TSP is not the only source of information, but I must say that they are, they have proved to be a very valuable source of information. (D0407, "personal communication," September 16, 2010)

One donor suggested data and information be used to guide interactions with MFIs aimed at providing a nonmonetary recognition for achievement that assists with building a sense of ownership in MFIs:

> Where quarterly reporting is not only submitted, but should be posted in the next month . . . So, quarterly, normally, when you receive that, the technical service providers should go through the set of target and achievement, and normally discuss with the microfinance institution . . . And if, for all of them we should issue letters saying that thank you, you are on targets, or thank you, you really made progress because you you've done better than what was expected. And then if they are below targets, you need to discuss the way to overcome obstacles. Maybe they are obstacles beyond the microfinance institution's management's control. We don't know. (D03-06, "personal communication," July 21, 2010)

De facto denial was an empirical category that labeled behavior hesitant to deny an MFI proposal, but instead approved the loan with conditions that appeared unrealistic. The donor below spoke to the challenge of reconciling the pressure to support MFIs with the organizational imperative to achieve impact with investments:

> It's often hard to estimate how long it will take an MFI to fulfill certain conditions. So, one is the necessity of the fulfillment and two is the realization or materialization of, of the fulfillment. If it's sent, if it matches with reality, if it's reachable and if it's de facto, is it true that it took too long in many cases, MFIs to fulfill conditions, and in that case we should have kind of all set more appropriate conditions, more realistic conditions. Or we should simply have cancelled the loan or the grant agreement because if you need too long, in some cases, this could also mean that an MFI was not ready for receiving a considerable amount of money and was maybe not enthusiastic enough and not sufficiently well performing. (D0609, "personal communication," July 14, 2010)

The persistent nascent status of the microfinance sector in Sierra Leone was a constant factor in efforts to develop MFIs. Capacity and paradigms were an integral part of developing the sector. Perhaps these were as important as industry practices and institutional financial performance. One official MITAF document records this observation in early 2010. "Given the nascent stage of the sector in Sierra Leone, capacity building of these institutions can take longer than anticipated" (MITAF Narrative Report-1st Quarter 2010). The MFI below expressed this view of the development machine:

> I say look, I came to this industry really with no knowledge of microfinance, a conviction brought me to this industry. A conviction that there is something our people are too dependent on handouts. I've done handouts. So, as Sierra Leoneans working directly with these different directors, I saw look, this has no meaning. They are just playing the game based on the new director. A new director comes in, he has his own position. If he comes for schools, gardens, that you do gardens. If he comes for latrines, we build latrines.
>
> Nothing really happens. Oh, a new director comes, he likes latrines, everybody moves. Ahh, the new director, he likes education and he likes school gardens, we start to plant trees behind schools. [laughter] I got mad at these. I say look, it's high time we start to question some of these people. (M0101, "personal communication," July 14, 2010)

H. George Frederickson (2005) references Fred Riggs in echoing the sentiments of this MFI representative in describing the interaction of local cultures and development efforts:

> Riggs brilliantly describes premodern, post-colonial developing countries and compares them to modern counties. In doing so he, like Weber, keeps a particularly keen eye on bureaucracies . . . I rejected the escalator model of the new modernization literature . . . in which "traditional" societies were expected to respond to the fresh breezes of "modernity" by embracing changes that would, sooner or later, bring them into the new world of opportunity. . . . It struck me that most societies would adhere tenaciously to many of their most valued ancient traditions and cultural norms while simultaneously importing and accepting a facade of practices and patterns that would, hopefully, enable them to maintain their distinctive cultures while benefiting from the autonomy and material goods offered by the outside world. (28–30)

Actors more dependent on others, often the MFIs and MITAF staff, may choose not to be trustworthy in order to avoid being abused (exploited) by the more powerful party, typically donors (Cook et al., 2005). Nonprofit organization research shows that organizations affect "an illusion of compliance" with government contract provisions when the organizations deem provisions unreasonable (Froelich, 1999, p. 257). When MITAF, or the disbursement conditions, were deemed abusive by MFIs then a veneer of action-patterns and discourse were embraced by MFIs to maintain a measure of power and access to resources. Such behavior creates an information asymmetry between participants in the deal. Power asymmetry in relationships, characterized as resource dependent, may result in distrust when powerful actors do not make "credible commitments" (Cook et al., 2005, p. 54). Local cultures and development efforts reflected MFI resource dependency as they shaped the donor perception and alignment assessment (Jurik & Cowgill, 2005).

The donor below described the importance of developing local interest by referencing an expected end to international support. The reference is to the role of the Bank of Sierra Leone in MITAF deliberations regarding investment deals and resource allocation.

> They are like the eye of the government to look at what is happening, I mean, how is going to benefit our people and all of that, you know. So, I think that their role has been very relevant because in the advisory committee meetings, these proposals are normally presented, and it is the Bank of Sierra Leone who chairs the advisory committee meetings. Because, at times, you know . . . the conditions we have of these MFIs meeting the criterias, they have to meet before they can access funding . . . for some of the local MFIs, you know they might need some capacity building in some area and so I see it is very relevant because the Bank of Sierra Leone then comes up with these issues that look, I mean this is an international MFI. They have the capacity to meet these criterias, but we still have our national MFIs who will need to build their capacity. Because I mean

> the internationals might decide to leave one day, you know. (D0311, "personal communication," March 3, 2011)

The difference was not in the desirability of disbursement conditions based on industry standards, but of the capacity of domestic MFIs to achieve them. The importance of adequate capacity of MFIs to perform is not the difference, but perhaps perceptions of the needed and appropriate time and effort to build sufficient capacity in a postconflict fragile state low income country.

How can the described contexts, intervening condition, complexity, and interconnectedness be viewed to make sense of it all? Deeply embedded in voice and archival data is a lens through which diversity and variableness can be viewed with understanding and clarity. I propose that

- when viewing efforts to produce a public good in postconflict fragile state Sierra Leone,
- where efforts are embedded in the context of an informal economy best understood as possessing survival and criminality properties, and
- rules define efforts by explicating what is required, prohibited, and permitted, as well as how to enter and exit the effort,

that the Collaboration Bureaucratic Triad (CBT) is the lens that makes sense of behavior-volatility linkages in collaborative mechanisms. It is a new bureaucracy and it is set forth in the next chapter.

NOTES

1. Two cross-connected loan deals totaling $952,000 USD involved the Finance Salone transformation. The third loan deal for $350,000 USD had complexities involving several contributing sources. Official records indicate the Agreement was not consummated for two years after agreement was reached. In addition, official documents report the conditions for disbursement were not satisfied. Finally, corroborating interviews suggest the application of the conditions did not consider the minimum acceptable performance, but was administered based on 100 percent compliance.

2. Precise data could not be located on disbursements that occurred early; however, interview data provided sufficient evidence to substantiate that it occurred.

3. Five loan deals were involved in 2008 (25 percent of deals) and eight in 2009 (47 percent of deals). Eight cross-connected deals were involved in 2008 (20 percent of deals) and one in 2009.

Chapter 7

The New Bureaucracy Defined

Collaboration Bureaucratic Triad

> In terms of releasing monies, I think once the investment committee has approved there was a commitment by these donors to transfer the tranches approved. What was not forthcoming was the MITAF green light [staff]. Because even if they have approved, the green light to transfer has to come from MITAF [staff]. And that's where the leadership of MITAF, if the leadership is not, well, for lack of a word, sympathetic to the aspirations to this particular MFI, it can hold on to these or raise the issue that the conditions have not yet been met. The third challenge of course, was the fact that the very investment committee made of donors, central bank, MITAF [staff]. I mean that all the bureaucracy of the investment committee itself was also a challenge. (MD0101, "personal communication," July 14, 2010)

> So now, when that institution, go back to their organization and decide to transfer this money there where the problems sometime come from. Because for instance, getting money from each organization is different. You know, sometimes . . . UNDP, UNCDF . . . system can be very bureaucratic because you have to get it approved here, it have to go through their lines and then they have to send it to HQ [headquarters]. HQ has to approve it. It comes back. They take some time before they transfer it to the bank. So, these are all hitches. (D0104, "personal communication," July 15, 2010)

How do data help make sense of linkages between organizational action/interaction and volatility? What approaches do different actors suggest to reduce volatility? How do different participants explain differences in capital disbursements? Embedded in numerous transactions, descriptive statistics on institutional performance, and official processes of training and technological improvements was extensive evidence of the ongoing struggle of collaboration, organizational imperatives, and the dual goal of serving the poor and performing in a financially sustainable manner. This struggle represents the linkage between organizational behavior and capital flow volatility. *Value of capital is affected by linkages between organizational behavior and capital volatility. Capital flow volatility is determined by the interactions of three properties of bureaucracy: collaboration; accountability; and effectiveness, efficiency, and responsiveness (impact). Capital value is a function of the level of volatility and MFI condition at disbursement: Collaboration Bureaucratic Triad (CBT).*

In a word it is *bureaucracy*, but this is not your father's bureaucracy. New paradigms are needed to better understand relationships between organizational behavior and capital volatility, especially when collaborative mechanisms are used. CBT aims to contribute to a better understanding. CBT theory defines bureaucracy as: *structures and processes employing collaboration to accountably serve the public effectively, efficiently, and responsively.*

In this chapter, I discuss implications of findings and results by connecting CBT theory with what we know about collaborations and bureaucracy, as well as the investigation's data. This is accomplished by moving from the abstract to specific, and from what we know to data. First, I provide an overview of CBT as an explanatory lens. The interaction of CBT properties, and properties interacting with capital, is emphasized as activity that affects both capital flow and properties. Drawing on the natural sciences, basic atomic theory is used to illustrate comparable phenomena in the physical world. CBT properties have proclivities toward constraining or enabling disbursements that function like ions in the physical world. Second, the CBT overview is followed by a brief description of each property's attributes. Seven central, though not exhaustive, CBT hypotheses (statements of relationships) are also presented. These grounded theory statement of relationships, are useful in predicting behavior-volatility connections in capital investment deals. Third, bureaucracy in CBT is connected to what we know about bureaucracy (i.e., the "Fathers" and others), placing collaborative behavior and structures in the bureaucratic theory camp. The collaborative property is set forth as the special CBT bureaucratic attribute, largely shaped by Institutional Analysis and Development (IAD) framework environmental variables. Classical comparative scholars and others are referenced to demonstrate collaboration has always been a tenet of bureaucratic literature, but in CBT it moves to a more prominent position.

Fourth, I move from connecting what we know and CBT to connecting CBT to data in the investigation. That is, CBT is shown as a data-driven method of understanding bureaucracy in collaborations. CBT is demonstrated as emerging from the data of this behavior-volatility research.

The MITAF case is presented as an analytic specimen. Framed by IAD, the presentation discusses MITAF's shaping by environmental variables: MFI regulation, informal economy, and rules. Also, MITAF participants are set. The presentation serves as the backdrop for an ensuing discussion utilizing CBT to view data linkages between behavior and capital volatility. The theory's three defining properties are detailed in terms of their attributes and dimensions, drawing on evidence from the analysis. CBT is a policymaking tool for examining capital investment deals to understand linkages between capital volatility and organizational behavior.

The more linkages are understood, the better volatility constraining measures can be developed.

A NEW LENS: OVERVIEW OF COLLABORATION BUREAUCRATIC TRIAD THEORY

I developed a substantive theory explaining the linkages of organizational behavior and capital flow in MITAF using data, not applying theories in the literature to the data. Although existing theories explain the phenomena in part, no one theory or framework of theories was located that explicated the diverse variance found in the MITAF case. External factors, individual organizational imperatives, collaborative commitments, and the structure of MITAF as a project are all components often seen in providing public services; however, this combination in one project has been rather infrequent. In 2003, MITAF was formed as the first sector development approach project of UNCDF with UNDP and KfW. It was an ambitious, adventuresome undertaking given environmental factors, a nascent microfinance sector, and administration required by this collaborative structure (Momo, Costa, Letho, Manzi, & Rebakis, 2011). The complexity and interconnectedness observed in MITAF deals held the key to making sense of linkages between behavior and capital volatility. It was a new bureaucracy.

The explanatory power of *coalescing and colliding* (i.e., interacting) in CBT theory provides clarity to complexity and interconnectedness in a manner similar to how atomic theory taught in U.S. high schools clarified relationships of interacting matter (Learning, 1960; Scott & Davis, 2003; Simon, 1996; Strauss & Corbin, 1998). Remember that in Einstein's theory of Special Relativity (i.e., E = mc2), he predicted the amount of energy physical matter would be equated to if it could be converted to energy. All physical matter is comprised of various combinations of elements. Each element consists of many identical atoms. An atoms' structure is unique to each element. For example, gas is different from diamonds. The structure includes specific combinations of three elementary particles: electronically neutral *neutrons* and positively charged *protons*, which make up a nucleus, surrounded by the negatively charged *electrons*. Modern atomic theory utilizes quantum mechanics to explain how these atoms act/interact. Observing behavior-volatility linkages at the level of the smallest, undividable unit allows for observations not visible at lower levels of magnification.

Quantum mechanics is a particularly appropriate simile because, like the combination of coalescing and colliding found in the MITAF case, it provides explanations that seem to be irrational. These are not considered flaws of the theory, but how matter behaves when examined at a subatomic level. At this level, typical concepts involving energy and motion do not apply the same. For example, traditional concepts cannot explain superconductivity.[1] I contend the classical, historic concepts of bureaucracy do not apply when employing the bureaucracy found in the MITAF-type of collaboration.

In more basic terms, I juxtapose the linkages in this investigation with the linkages between a river and conglomerate rock utilizing atomic theory. Atoms represent the three properties of CBT; each property is a different atom. Consequently, CBT is more like a mixture (e.g., conglomerate rock) than a compound (e.g., crayon) as the CBT properties can operate distinctively. Like the atom's elementary particles—positive, negative, and neutral—there are tendencies in CBT properties relative to capital flow. Positive or negative proclivities toward capital disbursement were found in the accountability and EEI properties.[2] In other words, properties have tendencies to constrain or enable disbursements.

Numerous considerations—such as stakeholders' evaluation, particulars of the deal, circumstances related to a tranche's disbursement, and individual organization characteristics—factor into constraining tendencies embedded in a CBT property that attach to a particular disbursement. This is similar to positively charged atoms transferring from conglomerate rock into a river. Not only does the conglomerate rock change the flow of the river, but the river changes the conglomerate rock (i.e., positively charged atoms, ions, transfer from the rock into the water). The linkage between the rock and the river illustrates the linkage between behavior and capital flow in this investigation. Linkages that reflect constraining tendencies are visible in deals with MFIs possessing different strengths. For example, financial performance as an EEI attribute tends to enable deal disbursements involving a financially strong MFI, while accountability to government stakeholders tends to enable deal disbursements involving a community focused, financially weak MFI.

Complexity is added to deal disbursement tendencies in CBT properties when quantum mechanics theory is introduced. For instance, the irrationality of quantum mechanics may be found in CBT explanations about donors relaxing disbursement conditions. Donors accept lower MFI financial performance as a condition for disbursement and this can result in MFI improving financial performance[3] because the MFI employs disbursed capital to hire additional staff and improve outreach. Staff and outreach improve performance by increasing interest income from more loans, and control of loan defaults (PaR) through increased staff attention to constraining late payments. Relaxing financial performance disbursement conditions may be perceived as an irrational act in efforts to improve microfinance institution financial performance.

Understanding how behavior and capital volatility affect each other is aided by the three properties (defining components of CBT bureaucracy), even when actions seem unrelated.

CBT THEORY: THREE AUTONOMOUS CONNECTED PROPERTIES

From Committee approval of an MFI investment package numerous, diverse, and complex organizational actions/interactions occurred that were linked to capital flow. Beginning with written notice of approval provided to the MFI by MITAF staff, through and until the last tranche of capital was disbursed, there were complex interactions between organizational behavior and capital flow. Some behaviors assisted timely capital flow, some delayed capital flow. Others caused premature capital flow. The variance in time is volatility. *The linkages between organizational behavior and capital volatility are explained by bureaucracy expressed as three interconnecting properties: collaboration; accountability; and effectiveness, efficiency, and responsiveness/impact. CBT theory defines bureaucracy as: structures and processes employing collaboration to accountably serve the public effectively, efficiently, and responsively.*

Grasping this autonomous connected aspect (Coleman & Tangermann, 1999) is essential to understanding bureaucracy in CBT, and how properties function in CBT. Properties, like atomic elements, are not exclusive to a mechanism. Accountability is found in both market and organizational mechanisms. Furthermore, properties are not to be viewed as a dichotomous variable. Rather, CBT properties have a range of dimensions. Observing different properties of bureaucracy at different dimensions does not make the observed something different than bureaucracy, just a different expression.

CBT assists this observation by better enabling close examination. When examining matter at the quantum level—the smallest, undividable unit—observations are seen that are not visible with less magnification. Similarly, CBT theory examines behavior-volatility linkages at the most basic levels, which is argued to be the three CBT properties, and finds explanations overlooked or undetected at higher levels.

CBT PROPERTY ATTRIBUTES

The three properties of CBT are briefly described below. The attributes provided reflect variances on a spectrum.

- *Bureaucracy of Collaboration.* This property provides for, and challenges, group commitment and individual organizational restraint. It involves coordinating resources in the context of tensions between individual organizational imperatives and collaborative commitment. It also requires flexibility to accommodate wide variation in goals. Effective coordination of complexity is important. The art of compromise through balance of power is important. Getting a given task done by utilizing any combination of several processes without one single authority is a challenge. For a transaction-intense industry such as financial services, where clear lines of authority and consistency in process are norms, this flexibility, complexity, and balancing power is problematic. MFIs work together to develop sector capacity and control losses. The MITAF staff works with donors, MFIs, Bank of Sierra Leone, and other resource providers, including consultants, to support Investment Committee activity and develop the sector on three levels: micro, meso, and macro. Donors make investment disbursement decisions by working together to comply with collaborative commitments, while remaining true to their respective organizational missions.
- *Bureaucracy of Accountability.* The attributes of serving with, and resisting, managerial oversight, governance, transparency, and various stakeholders constitute the accountability property. It often involves both top-down pressure and bottom-up pressure from various stakeholders. For example, disbursements to MFIs are tied to satisfying conditions, which involve pressure from MITAF to improve financial performance while communities pressure MFIs for deeper, broader access to financial resources. As goals vary so too do the results. In the process, accountability becomes less clear.
- *Bureaucracy of Effectiveness, Efficiency, and Impact.* Those features designed to produce quality outcomes at the least cost are challenged by forces pursing greater equality and broader, deeper access to financial services. Pursuing effectiveness, efficiency, and responsiveness/impact by utilizing any one of several processes without one single authority is a challenge. In this collaborative setting of shifting prevailing coalitions, whoever sets the goals determines the measurement of performance (e.g., effectiveness, efficiency, and impact).

Bureaucracy, as defined by these three properties, interacts with capital flow, shaping and being shaped like three-element conglomerate rock in a river. MITAF project participants acted bureaucratically to create, and respond to, capital flow. This determined the amount of delay and condition of the MFI at disbursement. The value of capital is a function of the level of volatility and MFI condition at the time capital is disbursed. Capital volatility is determined by the interaction of three bureaucracy-defining properties.

There are not three different bureaucracies, but three properties of CBT bureaucracy.

The concept is similar to triadic chords in music theory where three distinct notes combine as the substance of functional harmony. The properties are not only separate and distinct but overlap in practice. Property relationships are illustrated in figure 7.1, which presents the CBT model.

Relationship overlap is portrayed where the hexagons occupy common space. The property hexagons are designed to be applied in three dimensions: *x and y axes* portray pro/anti collaborative dimensions (*y*-axis), and alignment with individual imperatives (*x*-axis); individual relative layer indicates weight

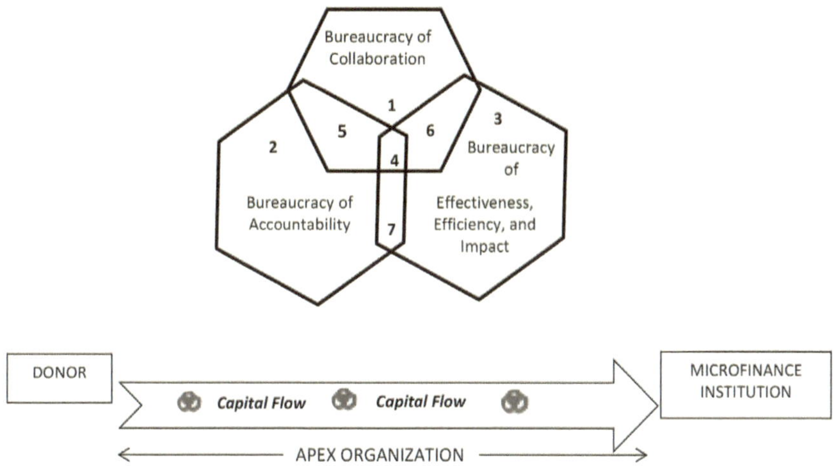

Bureaucracy Properties and Interactions

1. Bureaucracy of Collaboration within a participant organization and within MITAF.
2. Bureaucracy of Accountability within a participant organization.
3. Bureaucracy of Effectiveness, Efficiency, and Impact within a participant organization.
4. Interaction of 1, 2, and 3 where resources are being organized and employed in a collaborative structure to perform effectively, efficiently, and achieve social goals while being accountable to stakeholders of the individual organization, participants in MITAF, and MITAF stakeholders. Accountability within MITAF Collaboration is 5 (without 3), and Effectiveness, Efficiency, and Impact within MITAF Collaboration is 6 (without 2).
7. Interaction of 2 and 3 is where an organization's own process of employing resources for effectiveness, efficiency, and responsiveness to the target population—all of which may be defined differently than MITAF—are engaged while being accountable to its stakeholders.

Figure 7.1 Linkages Theory—Collaboration Bureaucratic Triad.

(upper level more weight, lower level less weight), and overlap reflects alignment of properties relative to collaboration and individual organizational imperatives. The properties operate like collinear variables; their combined contribution is not merely derived by addition. This overlap reflects the complexity and duality of a number of behaviors and characteristics of capital flow. Moreover, the Bureaucracy of Collaboration is the only property where the MITAF project is represented. This property's absence from the interconnection of the other two reflects bureaucratic dimensions within, rather than between, participant organizations. In essence, it is behavior outside of MITAF with unique costs and benefits. Conversely, when one or more of the other properties interconnect with the Bureaucracy of Collaboration the collaborative interests are added to those of a participant organization. CBT theory acknowledges behavior outside the collaborative; however, such behavior's capital value effects are not postulated.

Bureaucracy, as defined by these three properties and as illustrated in figure 7.1, interacts with capital flow, shaping and being shaped like three-element conglomerate rock in a river.

River and rock properties, as explained earlier, grow and strike together to change not only the flow of the river, but the chemical composition of both the river and the rock. Similarly, MITAF participants acted bureaucratically to create capital and in response to it, thereby determining the amount of delay and MFI condition at disbursement.

CBT STATEMENT OF RELATIONSHIPS: HYPOTHESES

My approach to grounded theory used the triad of analytical operations to identify preliminary hypotheses that evolved in developing an integrated theory that connects actions to capital flow. For instance, theoretical memos were used to record observed concept linkages early in the deductive process. I provide a brief summary in this section to consolidate major relationships observed by utilizing numbering that corresponds to that in figure 7.1. This summary can be used with CBT theory's complete presentation herein to serve policymaking in different contexts. These hypotheses are central to CBT bureaucratic theory and relate to an evolving tradition that explains bureaucratic behavior in public organizations.

In CBT theory, capital flow and its volatility were operationalized as variability in disbursement timing of each tranche from the time a deal was approved by the Committee and as measured against the structure of the deal and MITAF espoused disbursement rules. Capital volatility is a by-product of behavior involving all participant organizations: donors, apex, and MFIs. Behavioral factors included developing and satisfying disbursement conditions (including MFI condition at disbursement); donor bureaucratic activity; participants' routine response to daily business events; and strategic, premeditated actions in response to perceived problems linked with volatility.

CBT is a lens to view these factors and their linkages to capital disbursement with its associated volatility. As such, it is a descriptive theory to inform making sense of relationships between behavior and volatility in order to better attack the problem. Moreover, the model can also be used to predict volatility in certain contexts. Major relationships forming CBT are provided below:

1) Collaborative participants agreeing on a tranche disbursement's disposition will account for observed capital volatility. This is without regard to external stakeholders' interests or their EEI definition and measurement, especially when different from the collaborative. However, linkages between capital volatility and organizational behavior vary in dimensions deal-by-deal/package-by-package.
2) Capital volatility of a deal is affected by participant organizations' internal accountability tactics and strategies, including competitive considerations; regardless to whether it is prior or pursuant to a request for disbursement by the collaborative.
3) Stewardship of mission and resources in a financial sustainability manner is required for sustained financial sector effectiveness, efficiency, and responsiveness to the target population (impact).
4) Where bureaucratic behavior and capital disbursement involves all three properties, linkages with volatility are clear and agreed upon. Participants—MFIs, apex, and donors—have found balance between their respective organizational interests and the collaborative. Power is balanced by participants making credible commitments.
5) An organization's collaborative commitment reflects the interest(s) of its most powerful stakeholder(s) at the time of capital disbursement; perhaps deal-by-deal/package-by- package.
6) An organization's collaborative commitment is affected in capital disbursement considerations by the degree they have power to influence the collaborative definitions and measures of effectiveness, efficiency, and impact to align with their own.
7) Capital volatility of a deal is affected by participant organizations' internal definitions and measures of EEI combined with reflecting the interest(s) of its most powerful stakeholder(s). This is without regard to alignment with collaborative definitions and measures.

These statements of relationships, though not comprehensive, represent central hypotheses of CBT and were observed during the investigation. For example, Hypothesis 1 suggests that when the apex, donors, and an international MFI agree, as participants in a deal, there will be clarity on the action to be taken. This clarity is not affected by the beliefs of other MFIs or the central bank.

According to Hypothesis 2, MFIs with key stakeholders valuing social outcomes over financial performance may show leniency to people in default. Moreover, MFIs with a mission of providing credit to marginalized people may accept more credit risk than deemed consistent with sustainable operations. The target population holds MFIs accountable by selecting to do business with MFIs that most align with their needs. As such, competition is considered an accountability mechanism for MFI customer stakeholders.

Competition as an accountability mechanism may be foreign to some public organization researchers; however, it is found in public organization and business research. Research discusses public organizations where "accountability to the market" is expressly used to explain how citizens choose between government alternatives, describing the alternatives as competing to be selected by citizens (Adler, 2003, 2006). Government interjurisdictional competition is described as an external "mechanism for accountability" (e.g., IAD external environment) where citizens can exercise Hirschman's choice of exit (Bardhan & Mookherjee, 2006). The accountability relationship between government and business is addressed in the literature. One researcher examined the regulator-business relationship, arguing that accountability is turned upside down as governments compete for foreign direct investment (FDI) from transnational corporations (TNC). Competition for TNC's FDI makes the government accountable to TNCs through the market for their FDI (Koenig-Archibugi, 2004).

Markets are a context external to MFI organizations functioning as capital delivery mechanisms for poor people (i.e., financial services sector). Competition is viewed by many in economics as a market structure with properties. From this perspective competition is a mechanism. It also answers the three key accountability questions: accountable for what, to whom, and how. Competition has been useful to customer stakeholders for holding businesses accountable for responsive practices by choosing to exit and select another provider.

MITAF explicitly included in its formation document the goal of donors working together by investing in deals to support the government coordinating "activities in the micro-finance sector in order to avoid duplication and over-subscription" (UNCDF, 2004b, p. 6). Competition was viewed as a device to aid this avoidance by MITAF controlling investment capital, which is evidenced in MITAF Narrative Reports. It aligns with the work of Coase and Simon explaining that organizations are preferred over markets for much economic activity (Coase, 1937; Simon, 1996). MITAF was a powerful actor in shaping the structure of MFI competition, including competition for donor investment capital.

Hypothesis 3 contains a controversial concept as an explanation of behavior-volatility linkages when viewing powerful actors in MITAF. Stewardship is the antithesis of the node self-interest that emerged in data fragmentation and re-aggregation. Some scholars view stewardship as a normative construct and, therefore, problematic as an explicator and predictor. However, the relationship between stewardship and high performance in organizations is found in organizational theory research. In a world of limited resources, effective, efficient, and responsive financial service provision to the poor necessitates that MFIs perform at high levels to operate sustainably. MITAF data underscore that stewardship is related to sustainability and volatility levels. The volatility proclivity of the EEI property, however, can vary by deal. For example, individual organizations that value effective service delivery and responsiveness to targeted populations over efficiency will possess proclivities toward disbursing to MFIs so inclined, notwithstanding weak OSS and FSS performance. On the other hand, proclivities will be the opposite where organizations value OSS and FSS performance over social outcomes.

Stewardship theory is central to the EEI property that is foundational to Hypothesis 3 because it focuses on participant alignment of beliefs regarding mission and performance. Research has found stewardship is based on behavior motivated by goal alignment, rather than self-interest (Davis, Schoorman, & Donaldson, 1997). Stewardship theory research relates identification with organizational mission. Sustainability in stewardship theory assumes collaboration with organizations embracing similar visions. Credible commitments and trust are integral to stewardship theory. Moreover, stewardship research explains behavior seeks achievement at the highest level of collective commitment, thus satisfying most of the group.

Stewardship theory has not been studied extensively beyond the seminal work of Davis and his colleagues (Davis et al., 1997; Van Slyke, 2005). This accounts in part for its limited use in explaining organizational behavior and related controversy. One frequently cited empirical study looked at questions related to New York government agency contracting with nonprofit organizations for service delivery and the applicability of agency theory and stewardship theory (Van Slyke, 2005). The theories were found to be complementing, not opposing. In addition, it was suggested that length of relationship was particularly important to government agencies embracing stewardship views while nonprofit executives normally approached the relationship from a stewardship posture.

Stewardship concepts were operationalized in the Global Leadership and Organizational Behavior Effectiveness Research program (GLOBE), which added to the body of leadership knowledge by focusing on cross-cultural interactions. GLOBE utilized a theory-driven approach to develop question items to assess leadership values and practices across nations (Hanges & Dickson, 2004). Factor analysis was used to develop six factors that describe universal patterns of leadership traits and behaviors. The six factors were based on twenty-one factors, or subscales, describing specific leadership traits and behaviors. Table 7.1 provides some of the terms respondents rated regarding their importance to outstanding leadership (GLOBE, 2006).

Concepts expressed in these terms are integral to stewardship theory and thought.

Hypothesis 4 represents the ideal from MITAF's perspective. All three properties have equal weight, are in alignment relative to the collaboration's perspective, and have balance between individual organizational imperatives and collaborative goals. However, this does not necessarily mean constrained volatility. For example, all participants may be in agreement on targets to disburse capital only to experience MFIs taking longer to achieve the target. When a tranche is expected to be released within fourteen days of deal consummation, or within one year of consummation, conditions agreed to by all participants may have changed. Environmental conditions at consummation may have been radically different from the environment at the time a determination was to be made regarding tranche release. At this later point, the alignment may no longer exist. For example, environmental changes may have contributed to lower than expected MFI outreach growth and OSS. The MFI may believe this necessitates a wavier and leniency to provide support during a difficult period, while the investor may contend accountability to stakeholders necessitates a more careful use of investment capital. The state of properties with equal weight, alignment, and balance constrains volatility when beliefs and actual performance are aligned.

The assertion of Hypothesis 5 concerns effects of powerful stakeholders including instances when they are indifferent. Deals with powerful stakeholders perceived as indifferent often spawn a collaborative commitment by the organization that can have low costs and high value. This value includes securing other benefits (e.g., progress on donor/apex disbursement quotas)

Table 7.1 Stewardship Concepts Contained in GLOBE Survey

Self-sacrificial	Foregoes self-interests and makes personal sacrifices in the interest of a goal or vision.
Collaborative	Works jointly with others.
Group-oriented	Concerned with the welfare of the group.
Loyalty	Encourages group loyalty even if individual goals suffer.
Consultative	Consults with others before making plans or taking action.
Effective bargainer	Is able to negotiate effectively, able to make transactions with others on favorable terms.

and support of other stakeholders. Organizational self-interest was at times a central driver with MITAF participants. Moreover, external evaluation of the collaborative project can affect the amount of capital and number of deals approved, as well as the volatility of capital flow pursuant to those deals. Cooperation was enhanced during the midterm evaluation.

External evaluation may be viewed as a single stakeholder, though many stakeholders use the work product. It is important to note MITAF seemed to respond to the approaching evaluation with behavior not directly addressing a specific performance measurement; MITAF entered deals and disbursed capital. Underlying performance measures is the understanding it's about the money.

Hypothesis 6 asserts that an organization's collaborative commitment is affected by its ability to influence the group. This may come as no surprise. However, it is noteworthy that greater variances between MITAF and a donor results in a higher likelihood of de facto denial deals. Disbursement conditions that are likely to take a long time for an MFI to satisfy are the chief characteristics of de facto denial type deals. Rather than be on the record as vetoing an MFI capital investment proposal, an MFI that significantly deviates from the Committee member's EEI definition may be subject to certain MITAF disbursement policies that, in effect, relegates the deal to denial status. That is, the MFI condition is so far from disbursement conditions that MITAF disbursement expectations will not be satisfied (e.g., first tranche within 14 days, annual disbursements). As such, it will officially appear as if the disbursement was delayed to the MFI because it failed to satisfy disbursement conditions. For resource-dependent MFIs, it is important to have a noncollaborative capital source (e.g., donor), such as an international organization partner/sponsor to which they are accountable.

CBT theory is expressed in relations that link key concepts found in the investigation data. There are numerous relationships accounted for in CBT, including the seven key hypotheses presented above. These seven hypotheses are not comprehensive or sufficient in themselves to apply CBT. However, they are helpful in understanding the nature of CBT concepts used to explain behavior-volatility linkages and develop approaches to constrain volatility.

NOTES

1. Superconductivity is the state of no electrical resistance in certain material below a certain temperature, without gradual reduction in resistance before reaching that temperature.

2. Like neutrons, the collaborative property is neutral in MITAF and defines the collaboration/cooperation feature (Learning, 1960; UNCDF, 2004b).

3. Remember that Operational Self-Sustainability (OSS) and Financial Self-Sustainable (FSS) are organizational performance measurements computed by dividing the total revenue by total cost, and total revenue divided by total adjusted cost (inflation + subsidized cost of funding + in-kind subsidies), respectively. PaR (portfolio-at-risk) is a loan portfolio payment default measure. It normally involves balances with payments over thirty days late.

Chapter 8

The New Bureaucracy in Practice

CBT Applied to Data

> [T]he model now developed from the data is populated with the people who were involved, and their actions are described. Capital investment deals were part of a multi-faceted strategy to improve access to financial services for the poor and were in a context shaped by certain environmental factors. The Bureaucracy of Collaboration attributes were the basis for the espoused goals in commercial-based investment decisions where the project donors had political agendas. They also conflicted with those goals . . . the overarching goal of poverty alleviation required project stakeholders (i.e., donors, the project entity, MFIs) to cooperate. At the same time, each organization's mission was the primary compass guiding its work. The project's effectiveness was directly related to its ability to coordinate the complexity of various interests while working collaboratively. The collaborative property of the new bureaucracy is the distinguishing aspect that presents an alternative way of viewing bureaucratic authority relationships in the project, the new bureaucracy. (Preface)

The MITAF case portrays how organizational actions/interactions pursuant to capital investment deals related to capital volatility. Capital investment deals were part of a multifaceted strategy to improve access to financial services for the poor and were in a context shaped by certain environmental factors. Capital disbursements pursuant to deals experienced volatility ranging from substantially according to plan and expectations to substantial variance. The case helps make sense of complexity and interconnectedness because, at times, they seemed inconsistent with producing capital flows that improved access to financial services. Here I view case data through the CBT lens to connect defining properties to the data. *Whereas before the data was examined to excavate CBT, here CBT is used to view and understand the data.*

THE CASE WITHIN ITS ENVIRONMENT: REGULATION, INFORMAL ECONOMY, RULES

Data supports the claim that government regulation shaped the context where organization action/interaction was linked to capital flow from donors to microfinance institutions (MFIs). This included government activity that created, empowered, and constrained MFI behavior by institution and the entire sector. Specifically, regulatory activity involved monitoring both MFI risk and management. This activity also included access to information about MFIs that was used to define and promote socially accepted behavior by MFIs.

Understanding how MFI regulation shaped the context where behavior was linked to capital flow also required making sense of its postconflict and fragile state properties. In Sierra Leone, over a decade of civil war depleted and demolished much of the resident intellectual capital and bureaucratic infrastructure. "Infrastructure has been destroyed, institutions have disintegrated, people have fled" (English & Stryker, 2006, p. iv). Intellectual capital and infrastructure is integral to monitoring and reporting on (i.e., regulating) a growing, changing, diverse, and expansive MFI sector. As such, the postconflict property is closely related to the fragile state property. Limited human capital, scarce financial and material resources, and competing national and international priorities can make a fragile-state regulatory force one key resignation, or a couple of extended illnesses away, from substantive curtailment (Duval & Bendu, 2009; Miamidian & Khalaf, 2009). The threat of renewed conflict is another factor that helps shape the context where action/interaction is linked to capital flow.

Of civil wars that reignite, a substantial number do so within ten years of achieving peace. Armed conflict constrains government regulatory effectiveness. Sierra Leone has the unenviable distinction of hosting the largest UN peacekeeping force in history (Momo et al., 2011). Collapsing back into violence has significant ramifications for not only regulatory effectiveness, but well beyond the 71,740 square kilometers of this tropic nation. The government and donors believed the path to productive engagement, prosperity, and long-term peace and stability was accessible, to a large extent, by making financial resources available to the population-at-large. For many, their life was in the informal economy and financial services met them there.

Understanding the informal economy and its role in shaping the context where organizational action/interaction was linked to capital flow is extremely important. The informal economy is all economic activity not subject to government regulation or taxation. Making sense of how the informal economy forms the action/interaction context requires comprehending its survival and criminality properties. People and organizations are motivated to survive. This survival is both literal and ontological. Ever present are opportunities and pressures to engage in illicit activities. Sierra Leone has a substantial informal economy. Both licit and illicit forces work continually to capture and exploit the informal economy.

The linkage between organizational action/interaction and capital flow occurs in a context formed and shaped by rules. Rules were conceived, negotiated, and agreed upon by stakeholders possessing various amounts of power. Their respective amount of power was a function of numerous decisions and actions over many decades. It was also a function of then present constraints, urgencies, and resources. Rules shaped the context by determining what was required, forbidden, and permitted, as well as entering and exiting the context. Power vested in stakeholders was employed in the use of rules. Ostrom contends that "rules are the tools . . . that fallible humans can use to try to change situations to achieve better outcomes" (Ostrom, 2005, p. 132). History's lessons are stored in modified rules as an imperfect heuristic in the hands of fallible people.

THE PARTICIPANTS IN THE CASE: MFIS, DONORS, APEX

The MITAF project was a context shaped by rules, espoused and working (theories-in-use) rules, where organizational actions/interactions were linked to capital flow. One group of MITAF participants were MFIs. Participating MFIs were seen as possessing the best potential to lead and serve as a model for the sector. They were selected by the MITAF Committee, as recommended by the apex through application of rules (criteria) for selection. MFIs were broadly defined and have various structures, histories, and organizational missions.

Another set of participants was the Investment Committee (Committee) comprised of four donors that pledged at least the specific minimum capital amount to the project. Similar to MFI, donors represented various structures, histories, and organizational missions. These four donors were among the leading investors in sub-Saharan Africa microfinance sectors, measured in terms of number of nations and amount of capital.

The final participant is the apex, or MITAF staff (technical service provider). The apex organization was the functional apparatus of MITAF. It was charged with achieving broad outcomes that at times conflicted. The MITAF project collaboration involved different types of organizations, based in different nations, from different perspectives, committed to a common mission with separate individual missions that, at times, were in conflict with the collaborative commitment.

PROPERTIES AND DIMENSIONS OF BUREAUCRACY

Bureaucracy serves as helpful monocles in making sense of the MITAF collaboration's complexities and interconnectedness. Bureaucracy, however, has special attributes in MITAF. As noted earlier, this is not your father's bureaucracy. They provided a bureaucracy best understood by the administrative mechanism being replaced. Similarly, bureaucracy in MITAF took on attributes for this project shaped by particular environmental factors. The uniqueness was primarily found in the broad reaching effects of collaboration. Collaborative attributes at times were the basis for, and conflicted with, espoused goals in commercial-based investment decisions where actors had political agendas. Fragmentation and reaggregation of text data were combined with capital disbursement data to determine property combinations and predominance. Moreover, observed linkages were viewed as data points for dimensions within each property. The logical connection between CBT properties is discussed in the following sections. The attributes of the properties are connected to data, thereby providing the underlying case evidence.

BUREAUCRACY OF COLLABORATION

The overarching goal of poverty alleviation required MITAF stakeholders to cooperate. Specifically, members of the Investment Committee, MITAF staff, and MFIs needed to commit to the MITAF mission of providing "sustainable access to financial services for poor and low- income people" (UNCDF, 2004b, p. 6). At the same time, each organization's mission was the primary compass guiding its work. MITAF's effectiveness was directly related to its ability to coordinate the complexity of various interests while working collaboratively (For additional information on this aspect see Barnard, 1938; Gazley, 2010; Kearns, 2000; Kettl, 2007). Central to this coordination was balance of power. The collaborative property of CBT is the theory's distinguishing aspect that presents an alternative way of viewing bureaucratic authority relationships.

Compromise was important to balance power within MITAF. Within the Committee, compromise was important to developing disbursement conditions, notwithstanding policy set forth in various official documents. Compromise was important during interactions between Committee and MITAF staff, and apex maintenance of a "harmonious relationship" with the government and donors. This relationship qualifier was not explicitly contained in the UN Programme Support Document, but an implicit measure within MITAF, the government, donors, and other stakeholders (UNCDF, 2004b).

Compromise was important during interactions between MFI and MITAF staff, as well as between MFIs and donors (e.g., negotiation of loan performance based agreement conditions). Often compromise called upon one, or all parties, to both grant concessions and be confrontational.

Efficient, expeditious development of the Sierra Leone microfinance sector, and effective investment of public capital were explicit outcome goals strongly related to donor coordination. Donor coordination was deemed necessary to "guarantee" these outcomes (UNCDF, 2004b, p. 6). Technically and officially, MITAF was governed by UNDP rules and procedures. Practically, the Committee not only worked to coordinate donor investment in Sierra Leone and evaluate investment proposals but functioned as a governance mechanism. For example, the Committee would regularly have the MITAF staff give account of activities and provide direction under the broad authority of donor coordination. Yet the awareness that many actions may not have been official, and the practical reality that there was not an UNDP authority giving management direction to the project, represented a challenge for effective, efficient, impacting task execution. The dimensions of coordination ranged from broad donor activities in the sector to specific MITAF program direction, as in coordinating activities in the microfinance sector on the ground in Sierra Leone.

MITAF collaborative partners working to coordinate activities explicitly included "Government, Donors, Private Sector (Investors, Commercial Banks, Rating Agencies), MFIs" (UNCDF, 2004b, p. 12). The collaborators in MITAF agreed, by virtue of deciding to partner, to perform in line with, and optimally coordinate to advance, the government's microfinance policy (UNCDF, 2004b). Despite this, mutual agreement is subject to numerous interpretations. For example, MFIs "largely free from government and political interference" may be understood differently by various partners (UNCDF, 2004b, p. 22). This reference to partners agreeing to perform in line with the government microfinance policy illustrates the centrality of power in defining performance. Consider how government advocacy for domestic MFIs in Committee disbursement deliberations was deemed by some participants as unwanted political interference and by others as an important representative voice:

> Respondent: Yeah. It's true that the advisory committee, under MITAF, had a veto right which, in my view, and also in the view of [two other Committee members], after discussions, is not consistent of the idea what an advisory committee should do . . . Because the advisory committee is a political forum and we do, what we call sector dialogue within advisory committee forum and talk about the overall development of the microfinance sector and relate issues, but there are people from the government and from the Bank of Sierra Leone sitting

in the advisory committee in MITAF, which should not know any details about the submitted investments by individual MFIs. (D0609, "personal communication," October 13, 2011)

Below is a perspective of government involvement in MFI submitted investment opportunities, which seems to imply there are dimensions where involvement is not interference:

Investigator: When you run into that type of dynamic at the board meeting [strong influence over the direction of a meeting by a committee member], what's your response to that? How do you guide the meeting when that kind of activity is going on?
Respondent 2: I think there is also now central bank on the other side.
Respondent: Yes, central bank.
Respondent 2: Central bank tries to harmonize that because they try to balance when they see there is a lot of swaying this way they will try to put it in the middle, that's what I've seen at least. And you find that in most cases they are also pro-local institutions so that's where the balance comes in. (M-0303/04, "personal communication," July 20, 2010)

The donor below also refers to the central bank[1] as making a positive contribution to the meeting:

> The criterias they have to meet before they can access funding . . . for some of the local MFIs, you know they might need some capacity building in some area and so I see it is very relevant because the Bank of Sierra Leone then comes up with these issues that look, I mean this is an international MFI. They have the capacity to meet these criterias, but we still have our national MFIs who will need to build their capacity. (D0311, "personal communication," March 3, 2011)

More than the specific performance definition, who determines performance definition and measure is a central determinant of success. In MITAF, controlling power ranged from gridlock in the early years to in the final couple of years focusing on benefits from each partner's strengths and employing resources (including staff selection) appropriate for MITAF. One donor described Committee learning as reflecting expressions of distinctiveness and variableness (dimensions):

> [J]oint cooperation of six years and continuous meetings every six months in Sierra Leone, physical meetings, I think we learned to understand each other and to come to a consensus and to a joint vision of microfinance much better.

> . . . And of course, in the past, these different approaches or accentuations kind of clashed because we were not always of the same opinion, but I would say, that it is for the project and for the development of the microfinance sector in Sierra Leone that these different types of microfinance development approaches are complimentary to each other and are also enriching to each other and are conducive for the overall development in the microfinance sector. (D0609, "personal communication," October 13, 2011)

Capital flow was affected by collaborative behavior. This investigation discovered numerous examples. Empirically, MFIs not sharing information about borrowers (e.g., credit bureau) resulted in higher defaults and write-offs, which tended to cause disbursements to be later than expected in MFI business plans. This MFI behavior was related to competitive pressures, which were also visible in competition for staff. Such pressures illustrate both the limits of collaboration when providing services in a market context and dilatory effects of competition (Mollenkamp, 2011; Simon, 1996). In turn, disbursement conditions are not satisfied and capital is not disbursed. Within organization collaboration was illustrated in the reference to the donor with other programs in the nation that assisted with monitoring developments in client MFIs, which also had potential ramifications for capital disbursements. Donors experienced preference constraints by agreeing to use common performance indicators, reporting, and performance-based agreements, which simplified processes for MFIs that had multiple donors using different formats. Moreover, collaborative behavior, both within and between organizations, affected capital flow.

Interactions were often permitted and not required of participants. MITAF staff worked with MFIs to identify specific areas for targeted assistance and resulted in improved financial performance and outreach. MFIs were often not required to participate in MITAF trainings, and participation reflected a spirit of collaboration. This enabled MFIs to satisfy disbursement conditions and reduce the waiting time for capital investment. Also, MITAF staff negotiated disbursement condition waivers with donors that reduced volatility for MFIs that demonstrated improved performance but had not achieved industry standards. Similarly, donors negotiated directly with MFIs for disbursement conditions more lenient than MITAF policy. The result was disbursed capital with less volatility. Policies and Agreement provisions required first tranches to be disbursed within fourteen days of Agreement consummation and implicitly called for disbursement conditions compatible with the nascent MFI sector in Sierra Leone. Bureaucracy of collaboration is a property that provides insight into how collaboration is linked with capital volatility.

BUREAUCRACY OF ACCOUNTABILITY

The central determinant of success in Bureaucracy of Collaboration is also at the heart of key questions involving accountability: Accountable for what? Accountable to whom? Accountable how? (Slim, 2002). Answers to these questions, all related to power positions, determined what accountability meant in MITAF. Dimensions of accountability in almost any setting can range from laissez-faire to micro-managing. I found MITAF to be no different. However, making sense of accountability involves considering how various factors and dimensions applied to participants. MITAF partners' power relative to one another varied according to the measurement and mechanism assessing accountability. Accountability to commitments is central to creating the interdependence needed in collaborations. Making sense of accountability is aided by using three factors: effectiveness, reliability, and legitimacy.

In my article (2010) discussing accountability networks, literature on accountability mechanisms for nongovernmental organizations is used to develop a comprehensive construct helpful in viewing accountability in MITAF. As pointed out in this construct, core competencies and information enhances an organization's credibility and directly relate to *effective service deployment*. *Reliability* can be viewed in governance terms, such as board composition, financial stewardship, leadership, policies and procedures, and others. *Legitimacy* factors include "transparency, mission-focused activities, connection to the community" (p. 43). Legitimacy, reliability, and effective service deployment provide a robust explanation of accountability when added to dimensions of measurement.

Dimensions of accountability are explicit and implicit. For instance, explicit standards are found in MFI disbursement conditions. Implicit standards are found in MFIs expecting donors to be moved to faster action as they better understand the constraints of providing financial services to a particular population. Participants in MITAF had broad constituencies that occasionally encountered conflicting goals. As a result, goal clarification efforts (e.g., negotiated accountability) reflect the implicit and ill-defined shifting characteristics of certain measurements (Kearns, 1996; Slim, 2002). These dimensions of accountability and the three factors of accountability combine to provide a comprehensive construct: "serving in accordance with the negotiated explicit and implicit standards for effectiveness, reliability, and legitimacy in order to benefit clients, volunteers, employees, contributors/donors, and the public" (Bell, 2010, p. 43).

The construct serves as an organizing mechanism in the Bureaucracy of Accountability to making sense of the connections between behavior and capital flow. For example, in 2006, the midterm evaluation was an intervening condition related to the expeditious consummation and disbursement of many capital investment deals. On the other hand, the final evaluation in 2009 did not result in equal effectiveness. All three factors in the construct, according to explicit dimensions of measurement, were going to find MITAF broadly coming short at the midterm evaluation. The evaluation's focus, however, gave room for the implicit measure of demonstrated learning as a response to cited short-comings: "The mid-term evaluation will be forward looking offering lessons learned and recommendations to improve programme performance or national policy during the remaining project period" (UNCDF, 2004b, p. 10). The expeditious capital investment activity during the midterm evaluation year and immediately following demonstrates that learning was taking place and evidenced in action before the report was released. The 2009 final evaluation, on the other hand, was focused on the changes needed to remedy the continued difficulties of MITAF. Owning the discovered ongoing difficulties served as evidence in support of a proposed new structure. The dimensions in the final evaluation had an implied greater weight on the proposed response (MITAF 2) than on the summative assessment of the project that ended.

Bureaucracy of Accountability and various dimensions were also evident within organizations, as opposed to between MITAF participants. The struggle of MITAF's staff (technical service provider) to track and account for capital disbursements was fraught with bureaucratic complexity between the technical service provider's main office in Mexico and a difficult tracking mechanism in Sierra Leone. UNDP's decentralized, locally responsive bureaucracy illustrated one dimension of accountability, while the UNCDF centralized multilevel review and approval process demonstrated another. In addition, MITAF and each donor demonstrated a distinctive ability to consummate deals and disburse capital during the year an accountability mechanism was administered (midterm evaluation). Within-donor organization dimensions are reflected in one donor's response:

Person: Up to which extent you can make decisions that binds [donor] and that's a problem we had. You know, you can decide. You can say ok, let's say for example, the [a different donor] has a rank of director in [the different donor]. [Different donor representative] can make decisions right away, which is approved by the [the different donor] management. Which is not the case for [donor] . . . say oh, ok, I really would fund this and this because we think that this relevant and it makes sense to fund this. Ok? But then, they go back [to donor higher authority] . . . will say oh, no, no, no, we don't want to fund this . . .

Investigator: And that sense of uncertainty impacts things.

Person: Impacts, not only impacts things, but impacts also the behavior. If you are sitting across from someone from [donors] who fully represents the institutions, and you're not, it doesn't feel like you can represent the institution,

> you feel, you hesitating. You see? (D0306, "personal communication," July 22, 2010)

Donor representative behavior was affected by their organization's accountability mechanisms that were perceived to constrain and provide authority. Given that Committee meetings discussed new investment opportunities and tranche disbursement decisions, these perceptions impacted capital volatility (e.g., hesitating).

Within organization dimensions also existed in MFIs. Reporting outreach and financial performance data was a type of explicit, effective resource deployment accountability. MFI tactical decisions were observed to be directly tied to outreach and financial performance requirements for capital disbursements. Similarly, MFIs:

- answering credibility and
- representation questions for people in their community when expected capital was not available could be considered a type of implicit legitimacy accountability. Overlapping accountability with collaboration and effectiveness, as well as viewing behavior as acts of accountability alone within the organization, helps make sense of the behavior and capital flow in MITAF.

EFFECTIVENESS, EFFICIENCY, AND IMPACT (EEI)

EEI focuses on results and achievement through good stewardship. Stewardship is a concept central to public organizations, such as governments and NGOs. It involves judiciously employing resources to serve the public interests (Block, 1996; Davis et al., 1997; Meagher et al., 2006; Zietlow, Hankin, & Seidner, 2007). The oft cited work of Peter Block (1996) places EEI squarely in the discussion of stewardship:

> Stewardship can be most simply defined as giving order to the dispersion of power (p. 18) . . . the spiritual meaning of stewardship: to honor what has been given to us, to use power with a sense of grace, and to pursue purposes that transcend short-term self-interest (p. 22) . . . Part of the meaning of stewardship is to hold in trust the well-being of some larger entity—our organization, our community, the earth itself. To hold something of value in trust calls for placing service ahead of control. (p. 41)

Actions were directed by effectiveness, efficiency, and impact (or responsiveness) expressed as goals and performance measurements. MITAF focused heavily on explicit performance indicators designed into the project. Participants were highly responsive to these measures, though not always with expected and desired behaviors. Evaluation practitioners acknowledge that some important aspects of program performance are not defined a priori (Blakewell, 2007). Tactics and strategies were developed to guide assigning responsibilities with the aim of achieving results. Consequently, the important question is who defines EEI more than what the measures are. The answer reveals relative power positions. Dimensions are considered normative, ranging from impersonal operational assessments to expressions framed by missions, and characterize the dual-bottom line tension between commercial performance and social mission.

Actions within organizations, including tactics and strategies, are an important aspect of this property. Earlier I provided examples of various participants' actions directly related to capital volatility. These examples were drawn from Agreement consummation, MFI operations, and donor disbursement processes. Additional examples of unintended and undesired behavior to effectuate EEI are in the data. According to MFIs, their tactics and strategies (behavior) were in response to the incentives of performance indicators incorporated in deals as conditions for capital disbursement. For instance, the MFI below had an improved financial self-sustainability (FSS) but an extremely high caseload per credit officer, according to official documents,

> FSS [financial self-sustainability] improved to 93.03% from 84.71% last quarter and OSS [operational self-sustainability] is 106.15%, increasing from 103.27% last quarter. The increase in FSS is a result of fewer adjustments for TA [technical assistance] as [the MFI] received no TA from MITAF this quarter. The high PaR30 is attributed to the high case load per loan officer. (MITAF Narrative Report-1st Quarter 2010, p. 7)

Although MITAF staff attributes the improved financial performance to fewer TA adjustments, the managing director of this MFI discussed using the strategy of increasing caseloads to satisfy capital disbursement conditions. There were numerous examples of improved EEI due to MFI operational changes implemented through MITAF provided technical assistance. The MFI below, which received onsite technical assistance in 2008 and 2009, referred to the resulting procedures,

> Because MITAF, they have provided a lot of facilities for us. . . . We don't know what operational manner or financial manner but they recommended a RTA [resident technical assistant] to us who worked with us for almost a year. He put up all this assembly. (M0305, "personal communication," July 16, 2010)

The resulting organizational intelligence (enhanced performance) withstands tendencies toward increased capital volatility.

The definition and measure of EEI expresses and reflects power. In MITAF, and the broader Sierra Leone microfinance sector, the EEI property illustrates the weakness of the commercial-political dichotomy contained in the UN Programme Support Document. Power illuminates aspects of the property's dimensions when commercial based key performance indicators focused on market share and financial performance are juxtaposed to social indicators focused on impact to Sierra Leoneans' quality of life. Rules that defined what was required to be classified as effective, efficient, or impacting were legitimized based on stakeholder's perceptions regarding the relevance of distinctions and importance of measurements. The tensions found in demands for universal treatment while working in an environment requiring innovation and contextual adaptation involved judgments by those in power.

Judgments resulted in variations in the use of key performance indicators as conditions for capital disbursements and were presented in the prior chapter. Capital investment decisions and disbursements in 2006 and 2008 were analyzed utilizing performance criteria espoused and included in Agreements compared to actual performance. The different situational contexts of those deals (i.e., midterm evaluation and Agreement consummation) illustrated the power of external (transparent evaluation) and internal (a donor participant) forces affecting the linkages between behavior and capital flow. Use of key performance indicators were recognized as expressing EEI dimensions as self-interest (self over organization) shrouded as stewardship (organization over self) because of MITAF's structure:

> So, institutional development was kind of hindered by, or at the expense of . . . fulfilling the MITAF criteria. (D0609, "personal communication," October 13, 2011)

> I must say that these type of indicators [institutional disbursement conditions] were not very often proposed by the TSP [MITAF staff]. These were the type of things that we came up later, with making really the contract. (D0407, "personal communication," September 16, 2011)

> So, let's say the project document is drafted in 2003, by 2006, the total sector has changed, everything has changed. So, the TSP [MITAF staff] sticks with what was asked from him, within the document, he would miss a lot of what's going on. That's true. And it happens . . . But, that's why they have this midterm review. Ok? So, the midterm reviews should really, really help fine tune some of the outcomes. And then, so that we can say to the TSP [MITAF staff], Ok, now, here are the real outcomes you have to look at. But it's not sufficient, I think

> . . . They [donors] will ask him [TSP] and say, ok send us an annual report. And the annual report will say ok, we've done this. For outcome 1, this is what we have done. For outcome 2, this is what we have done. But for all the rest that are not specifically in the document, the project document, or even in the contract, it could be missed . . . But at the same time, the question is, do you think that as a TSP, as . . . a donor contractor, you could ask the consultant to come up with something that is not in the terms of reference [TOR], or . . . come up with different structuring of the TORs, in terms of referencing? That's, you know, difficult actually. (D03-06, "personal communication," July 22, 2010)

> This conflict of interest was exacerbated by the fact that the TSP's contract was performance-based and its compensation was contingent upon achieving project targets an inherent tension was created between encouraging PLIs [partner lending institutions-MFIs] to expand and helping them to build capacity. Further, ambitious project goals dictated that the TSP also identify and ensure capacity-building for numerous other local recipient institutions at meso and macro levels as well as administer the project overall. Fulfilling these multiple roles exceeds the capacity of one consulting firm and contributed to limited results at the meso and macro levels. (Duval & Bendu, 2009, pp. 9, 10)

Data reflects a strong awareness and belief that MFI institutional development was inadequate, thus threatening MFI sector sustainability, regardless of aggregate measures of outreach and financial performance suggesting success. Power to define EEI is a substantial consideration in researching behavior-volatility connections.

Linkages between behavior and capital flow volatility can positively impact social performance by *utilizing* bureaucracy, not for *replacing* social performance as the driver, but as a mechanism guided by the same mission (Hummel, 2008). Mission is about values. It is an expression of values as a statement involving dedicated time, talent, and treasure focused on a pursuit or end. Impact, or a responsive orientation, in human services initiatives is distrusting of effectiveness and efficiency due to the danger in focusing on achievement without meaning.

Profit without social purpose captures impact to masquerade as altruistic when, in fact, success is defined as sustainably operating as measured by commercially framed indicators, such as market share in the façade of outreach. This aspect of the property reflects dimensions embedded in sustainability-social performance ontological tensions.

The EEI dimensional epicenter focuses on sustainability. Sustainability, at the core, is about reliability and stability. It has been decided the people of Sierra Leone need reliable access to financial services. Commercial banking institutions are accessible to relatively few. Microfinance institutions have proven to be reliable and accessible to many people in developing nations throughout the world; however, this requires a certain level of capital and consistently operating with revenues exceeding expenses (i.e., profit). Although the magnitude of capital and profit is hotly debated, it is generally agreed by stakeholders from all persuasions throughout the world that both are required for microfinance to provide people reliable, stable access to financial services. The MITAF project aimed to develop financially sustainable MFIs.

However, it struggled in developing strategies to enhance institutional capacity while incorporating trends toward industry standards rather than strategies focused exclusively on MFIs *reaching* industry standard targets.

VIEWING MITAF DEALS THROUGH CBT

CBT theory provides a perspective of behavior-volatility relationships to make sense of observations and predicting behavior and volatility in certain contexts. Aggregation of deals in 2006 and 2008 are used in this section to apply the theory. In addition, unique outlier deals are used to demonstrate CBT's limits. There are three basic questions involved when applying the model to capital investment deals:

- What is the prevailing relative weight of CBT properties?
- What is the prevailing alignment of the properties relative to:
    - Commitment to collaboration compared to individual organization imperatives?
    - Alignment with individual organization imperatives (i.e., degree of responsiveness to organization stakeholders and targets of performance)?
- What are the proclivities toward capital flow in the deal?
    - Relevance and nature of stakeholders' interest.
    - Deal particulars (e.g., grant or loan; purpose of the investment-operating capital, technical assistance, loan capital; conditions for disbursement-industry standards, condition relative to MFI status).
    - Conditions related to a tranche's disbursement (e.g., pending external program evaluation, any target imperatives of funding source).
    - Individual organization characteristics (e.g., level of MFI dependence on MITAF, donor preference for type of MFI, length of relationships).
    - Considering these key factors, utilize a scale with "perform then payment" at one end and "payment then perform" at the other.

Remember, capital flow is the outcome of interactions in this collaboration. In general, think in terms of the collaborations outcome being examined.

In the following I demonstrate using the model, reflecting analysis presented earlier.

2006 DEALS: COLLABORATION, ACCOUNTABILITY, EEI

Close examination revealed 2006 deals were disbursed quickly: fifty-nine percent disbursed in both 2006 and 2007. Volatility was primarily related to self-interested behavior (the stewardship antithesis).

This disbursement observation is associated with accountability. The most outstanding difference between 2006 and other years was the MITAF mid-term evaluation, which is an accountability mechanism. The capital investment machine worked to demonstrate and create an empirical record that MITAF, as of 2006, was an improved, learning organization. Behavior in 2006 proved to be the touchstone illuminating linkages with capital volatility. CBT properties aligned to reflect a primary emphasis on collaboration and accountability, with less emphasis on EEI.

CBT properties in practice are separate and distinct, but also overlap. The overlap reflects the complexity and duality observed in interactions involving behavior and capital flow. The alignment of collaboration and accountability is reflected in their overlap in figure 8.1. The respective weight is viewed three dimensionally with accountability in the forefront, followed by collaboration, then EEI. EEI is slightly aligned with accountability-collaboration combination, and slightly with accountability without collaboration. The alignment is reflected by the hexagons relative placement whereas the dimension of each property is reflected by placement on the axes.

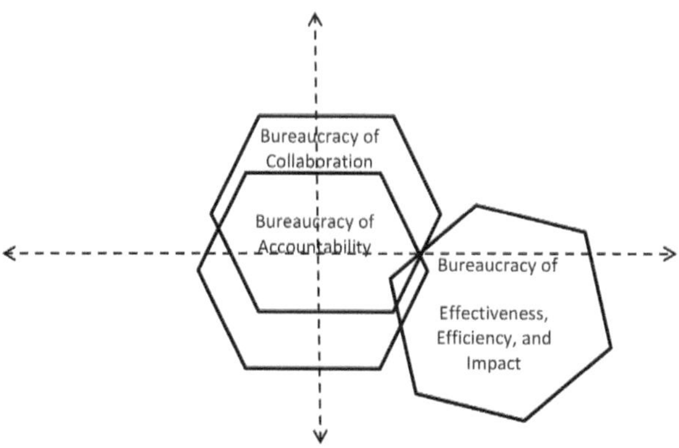

Figure 8.1 2006 Deals—Collaboration, Accountability, EEI.

The *x and y axes* are used to reflect the dimension of the property on a range. Placement on the *y-axis* (vertical) reflects location on the collaboration properties scale. High scales represent dimensions of activity aimed to relatively more align with MITAF, lower dimensions represent an aim relatively less aligned with MITAF. Placement on *x-axis* (horizontal) reflects location on the scale for accountability and EEI. These two properties can be observed independently of the MITAF collaborative (i.e., individual organizational activity). Left of the scale represents dimensions of activity aimed to relatively *more* align with individual imperatives, while dimensions on the right aims to represent relatively *less* responsiveness to individual organizational imperatives (e.g., considered not responsive to the organization's stakeholders). For all three properties, the center represents ideal alignment where the intension is MITAF and individual participant imperatives to be equally satisfied.

As described earlier, 2006 deals did not give substantial consideration to MFI performance considerations (e.g., MITAF espoused EEI). However, there was remarkable collaboration in consummating deals and disbursing capital. This was determined to primarily be driven by the MITAF midterm evaluation as an intervening condition. This explains observations of constrained volatility. Moreover, disbursement deliberations on deals in similar conditions (e.g., impending external evaluation, constrained disbursements to-date) with CBT properties configured similar to figure 8.1 will likely find a bureaucratic mechanism that constrains volatility. This can be stated with greater certainty provided the proclivity of the property is toward disbursement.

2008 UNDP/YES DEALS: EEI, ACCOUNTABILITY, COLLABORATION

Youth Employment Secretariat (YES), a UNDP program, provided capital used to invest in 50 percent of 2008 MFIs receiving Committee approval. YES capital was invested by UNDP as a MITAF Committee member. As explained earlier, deals involving YES capital were distinctive in part because there was no evidence of:

- Delay in Agreement consummation,
- Dispute on disbursement conditions,
- Post-Agreement consummation disbursement delay, or
- Premature disbursement criticism.

Capital volatility was constrained, and loan portfolio quality improved into 2010. Figure 8.2 presents the model assessing behavior-volatility linkages in 2008 YES deals.

YES deals reflected an emphasis on individual organizational imperatives, but not to the exclusion of collaborative commitment. The alignment of EEI and accountability is reflected in their overlap in figure 8.2. Collaboration also overlaps with EEI-accountability combination, and to some degree with EEI without accountability. There are, however, substantial areas of nonalignment. Viewed three-dimensionally, EEI and accountability are on the same level followed by collaboration at a deeper level. The relatively decreased emphasis on collaborative commitment is reflected in the property's relative level and relative small amount of hexagon overlap.

YES deals were distinct in the EEI property due to an apparent emphasis on program targets different from MITAF and actions taken to be accountable to YES program aims. The YES-MITAF memorandums of Agreement and Understanding were not obtained for this investigation. Nevertheless, evidence of their execution and observed capital flow and organizational behavior support the conclusion that each organization agreed to collaborate and accept some level of cost (e.g., MITAF accepted industry standards subordinate to YES social goals for disbursement decisions, YES accepting MITAF Committee process for selection of MFIs receiving investment). Development agencies and the Sierra Leone government considered incessant and ubiquitous unemployment among youth a serious threat to stability (UN-Sierra Leone, 2008). Weakness in youth empowerment and employment was considered the greatest peril to peace of several concerns identified. Official documents underscored the importance of urgency, "realizing immediate and quick impacts that will help bring visible and tangible peace dividends to the population" (UN-Sierra Leone, 2008, p. 2). The urgency imperative was addressed by several initiatives, including the Youth Employment Scheme (a.k.a., Youth Employment Secretariat, Youth Enterprise Development, and Empowerment Scheme). EEI for YES shared MITAF's espoused urgency

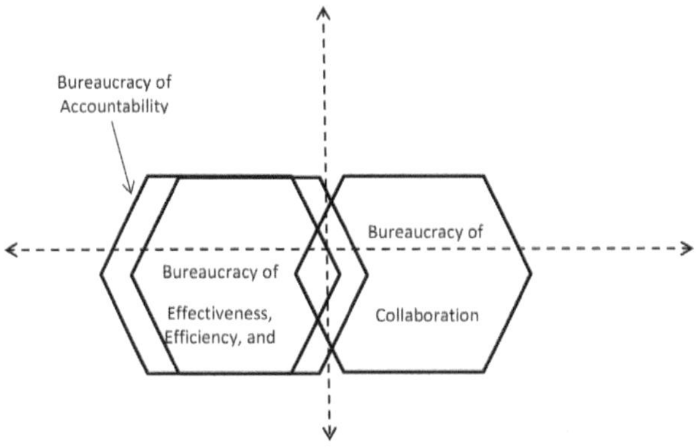

Figure 8.2 2008 UNDP/YES Deals—EEI, Accountability, Collaboration.

imperative; however, it also focused on a population segment (i.e., youth) and did not give considerable weight to the capital delivery mechanism's capacity to be self-sustainable.

YES was a three-year project created to immediately provide support to existing and new businesses owned by young people. It provided start-up capital, training, and other services to empower youth operating in both the formal and informal sectors. But, as discussed before, a central challenge in poverty alleviation efforts was an effective capital delivery mechanism. One such mechanism in Sierra Leone was microfinance institutions. However, it was recognized the microfinance sector was capacity challenged and also required an appropriate capital delivery mechanism. YES looked to MITAF as an effective capital delivery mechanism for MFIs.

United Nations-Sierra Leone utilized its UNDP membership on the MITAF Committee in a strategy to effectively and urgently disburse capital to unemployed young people interested in developing businesses. It seems MITAF, in turn, accommodated the YES initiative's definitions and measures of EEI while using MITAF's EEI definition and measures as subordinate criteria in making deals. More importantly to this investigation, it seems MITAF's EEI was also subordinate in capital disbursement decisions. This subordination is reflected in the model by the collaborative property at a lower depth level, overlapping less with the other two properties, lower position on the *y*-axis, and rightward positioning on the x-axis.

OUTLIER DEALS

The collaboration property is the only property where MITAF is represented. Capital disbursements not exhibiting this property reflect bureaucratic dimensions of organizational participation in the deal. That is, MITAF espoused rules had no effect. Participating organizations may share some of the same rules and reflect behavior that would have been observed if MITAF was involved. Such outlier behavior can be modeled with CBT theory and is reflected in figure 8.3. Activity outside the collaborative by collaborative-participating organizations is not reflected in the collaborative official records. That said, to the degree behavior was outside of MITAF, it had low to no associated costs and benefits. CBT theory acknowledges behavior outside the collaborative (Hypotheses 2, 3, 7); however, such behavior's capital value affects are not postulated.

There were deals consummated outside of MITAF that were attributed to it. This is reflected in figure 8.3 by the collaboration hexagon placed low, and to the far right. Each Committee member engaged in this activity, though it was rare. As mentioned earlier, there were capital investments made without prior

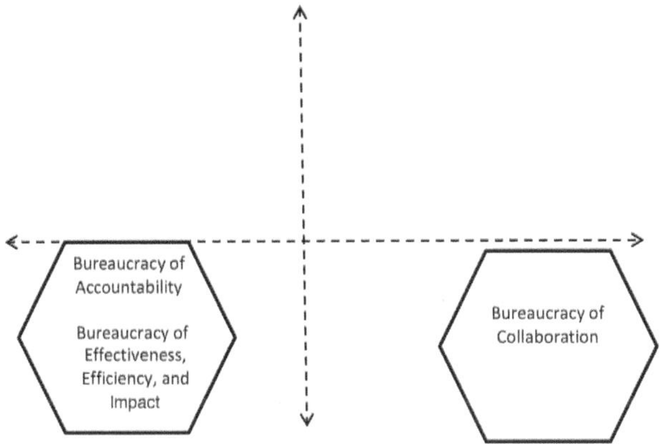

Figure 8.3 Outliers—Accountability, EEI, Collaboration.

Committee approval by a Committee member. Subsequently, the deals were added to the MITAF portfolio of commitments and data in official records. Data is insufficient to determine organization disbursement activity with a high level of confidence. For example, it is not clear what role the apex had in determining the MFI's satisfaction of disbursement conditions and request for disbursement of tranche(s). Official records seem to reflect one deal consummation in 60 days, at the latest. Also, records seem to reflect it was fully disbursed five months after consummation, at the latest. Data at consummation reported the MFI's loan defaults (i.e., PaR, portfolio-at-risk) was more than double industry standards; therefore, it did not conform to MITAF's financial performance standards. Later, PaR decreased approximately 20 percent during the following two quarters. Also, outreach went down during the quarter of consummation, but increased slightly the following quarter. Data available suggests this outside deal disbursed with low volatility to an MFI that did not perform at MITAF's EEI standards. The accountability and EEI hexagon overlap reflects perfect property alignment, but lack of collaboration overlap and placement low and far right indicates the deal was outside of MITAF. Once capital flow leaves the collaboration certain dynamics come into play. Some dynamics are outside the scope of focused analysis in this investigation. For example, capital flow viewed through CBT as substantially outside the collaboration may experience low volatility. However, CBT theory realizes there are devaluing effects of being outside the collaboration. Though devaluing effects other than volatility are outside this investigation, the MITAF collaboration attribute is associated with constraining transaction costs. Numerous transaction costs are increased outside the collaboration, such as learning and obtaining capital by MFIs. The value-preserving effects of low volatility of a deal outside of MITAF may be offset by transaction costs related to capital flow activity outside the collaboration.

These three examples illustrate how to apply the CBT model. It can be applied to aggregate deals, such as 2006 and 2007. The model can also be applied to individual deals, such as the outlier deals. Applying the model allows linkages to be viewed in a manner to examine effects and assists developing responses to certain behavior-volatility linkage configurations. In addition, the model can be used to configure *what-if* scenarios to aid program design.

I described accountability as involving effectiveness, reliability, and legitimacy measured by implicit and explicit standards. Accountability in MITAF ranged from within the collaborative to totally outside the collaborative. When it was within in some measure, volatility was constrained to varying degrees. In deals when collaborative accountability was given no weight, volatility was also constrained to varying degrees; however, transaction costs associated with noncollaborative behavior had capital devaluing effects. Similarly, deals where EEI was defined and measured within the collaborative experienced volatility to varying degrees. Also, deals that gave less weight to the collaborative experienced volatility to varying degrees. However, when the collaboration was given no weight or activity occurred outside the collaborative, there were capital devaluing effects.

Comprehensively, CBT was demonstrated to be grounded in data by applying the model to phenomena observed in MITAF. The property hexagons of the model were applied to observed behavior I detailed earlier. Capital flow experiencing varying degrees of volatility involving MFIs with varying conditions (e.g., outreach, financial performance, governance) were associated with the different hexagon patterns. Linkages between organizational behavior and capital volatility are explained by the CBT theory, which informed development of several policy recommendations. I set forth these policy recommendations in the next chapter.

NOTE

1. Originally a central bank representative chaired the Investment Committee. In 2008, the project document was amended to change the role to chairing a newly created Advisory Committee, with no direct participation during Investment Committee deliberations.

Chapter 9

Policy Implications

Recommendations and Future Research

> Its [bureaucracy] motives, its objects, its policy, its standards, must be bureaucratic. It would be difficult to point out any examples of impudent exclusiveness and arbitrariness on the part of officials doing service under a chief of department who really served the people, as all our chiefs of departments must be made to do . . . The ideal for us is a civil service cultured and self- sufficient enough to act with sense and vigor, and yet so intimately connected with the popular thought . . . as to find arbitrariness or class spirit quite out of the question. (Wilson, 1887, p. 217)

> [J]oint cooperation of six years and continuous meetings every six months in Sierra Leone, physical meetings, I think we learned to understand each other and to come to a consensus and to a joint vision of microfinance much better. . . . I would say, that it is for the project and for the development of the microfinance sector in Sierra Leone that these different types of microfinance development approaches are complimentary to each other and are also enriching to each other. (D0609, "personal communication," October 13, 2011)

What does MITAF teach that will inform bureaucratic organizational behavior and capital flow within collaborative arrangements? The biggest challenge in the collaborative effort, within and between organizational group types, was demonstrated clarity of a common perspective and the ability to rapidly locate the effort in a place of agreement such that outcome values were not diminished by capital volatility. Evolving perspectives on the properties and dimensions of key MITAF outcomes and assessment methods was particularly important. Where and how to move in adjusting various perspectives was central to initiating organizational actions and disbursing capital investments such that all were equally uncomfortable, but all agreed there was progress. It is a bureaucracy inclusive, not separate, of individual organizational identities.

I start this chapter by providing recommendations about how to affect organizational actions and capital disbursements. In other words, how to accountably employ collaborative processes in organization behavior and capital flow. Five strategic take-aways are provided from examining MITAF:

- Directly address exogenous variables, or environmental factors, to minimize delays in capital disbursements.
- Employ the combined skill sets of the team to expeditiously assess the situational context, detect and assess contextual changes, and maintain a calculated action orientation.
- Provide sufficient funding and marshal sufficient resources to collect data and employ the rigorous processes required to inform learning and make thoughtful, nuanced, strategic decisions as the program progresses.
- Account for the project's commitments; tracking money is only part of accounting.
- Entering collaboration makes transactions consummated one-on-one between donors and MFIs subject to additional commitments that must be accounted for.

The four strategic recommendations affecting public organization actions and capital disbursements are based on the premise that public policy administration is the actual expression of policy and it speaks to espoused theories' relevance in attacking societal problems.

Next, the chapter outlines a research agenda. Exploring accountability as effectiveness, reliability, and legitimacy to better understand MITAF participants' views and constructs for ranking the importance of various strategies can improve efforts to bridge communication and performance gaps. Moreover, examining how MITAF participants perceive how their views have changed in defining and measuring effectiveness, efficiency, and responsiveness can help explain and assess organizational learning related to constrained capital volatility. The agenda presented aims to tackle the complex organizational behavior associated with development in sub-Saharan Africa and postconflict areas.

ENVIRONMENTAL FACTORS AND CHANGE

One of my unanticipated findings is how various development programs in Sierra Leone underestimate the depletion and devastation caused by colonialism and the war. The human potential in Sierra Leone is remarkable;

however, the aggregate human talent was desperately low. In addition, the structure and resources needed to engage human capital is very often absent or remarkably inadequate. One Sierra Leone government agency concept paper prepared in early 2011 (not directly related to this research) requested assistance from civil society organizations by explaining that government staff was inadequate and unmotivated. Encouraging gains in MFI organizational intelligence can be stifled or completely reversed in short order without proper attention to environmental factors that shape collaborative human development projects.

The Institutional Analysis and Development framework I used to organize this presentation contends that outcomes from interactions can, over time, change environmental variables (Ostrom, 2005). The framework did not suggest the impact is as direct as environmental factors on the arena where organizations interact; only that as interactions continue to produce results, the factors shaping the interaction can change. My concern here is that outcomes are excessively relied on to change environmental factors (e.g., MFI regulation and informal economy) that shape the arena of interactions, such as a collaborative development project. *Exogenous variables, or environmental factors, must be directly addressed to minimize delays in capital disbursements.* Project outcomes, often reflected as investment deal disbursement conditions, can be severely constrained when market incentives and punishments operate unchecked in an imperfect market environment, and when market-regulating institutions are weak. This seems to be especially the case in a postconflict, fragile-state setting. It can take considerable time to observe substantial shaping of environmental factors by outcomes from organizational interactions; direct action is needed to shape environmental factors.

Meso and macro institutions are environmental-level factors that are vital to maintain and improve microlevel outcomes. MITAF had the right idea. *Mesolevel institutions, such as industry associations, credit exchange agencies, and support services like independent audit firms are important to developing a sustainable pro-poor financial sector in Sierra Leone.*

Unfortunately, MITAF was not able to completely achieve the galactically huge project mandate, which included mesolevel development. An important item for future exploration is how these environmental factors affect MFIs that have experienced a period of sustained growth and financial performance. Do MFIs continue the positive trend without development of mesolevel institutions? Does stagnation set in? Do MFIs experience decline? How is capital volatility affected? Similarly, what is observed when mesolevel institutions are present and vibrant?

Apex organizations are also vital mesolevel institutions. Mesolevel institutions that provide capital are especially germane. The Rules on capital flow that shaped MITAF are best understood in terms of organizational theories than market theories. Research reviewed suggested that Sierra Leone's underdeveloped markets and propoor financial sectors did not provide the capital the country urgently needed. Simon (1996) explains that economist suse externalities and uncertainty to explain the benefits of organizations over markets for a lot of economic activity. The more important reason, according to Simon, is actors provide additional effort to benefit the collaborative because they benefit more from collaborative learning than by incurring the cost of learning independently. Both capital investors and MFIs benefit in critical ways from mesolevel capital-providing institutions, thus minimizing factors that increase capital volatility.

Monitoring external factors closely is important to developing a propoor financial sector in a context like Sierra Leone. The metaphor of the frog in the water pot with the heat continually, gradually rising is *apropos* to maintaining focus on environmental factors. If external factors are not given careful, consistent attention the same factors that constrained the sector's development will inhibit its growth or worse.

LEADERSHIP AND TEAM SKILL-SETS

An important strategic take-away involves people. Each organization, group of organizations, and the project as a whole should invest considerable attention toward the people selected to be involved with projects (primarily and secondary),[1] especially at the outset. Although these strategic recommendations aim to inform the collaboration, the individual organizations must be strategic in team compilation also. The evidence showed team compilation made a difference in capital volatility. People must work to diligently understand the perspective of other players and find an initial place of agreement where action can, and does, take place; "Great vision without great people is irrelevant" (Collins, 2001, p. 42). System knowledge and expertise enable administrative tasks to be completed without delay and prevent bottlenecks due to carelessness and inattention to detail. The ability to ascertain and appreciate, within and between, organizational differences aids in minimizing behaviors that contribute to capital disbursement delays. *The multicultural team each organization brings to function within the collaboration will account for the variance experienced in behavior and capital volatility, within a context.*

The effect of leadership and team composition on behavior and capital flow was visible from the midterm evaluation, responses in interviews, and records of disbursement activity. The midterm evaluation suggested capital investment decisions did not reflect sufficient risk-taking in smaller MFIs. The evaluation and my interviews reflected the need for MFI capacity building, including training, procedures, policies, tools, and systems. Quick, targeted, measured capital investments were needed for training, operating capital, and on-site technical assistance (which could also serve as a monitoring function). The record reflects meaningful capacity enhancement in MFIs early on; however, they were deemed to still have substantial weaknesses (Duval & Bendu, 2006). Initial MFI trainings could have created more awareness and general knowledge diffusion than behavioral modification.

Trainings are also opportunities to gain insight into perspectives by all parties. Regional and on-site trainings could have assisted in encouraging participation. MITAF on-the-ground staff members varied in attributes to assess and monitor the environment with the intent of disbursing capital to MFIs in a targeted manner utilizing appropriate disbursement techniques (e.g., pre/post utilization documentation, direct/indirect to MFI/supplier). Collaborating organizations that select team members who are able to quickly assess the environment, continually monitor it, and with a *freedom* and *propensity for action* is vital to their ability to constrain and minimize capital volatility. This is especially important in the crucial first 18 to 24 months. In postconflict fragile state collaborations, organizational learning and intelligence is not facilitated by selecting a team *before* the organizational structure is complete *but* selecting a team with freedom and a propensity to act (Collins, 2001, 2005; March, 1999; Picard & Buss, 2009).

People who are able to assess and respond effectively to the performance orientation of their team and collaborative partners are vital, especially during the beginning of a project. These people, regardless to title or rank, are leaders. These leaders, including formal leaders (e.g., authority positions) can potentially facilitate mutually agreed progress that creates momentum for performance rapidity, such as MITAF mandated. One party involved in MFI assessment provided support for this point by discussing leadership and management as roles:

Person: No, frankly speaking, from the management cohort, leadership and management are different, they are two different. You can be a manager and not a leader. You can be a leader but not a manager but we aren't going to treat it the same. But we are normally, in many cases we have, like in the community bank we have identified already the leader in the bank.

Investigator: And a leader in that bank, what would a leader look like as an example?

Person: The leader is the guy who inspires everyone, the guy who motivates people, he might not be the manager himself.

Person: Believing

Investigator: Believing?

Person: People believing, you're a team player.

Investigator: Ok

Person: If I could give you an example, most of the community bank you discover that the person who is really up and running some of them are the accountants, not the manager himself. Maybe it's an accountant, maybe it's operations manager, even at [MFI] for example. The guy who I thought was the leader there was the operations manager, apparently had just left. Yesterday, four other people just left. But if the CEO, the chief executive officer who is the manager, but people don't believe in him. (M-0304, "personal communication," July 20, 2010)

These observations were also found in the Global Leadership and Organizational Behavior Effectiveness Research program (GLOBE), which investigated *performance orientation* in organizations and societies. GLOBE was created to add to the body of knowledge pertaining to cross-cultural interactions. The study found that performance orientation was the most valued of seven scales by societies around the world. This scale includes encouraging and rewarding "innovation, challenging goals, and improvement" (Javidan, 2004, p. 248). A performance-oriented society is *desired* across societies; however, the desire does not always positively correlate with *perceived practice*.

An example of differences between desire and perceived practice can be found between sub-Saharan African nations and Germanic Europe region nations.[2] Sub-Saharan African nations scored higher than Germany and the Netherlands on the importance they place on performance orientation; however, they scored generally lower on the assessment of *perceived practice*.[3] Interestingly, the study found finance industry respondents on performance orientation to be most correlated with overall society, both in terms of perceptions of what is valued and practiced, than those in other industry groups sampled. Consider the possibility of a person from a high-performance oriented society, as reflected in perceived *values* and *practice*, interacting in a collaborative with people from another nation with a greater variance between perceived value and practice than those in their own nation. Such an experience may cause the person confusion and frustration as the talk-and-the-walk of people from nations with a higher variance does not seem in alignment. For some people, observing misalignment between talk and action results in certain value judgments that are prone to divide more than unify. For example, such an observation could be interpreted as being intentionally misleading. A global orientation, such as understanding the perspective of others, can go a long way to minimize behaviors that promote capital volatility, such as division between collaborative actors.

An example from MITAF can illustrate a challenge of perceptions and perspectives. An interview excerpt presented earlier expressed a perspective regarding a divide in north-south development paradigms that were perceived to affect behaviors in MITAF in ways that were linked to capital volatility. I interviewed another respondent who provided an enlightening response regarding the suggestion of a north-south divide affecting capital flow,

Investigator: For example, I visited with an MFI, and they said to me that the TSP at one point did not understand how business operated in Sierra Leone. I paraphrased there.

They said the Chief of Party had a northern mindset. But that there was a change to someone who understood southern paradigms.

Person: I would not agree to this statement . . . the question is really what does this MFI member, or do the people that think, in the same direction, what do they think the south paradigm and the Sierra Leonean business paradigm is about? I mean microfinance is a pretty clear exercise, a pretty clear business, and although there are of course significant differences in local and national contexts, I would say that microfinance from Bangladesh and from India and from America does not differ very much from microfinance in Sierra Leone. Of course, Sierra Leone has its particular challenges and some national requirements or whatever, but the core business of microfinance still remains the same.

So, I really wonder what these people that think that we are dealing here or we are having a north-south discrepancy will be meaning as they say it. I mean of course we have a zero-tolerance—that means we do not accept any extra . . . bribes. (D0609, "personal communication," October 13, 2011)

Differences in experience and perception are important factors when team members and leadership can make an immediate and project-long difference (Harvey, Novicevic, & Kiessling, 2002). There is an extensive body of knowledge on north-south perspectives on development in collaborative arrangements (Ashman, 2001; Derksen & Verhallen, 2008). The MFI spoke of the north-south divide in reference to access to resources, or capital disbursement. The other respondent seemed puzzled by the idea and queried what the MFI thought the Sierra Leonean business paradigm consisted of in the context of microfinance. In addition to reduced tension between the government and the TSP, the most empirically clear difference from the chief of party change in the excerpt is the timing of disbursements.

The team and leadership, with various backgrounds and points of view, are vital to developing mutually agreed goals and achieving them. *The combined skill sets of the team should expeditiously assess the situational context, detect and assess contextual changes, and maintain a calculated action-orientation while realizing changes in human behavior and life style status are long-term propositions.* Observations from a study in Sierra Leone underscore this point:

> Development is obviously perceived as a vital factor in preventing and combating violent instability. But it is also extremely important to keep in mind that in post-conflict situations, goals such as development, sustainable growth, social stability and political accountability may take some time to be implemented, and the professionalism, commitment and quality of the work of NGOs' staff becomes a key element in the path to rebuilding the nation and guaranteeing its future stability. (Momo et al., 2011, p. 1)

Attributes of staff and their freedom to act affects the power aspect in the Bureaucracy of Collaboration property where performance (mutually agreed to goals) is defined.

Action requires leadership. Skill sets are key elements in international collaborations, like MITAF, that involve market mechanisms and financial institutions/rules with social and cultural ramifications. In addition, complementing skill sets are important. Remember the donor representative that shared how the Investment Committee gained organizational intelligence by capturing the learning from teams interacting,

> [J]oint cooperation of six years and continuous meetings every six months in Sierra Leone, physical meetings, I think we learned to understand each other and to come to a consensus and to a joint vision of microfinance much better. . . . I would say, that it is for the project and for the development of the microfinance sector in Sierra Leone that these different types of microfinance development approaches are complimentary to each other and are also enriching to each other. (D0609, "personal communication," October 13, 2011)

Freedom to employ approaches, including skill sets that distinguish each participating organization, allowed for the benefits of complementary synergy to be realized by MITAF. Freedom to act speaks to the centrality of organizations having an orientation and environment that thrives on cultural and generational diversity (Springer, 2011). The leadership and staff in the collaboration who understand each other, reach agreement on goals, and operationalize a joint vision can help minimize capital volatility.

DEFINITION CHANGES AND DATA

As important as the team composition decisions are, so are the actions and decisions involving key definitions and data. From inception, MITAF placed a high priority on data (Duval & Bendu, 2006; UNCDF, 2004b). Key definitions are important information developed from data, whereas data are building blocks, a substance of information (Blair, 2001; Hendrick, 1994).

Organizational learning and intelligence are based on actions and decisions informed by key definitions and data. In other words, data are processed and organized to develop key definitions. In turn, key definitions are used as information employed by actors in decision making and actions. Following are the examples of producers and reservoirs of huge amounts of data:

- environmental factors
- MITAF actors
- capital flow
- actor interactions
- credit history and lifestyle indicators of borrowers

Data are processed into information-servicing actions and decisions are shaped by, and shape, key definitions.

As understandings improve and new levels of agreement are reached (information), definitions change. Definitions of acceptable performance standards change. Definitions of what constitutes a waiver changes. *A focus on trends, while developing the sector to operate in accordance with industry standards, can result in definition changes. It is important to provide sufficient funding and marshal sufficient resources to collect data and employ the rigorous processes required to inform learning and make thoughtful, nuanced, strategic decisions as the program progresses.* This is money beyond capital investments to service delivery organizations (MFIs). Developing microfinance sectors in contexts like Sierra Leone requires aggressively attacking information asymmetries, including data acquisition-dissemination and organizational learning translated to organizational intelligence, thus connecting data and action.

Two points forcefully made during my investigation connected data and action: the importance of trends reflecting performance direction *and* assessing progress toward the overarching goal of reducing poverty. Two interviews drive these points home for me:

> What I'm interested in, in any commitment, are the trends. Are the trends positive or not? And this is an important statement because, I can give you an example, which is not even Sierra Leone, they had that. We had that discussion even during the last Investment Committee. . . . So, are we going to relax a little bit the portfolio at risk [load default measure] that we expected MFIs to have because of some contextual factors that could impact negatively? Yes, we can. We can discuss that because usually we are talking about 5 percent but in some contexts, up to 10 percent. (D03-06, "personal communication," July 21, 2010)

> From my point of view, the biggest question mark and the greatest interest is certainly in the IMPACT of donor contributions to the microfinance client. Do

> all these capital flows really help poor people? . . . With targeted interviews and field research, one could find out the different impacts of diverse types of microfinance interventions, e.g. comparing BRAC with other types of MFIs and deposit-taking/ non-deposit taking institutions.
>
> Besides the practical relevance, impact of microfinance capital flows in Sub-Saharan Africa is of great interest in science. (D0609, "personal communication," September 13, 2010)

These comments reflect dynamics of a learning organization in a challenging context. Although a key goal was to have MFIs operating according to industry standards, MITAF underscored the importance of organizational intelligence reflected by MFI positive performance trends in a nascent situation like Sierra Leone. MITAF also highlights the importance of performance reflected in deals containing terms and conditions that align with data-supported, unique attributes of MFIs and the target population. Investment Committee interviews and, at times, MITAF actions demonstrated more consideration of MFI uniqueness rather than inflexible homogenization to implement industry standards. Organizational intelligence (sustained improvement in performance) resulted from learning and employs a systemic view informed by data beyond the specific MFI performance indicators and MITAF outcome measures (e.g., implementing industry standards in MFI operations). Included is understanding the importance of trends developed by sufficient, relevant data, beyond *what* to *why* (Collins, 2009; DiMaggio & Powell, 1983; Jurik & Cowgill, 2005).

Dynamics harnessed to inform actions can result in an empirical record of learning and organization intelligence. This learning and intelligence is important to future development efforts, including work to reduce capital volatility. The subtleties and undercurrents associated with creating an atmosphere of collaboration, hope, and expected success (i.e., confidence) are exploited by praising and rewarding achievement. This is done while also understanding and responding to nonimproving trends and questionable impact. A response from a donor discussed positive re-enforcement for achievement, and assistance for those performing below targets (D03-06, "personal communication," September 23, 2010). While an initiative may have sound mechanisms for formal legitimacy, confidence of participants and intended beneficiaries is also required for public organizations to perform effectively (The World Bank, 2000). Confidence and successful performance are important considerations in an accountability ethos supported by credible information from quality, relevant data.

One MFI shared with me a very telling thought that speaks to subtleties and undercurrents resident in an environment of hope and expected success that affects capital disbursement:

> You know microfinance is very new program in this country. We are used to sending a proposal, but a proposal is quite different from a business plan. So, sometimes we have to take time actually to [create] a business plan. We have to finish a projection. That is very much important. We have to set our target. We are to go from here before the end of 2010s from where will you be. So, you have to talk of all of those things. If they are not in place, no way [no capital disbursement]. So, these are some of our challenges. But *with that*, [emphasis added] they [MITAF] have been conducting a series of trainings actually. Yeah. (M0305, "personal communication," July 16, 2010)

Challenges and obstacles accompanied "with that" believed to be sufficient to overcome creates an expectation of success and greater confidence when confronted in the future with the unknown and unfamiliar. *The learner believing and buying into the lessons and practices taught is important to increased knowledge and awareness (e.g., key definitions). These aspects of the learner are also important to changes in behavior (actions and decisions) that improve performance and reduce capital volatility, especially after behavior is directly connected to specific capital investments.*

The following excerpts from interviews and the MITAF final evaluation underscore this recommendation:

> But believe me, when we went through it [adding a branch office], and I said this was what (MITAF) deprived us of, the ability to learn, to know. You know. When people are given the opportunity to learn, to know, to test, the learning is stronger. Hmm? (M0101, "personal communication," July 14, 2010)

> I like Sierra Leone. But we spend a lot of money on training and in many cases, many people who we trained, very many, 10 percent of the people we have trained, they have come back and applied what they learned. We need a lot of training of trainers but . . . out of maybe 20 people only two people that I can identify and say I can even use them. . . . The rest, it's a country problem. There's no label; now the standards are gone. I can't blame them for that. So that's what we need. . . . On one hand we try to bring in new discipline into the sector to enforce best practice, we call them performance-based agreements and they work to enforce best practice in the sector. But if you look on the other side, your enforcing [is] forcing the horse [MFIs] to drink water. (M-0304, "personal communication," July 20, 2010)

> The TSP is to be particularly commended for identifying many regional consultants to act as RTAs [resident technical assistance] for the MFIs. However, the technical assistance provided by both ESGC [the TSP] staff and the RTAs identified by the TSP and financed by the project seem to have had little lasting impact on many of the MFIs. Although the assistance generally was appreciated by the PLIs [partner lending institutions, MFIs], few of the institutions seem to be applying the systems and policies developed by the RTAs. In the estimation of the evaluation team based on discussions with the PLIs in question, this is partly due to . . . the fact that ESGC staff and the RTAs tended to develop manuals and plans for the institutions rather than guide them in developing these materials for themselves. (Duval & Bendu, 2009, p. 29)

Quality, relevant data is vital to developing credible information used to increase performance—organizational intelligence. MFIs selected for leadership development in the sector and presented as models need to be substantive partners in shaping a systemic leadership model. However, a leadership model shaped by MFI superficial conformance to certain output measures without strong, deep controls can experience failure, exemplified by ProCredit discussed earlier. This view of data and leadership development (changing, adapting) is central to organizational learning in CBT. Quality data is important to develop credible information used in learning that is shaped and embraced by MFIs. In practice, MITAF redefined performance (to some degree) as new and better data emerged.

RECORDKEEPING AND ACTION: IT'S ABOUT THE MONEY, AND MORE!

MITAF struggled with maintaining records of capital investment activity. The challenge was exacerbated by donors remitting directly to MFIs without notice and before disbursement requests were submitted by the MITAF staff. Delays in consummating a performance-based agreement similarly impacted disbursement recordkeeping. The structure of the MITAF project, though expedient and helpful in the beginning, contributed in some measure to the struggles.

The diversity and complexity of activity made recordkeeping a significant challenge for the MITAF staff's approach to the task. Nevertheless, it was empirically demonstrated that challenges were manageable when there was sufficient motivation for the parties involved. *It is important to account for the project's commitments; tracking money is only part of accounting.*

Stewardship requires accounting for MITAF commitments. *UNDP in Action: Delivering on Our Commitment to Development*, references their 2007 strategic plan and underscores the importance of this strategic recommendation: "The plan stressed the importance of delivering programming in an effective and accountable manner with measurable and transformative results" (p. 2). The stewardship mandate associated with delivering on commitments is akin to promises that are integral to economic systems. When capital flows directly from a donor to the MFI, it is less a financial accounting issue because it employs resources to effectively satisfy the MITAF commitment. However, a deal between a donor and an MFI was not just that; it was also an MITAF commitment. The investment package was presented to the Investment Committee,[4] which first acts on the investment opportunity. Only then did an individual donor got involved to varying degrees through completion of the performance-based agreement and disbursement of all the capital, in accordance with the MITAF commitment. *Collaboration begets one-on-one transactions between donors and MFIs that are subject to additional commitments that must be accounted for.*

MFI understanding of capital investment commitments, and how they perceive donor and MITAF staff behavior relative to those commitments, should be expected to inform MFI actions. Although capital market development is environmentally important and centrally necessary for developing an inclusive financial sector in developing countries (Imboden et al., 2006), it is not best employed as the primary mechanism in postconflict fragile states. Governments and donor communities would be wise to not rush quickly to the normative framework visible in today's huge, tech-savvy capital markets. Initiatives like MITAF function as financial intermediaries[5] and should not employ less people-centric, more big-technology-centric mechanisms that assume behavioral reputations matter less (Davidoff, 2011; Van Slyke, 2005). Not only is reputation an "important enforcement mechanism" (Davidoff, 2011), but it is used in asymmetrical power relationships by less powerful actors, such as MFIs in many capital investment deals, to protect against exploitation (Cook et al., 2005). MFI reporting and capital disbursement behavior is an important recordkeeping-capital volatility connection.

For the MFI, the deal included both MITAF and at least one donor from the start.

Resource-dependent MFIs may agree to the deal even if they believe it is unlikely they will satisfy the conditions committed to. What do they have to lose? If they do not enter the deal they are without the capital investment. If they enter the deal and default on their obligations, they are without the capital investment. If they enter the deal, there is a chance they will satisfy the conditions, or that a wavier may be granted. For MFIs, the commitments are often about a survival sense; the motivation is the desperate need to acquire capital that consumed 50 to 60 percent of the director's time prior to MITAF (Tucker email, March 2011). *Accounting for MITAF commitments is about the money, but it is also about stewardship of promise keeping.*

The motivation for MITAF, including specifically donors, to manage the challenges of accounting for capital disbursements is that *MITAF made a promise*. A normative, intrinsically motivating, promise was provided in a communiqué after an Investment Committee meeting informing the MFI that a decision was made to enter a capital investment deal. With that notification delivery, time started and commitments were made. In addition, MITAF did not have viable alternative means of accomplishing its mission. Making credible commitments was so important to MITAF's mission that not transparently accounting for activity related to each promise carried the potential to reduce the value of its capital investment.

Cook and her colleagues (2005) contend that transactions involving bankers, absent power equality, often use "reputation systems" as a source of information to assess actors' reliability and trustworthiness. Reputation not only has properties that encourage reliable behavior to preserve future business opportunities (Davidoff, 2011), but it is an important assessment tool for the less powerful to avoid being exploited (Cook et al., 2005). Research involving relationships with power asymmetry has found that if the more powerful party makes a commitment sufficient enough to convince the less powerful party that their desire for trust is genuine, then balance of power can be adjusted. In essence, power relations can reflect interdependence where more trust can be realized with associated benefits.

The interdependence of this collaborative necessitated that donor and MITAF staff actions were consistent with rhetoric involving rapidity in the MITAF commitment, or mission. The contextualized importance of timeframes in Sierra Leone capital investment commitments has been made clear. The UNCDF Results-Oriented Annual Report 2007 characterized MITAF as a "high risk niche," a reflection of the donor's "risk-taking nature" (p. 2). *It is important that there is consistency between committing capital investment to rapidly develop the sector and the conditions employed for disbursement.* A key goal is for MFIs to perform in accordance with industry best practice. However, providing capital to a sector considered nascent and high risk, while imposing disbursement standards of best practice during the first 36 to 48 months, is not always consistent with a commitment to rapidly develop the sector. Entering a deal with disbursement conditions that are substantially inconsistent with the performance trend is inherently problematic.

A microfinance study in Sierra Leone addresses timing and best practices. It suggested the following strategies for MFIs: "Do not abandon best practices. In post-conflict environments, sustainability may take longer to reach, and the repayments especially in the earliest phase of the programme may be lower than usual" (Momo et al., 2011, p. 8). The goal to perform in accordance to MFI industry standards is advanced by *mission accountability tracking* of capital invested and disbursed, including when and to whom. A donor's response provided earlier underscored that MITAF capital investments are venture capital. Though not a license for carelessness, it is not unexpected to write off over 20 percent of the deals. Advancing the mission in Sierra Leone placed a strong demand on donor's risk-taking predisposition.

My four strategic recommendations are as follows:

1. Monitor external factors to ensure the environment is conducive for sustainable growth of the financial sector. This is important to minimize capital volatility and ensure organization learning is retained as intelligence reflected in enhanced performance. Ensuring conduciveness requires direct action that impacts the environment and employs meso-level organizations.
2. Effective leadership and competent staff should be given early attention. Thoughtfully consider the people selected to be involved throughout the project (in project location and elsewhere), especially at the outset. A multicultural team embodies the organizational attributes and intelligence need to account for variance in behavior within a context, and in capital volatility. The organization with an orientation and environment that thrives off cultural and generational diversity achieves high-level performance. People who can assess and respond effectively to the performance orientation of their team and collaborative partners are vital, especially during the beginning of the project. The combined skill sets should expeditiously assess the situational context, detect and assess contextual changes, and maintain a calculated action orientation while realizing changes in human behavior and life style status are long-term propositions.
3. Provide sufficient funding and marshal sufficient resources to collect data required to inform learning and make thoughtful, nuanced, strategic decisions as the program progresses. Definitions change as organizational intelligence grows and new agreements are reached among collaborators. Organizational intelligence, sustained improvement in performance resulting from learning, employs a systemic view informed by data beyond the specific MFI performance indicators and MITAF outcome measures, including understanding the importance of trends. Aggressively attacking information asymmetries and making changes that a dynamic context requires is central to creating and maintaining a sense of hope among participants. Quality, relevant data are vital to developing credible information used in learning that increases performance—organizational intelligence. The learning organization that believes and buys into the lessons and practices taught is important to increased knowledge and awareness, and to changes in behavior that improve performance.

4. The project's commitments must be timely and accurately accounted for. Stewardship requires accounting of MITAF commitments. Credible commitments have value, similar to loan notes discussed in Chapter 1. Entering collaboration makes one-on-one commitments between donors and MFIs subject to additional commitments that must be accounted for. Accounting for MITAF commitments is about the money, but it is also about stewardship of promise keeping. It is important that there is consistency between committing capital investments to rapidly develop the sector and the conditions employed for disbursement. Tracking money is only part of accounting. It also includes accounting for commitment stewardship, such as stipulated timeframes to process performance-based agreements.

CONCLUSION AND FUTURE RESEARCH

Understanding the bureaucracy of collaborative development projects, as observed in my examination of behavior-volatility linkages, is important for both industrialized nations and the developing world. Minimizing outcome-devaluing linkages is vital for effective performance and organizational intelligence. This is critical for developing nations where the devaluing impact of volatility is multiples of industrialized nations. Moreover, volatility in resource-dependent relationships requires those in power to be highly sensitive to the importance of credible commitments. Underdevelopment and destabilization often hang in the balance of making sense of the connection between behavior and capital flow.

There is much to learn beyond the insights from this investigation. A similar investigation exploring other collaborative projects can test the CBT lens and yield additional insights. Further investigating legitimacy, reliability, and effectiveness in MITAF can excavate important variances that can inform sense making of behavior and volatility, as well as other important linkages. For example, obtaining data from key stakeholders can provide valuable insights into evaluative construct differences. In addition, deeply exploring these relationships to identify and assess "accountability fatigue" can provide insights to undesirable effects (ECOSOC, 2010, p. 6). Additional research analyzing tensions between volatility, effectiveness, efficiency, and impact can provide interesting, rich insights on perceptions and beliefs regarding trade-offs. Furthermore, constructs used by different participants in measuring Effectiveness, Efficiency, and Impact, including relative weights, can help identify and bridge gaps that exacerbate outcome-constraining factors. Measuring impact of microfinance has been a difficult challenge that arguably begins with understanding different perspectives and measures of impact. This future research agenda suggests that there is complexity associated in combining aid with organizational behavior in collaborations in sub-Saharan Africa.

Organizational learning is found in cognizance of environmental factors, organizational and contextual histories, relative importance of individual and collaborative imperatives, and developments on the ground. Monitoring environmental factors and taking direct action are important. Leadership and team are important, as are valuing and committing data to eliminate crippling information asymmetries. Intrinsic motivation to embrace commitment stewardship is another important property that is linked with capital volatility.

The bureaucracy found in collaborations that contextualizes linkages between behaviors and capital volatility can easily overwhelm anyone seeking to understand the relationship. Intransigence, stubbornness, bullying, and dishonesty are examples of the easily available unpalatable explanations that lead to simple prescriptions. On the other hand, viewing complexity and interconnectedness through the Collaboration Bureaucratic Triad lens can subside the overwhelming waves. Collaboration, accountability, and effectiveness, efficiency, and impact combine to make sense of dedicated organizations that work to make substantive differences and remain relevant in an increasing perilous, dynamic, and challenging world.

NOTES

1. Organizations have people directly involved in the collaboration, such as donor representatives attending Investment Committee meetings, TSP staff managing day-to-day operations, and MFI staff in direct communication with MITAF/TSP. There are also people involved indirectly, such as those who process requests for disbursements at the donor, MFI staff who prepare MITAF reports, and MITAF staff who perform certain financial tasks at the home-office.
2. The Germanic Europe cluster of nations was based on research conducted and published by Simcha Ronen and Obed Shenkar (1985), "Clustering Countries on Attitudinal Dimensions: A Review and Synthesis," *Academy of Management Review,* 10(3), 435–454. The sub-Saharan Africa group, as used by GLOBE, was not established by prior empirical research. Characteristics of the group include values of "reciprocity, suppression of self-interest, the virtue of symbiosis, and human interdependence" (Gupta & Hanges, 2004, pp. 187, 188).
3. Also, *Tropical Wet and Dry* climates, like Sierra Leone, had a variance of over 60 percent between society values and society practices for performance orientation; however, *Marine West Coast* climates, such as Germany and the Netherlands, had a variance almost half as much (Javidan, 2004, pp. 260, 261).
4. In a very few instances it appears donors invested directly in MFIs without IC approval and MITAF was credited with the investment.
5. See the discussion of apex organizations in Chapter 2.

Bibliography

Adler, M. (2003). A Socio-Legal Approach to Administrative Justice. *Law & Policy*, 25(4), 323–352.

Adler, M. (2006). Fairness in Context. *Journal of Law and Society*, 33(4), 615–638.

Alesina, A., & Dollar, D. (2000). Who Gives Foreign Aid to Whom and Why? *Journal of Economic Growth*, 5(1), 33–63.

Amin, S. (1972). Underdevelopment and Dependence in Black Africa-Origins and Contemporary Forms. *The Journal of Modern African Studies*, 10(4), 503–524.

Armendariz de Aghion, B., & Morduch, J. (2005). *The Economics of Microfinance*. Cambridge, MA: The MIT Press.

Ashman, D. (2001). Strengthening North-South Partnerships for Sustainable Development. *Nonprofit and Voluntary Sector Quarterly*, 30(1), 74–98.

Bardhan, P., & Mookherjee, D. (2006). Decentralization, Corruption, and Government Accountability. In S. Rose-Ackerman (Ed.), *International Handbook on the Economics of Corruption* (pp. 161–188). Cheltenham, UK: Edward Elgar Publishing Limited.

Barnard, C. I. (1938). *The Functions of the Executive*. Cambridge, MA: Harvard University Press.

Beck, T., Demirguc-Kunt, A., & Levine, R. (2007). Finance, Inequality and the Poor. *Journal of Economic Growth*, 12, 27–49.

Bell, D. (2010). Who Is Watching the Watcher? Voluntary Networks as an Accountability Mechanism for Civil Society Organizations. *Pitt Political Review*: GSPIA Edition, 2(Summer 2010), 42–47.

Bell, D. (2017). Evaluation Influence: The Evaluation Event and Capital Flow in International Development. *Evaluation Review*, 41(6), 568–592.

Benson, J. K. (1975). The Interorganizational Network as a Political Economy. *Administrative Science Quarterly*, 20(2), 229–249.

Bhattacharjee, Y. (2015, March 17). The Sting: An American Drugs Bust in West Africa. *The Guardian*.

Bigombe, B., Collier, P., & Sambanis, N. (2000). Policies for Building Post-Conflict Peace. *Journal of African Economies*, 9(3), 323–348.

Blair, D. C. (2001). Knowledge Management: Hype, Hope, or Help? *Journal of the American Society for Information Science and Technology*, 53(12), 1019–1028.

Blakewell, O. (2007). Breaching the Borders Between Research and Practice: Development NGOs and Qualitative Data. In M. Smith (Ed.), *Negotiating Boundaries and Borders: Qualitative Methodology and Development Research Studies in Qualitative Methodology* (Vol. 8, pp. 217–238). Oxford, UK: Elsevier Ltd.

Blau, P. M. (1963). *The Dynamics of Bureaucracy: A Study of Interpersonal Relations in Two Government Agencies*. Chicago: University of Chicago Press.

Block, P. (1996). *Stewardship: Choosing Service Over Self Interest*. San Francisco: Berrett-Koehler Publishers, Inc.

BRAC. (2010). *Evaluation of BRAC West Africa Microfinance Program*. Bangladesh: BRAC.

Brunnermeier, M. K. (2009). Deciphering the Liquidity and Credit Crunch 2007–2008. *Journal of Economic Perspectives*, 23(1), 77–100.

Cai, H., & Theisman, D. (2005). Does Competition for Capital Discipline Governments? Decentralization, Globalization, and Public Policy. *The American Economic Review*, 95(3), 817–830.

Celasun, O., & Walliser, J. (2008). Predictability of Aid: Do Fickle Donors Undermine Aid Effectiveness? *Economic Policy*, 545–594.

CGAP. (2004). *How the Netherlands Government Fostered Successful Public-Private Partnerships for Financing MFIs Case Studies in Donor Good Practices* (Vol., No. 17). Washington, DC: CGAP.

CGAP. (2006). *Good Practice Guidelines for Funders: Microfinance Consensus Guidelines*. Washington, DC: Consultative Group to Assist the Poor/The World Bank.

CGAP. (2009). *Microfinance Funder Survey: Sub-Saharan Africa (SSA) Annual Survey of Microfinance Portfolios of Leading Dorons and Investors*. Washington, DC: Consultative Group for Assisting the Poor.

Chouvy, P.-A., & Laniel, L. R. (2007). Agricultural Drug Economies: Cause or Alternative to Intra-State Conflicts? *Crime Law Social Change*, 48, 133–150.

Clarke, M. (2006). Aid and Development in Conflict Environments: An Introduction and Summary. In M. Clarke (Ed.), *Aid in Conflict* (pp. 1–8). New York: Nova Science Publishers, Inc.

Clarke, G. R. G., Xu, L. C., & Zou, H.-F. (2006). Finance and Income Inequality: What do the Data Tell Us? *Southern Economic Journal*, 72(3), 578–596.

Coase, R. H. (1937). The Nature of the Firm. *Economica*, New Series, 4(16), 386–405.

Coleman, W. D., & Tangermann, S. (1999). The 1992 CAP Reform, the Uruguay Round and the Commission: Conceptualizing Linked Policy Games. *Journal of Common Market Studies*, 37(3), 385–405.

Collier, P., & Hoeffler, A. (2002). *Aid, Policy, and Growth in Post-Conflict Societies Policy Research Working Paper*. Washington, DC: World Bank.

Collier, P., Dollar, D., & Stern, N. (2000). *Fifty Years of Development*. Washington, DC: The World Bank.

Collins, J. (2001). *Good to Great*. New York: HarperCollins Publishers.

Collins, J. (2005). *Good to Great and the Social Sectors: A Monograph to Accompany Good to Great*. Boulder, CO: Jim Collins.

Collins, J. (2009). *How The Might Fall: And Why Some Companies Never Give In*. New York: HarperCollins Publishers Inc.

Cook, K. S., Hardin, R., & Levi, M. (2005). *Cooperation Without Trust?* (Vol. IX). New York: Russell Sage Foundation.

Cull, R., Demirguc-Kunt, A., & Morduch, J. (2008). *Microfinance Meets the Market Policy Research Working Paper*. Washington, DC: The World Bank.

Davidoff, S. M. (2011, April 27). The Declining Worth of a Good Name: Window on Wall Street. *The New York Times*, p. 17.

Davis, J., Schoorman, F. D., & Donaldson, L. (1997). Toward a Stewardship Theory of Management. *Academy of Management Review*, 22(1), 20–47.

Demir, F. (2009). Capital Market Imperfections and Financialization of Real Sectors in Emerging Markets: Private Investment and Cash Flow Relationship Revistited. *World Development*, 37(5), 953–964.

Derksen, H., & Verhallen, P. (2008). Reinventing International NGOs: A View From the Dutch Co-Financing System. In A. J. Bebbington, S. Hickey, & D. C. Mitlin (Eds.), *Can NGOs Make a Difference? The Challenge of Development Alternatives* (pp. 221–239). London: Zed Books.

Deutscher, E. (2010). *Development Co-operation Report 2010*. Paris: Organisation for Economic Co-Operation and Development.

DFID. (2009). *Annual Report and Resource Accounts 2008–2009* (Vol. II). London: Department of International Development.

Dichter, T. (2007). Can Microcredit Make an Already Slippery Slope More Slippery? Some Lessons From the Social Meaning of Debt. In T. Dichter & M. Harper (Eds.), *What's Wrong With Microfinance?* (pp. 9–17). Warwickshire, UK: Practical Action Publishing, Ltd.

DiMaggio, P., & Powell, W. (1983). The Iron Cage Revisited: Institutional Isomorphism and Collective Rationality in Organizational Fields. *American Sociological Review*, 48(2), 147–160.

Doyle, K. (1998). *Microfinance in the Wake of Conflict: Challenges and Opportunities*. Bethesda, MD: The SEEP Network.

Dunion, G. (2010, October–December). "Are the Achievement of the Goals Still a Viable Prospect?" No. *Focus on Africa*, 21, 20.

Duval, A., & Bendu, F. (2006). Mid-Term Evaluation September 2006: Development of a Sustainable Pro-Poor Financial Sector in Sierra Leone Project SIL/03/C01.

Duval, A., & Bendu, F. (2009). *Final Evaluation: Development of a Sustainable Pro-Poor Financial Sector in Sierra Leone*. New York: United Nations Capital Development Fund.

ECOSOC. (2010). *Report of the 2010 ECOSOC Development Cooperation Forum*. New York: United Nations Economic and Social Council.

English, P., & Stryker, D. (2006). *Sierra Leone: Adding Value through Trade for Poverty Reduction*. Geneva, Switzerland: Integrated Framework for Trade Related Technical Assistance to Least Developed Countries.

Eyben, R. (2012). Relationships: A New Perspective on International Aid. In R. Eyben (Ed.), *Relationships for Aid* (pp. 1–18). Sterling: Earthscan.

Ferguson, J. (1994). *The Anti-Politics Machine: "Development," Depoliticizatin, and Bureaucratic Power in Lesotho*. Minneapolis: University of Minnesota Press.

Frederickson, H. G. (2005). *Public Administration with an Attitude*. Washington, DC: American Society of Public Administration.

Froelich, K. (1999). Diversification of Revenue Strategies: Evolving Resource Dependence in Nonprofit Organizations *Nonprofit and Voluntary Sector Quarterly*, 28(3), 246–268.

Gazley, B. (2010). Linking Collaborative Capacity to Performance Measurement in Government- Nonprofit Partnerships. *Nonprofit and Voluntary Sector Quarterly*, 39(4), 653–673.

Gazley, B., & Brudney, J. L. (2007). The Purpose (and Perils) of Government-Nonprofit Partnership. *Nonprofit and Voluntary Sector Quarterly*, 36(3), 389–415.

GLOBE. (2006). *Research Survey-Form Beta*. Vancourver, Canada: GLOBE Foundation.

Goodnow, F. J. (1900). *Politics and Administration: A Study in Government*. New York: The Macmillan Company.

Gries, T., Kraft, M., & Meierrieks, D. (2009). Linkages Between Financial Deepening, Trade Openness, and Economic Development: Causality Evidence from Sub-Saharan Africa. *World Development*, 37(12), 1849–1860.

Gulick, L. (1937). Notes on the Theory of Organization. In L. Gulick & L. Urwick (Eds.), *Papers on the Science of Administration* (pp. 3–13). New York: Institute of Public Administration.

Guo, C., & Acar, M. (2005). Understanding Collaboration Among Nonprofit Organizations: Combining Resource Dependency, Institutional, and Network Perspectives. *Nonprofit and Voluntary Sector Quarterly*, 34(3), 340–361.

Gupta, V., & Hanges, P. J. (2004). Regional and Climate Clustering of Societal Cultures. In R. J. House, P. J. Hanges, M. Javidan, P. W. Dorfman & V. Gupta (Eds.), *Culture, Leadership, and Organizations: The GLOBE Study of 62 Societies* (pp. 178–218). Thousand Oaks, CA: Sage Publications, Inc.

Gutierrez-Nieto, B., & Serrano-Cinca, C. (2010). Factors Influencing Funder Loyalty to Microfinance Institutions. *Nonprofit and Voluntary Sector Quarterly*, 39(2), 302–320.

Hanges, P., & Dickson, M. W. (2004). *The Development and Validation of the GLOBE Culture and Leadership Scales Culture, Leadership, and Organizations: The GLOBE Study of 62 Societies* (pp. 122–153). Thousand Oaks, CA: Sage Publishing.

Hartarska, V. (2009). The Impact of Outside Control in Microfinance. *Managerial Finance*, 35(12), 975–989.

Harvey, M., Novicevic, M. M., & Kiessling, T. (2002). Development of Multiple IQ Maps for Use in the Selection of Inpatriate Managers: A Practical Theory. *International Journal of Intercultural Relations*, 26, 493–524.

Heady, F. (2001). *Public Administration: A Comparative Perspective* (Sixth ed.). Boca Raton, FL: CRC Press.

Hendrick, R. (1994). An Information Infrastructure for Innovative Management of Government. *Public Administration Review*, 54(6), 543–550.

Hinton, R., & Groves, L. (2004). The Complexity of Inclusive Aid. In R. Hinton & L. Groves (Eds.), *Inclusive Aid: Changing Power and Relationships in International Development* (pp. 17–30). Sterling: Earthscan.

Honohan, P., & Beck, T. (2007). *Making Finance Work for Africa*. Washington, DC: The World Bank.

Hulme, D. (2007). Is Microdebt Good for Poor People? A Note on the Dark Side of Microfinance. In T. Dichter & M. Harper (Eds.), *What's Wrong With Microfinance?* (pp. 19–22). Warwickshire, UK: Practical Action Publishing, Ltd.

Hummel, R. P. (2008). *The Bureaucratic Experience: The Post-Modern Challenge*. New York: M. E. Sharpe, Inc.

Imboden, K., Clark, H., & Herman, B. (2006). *Building Inclusive Financial Sectors for Development*. New York: United Nations Department of Economic and Social Affairs; United Nations Capital Development Fund.

IMF. (2009). *Sierra Leone: Fourth Review Under the Three-Year Arrangement Under the Poverty Reduction and Growth Facility*. Washington, DC: International Monetary Fund.

Isidore, C. (2008, December 1). It's Official: Recession Since Dec. '07 Retrieved November 11, 2011, from http://money.cnn.com/2008/12/01/news/economy/recession/index.htm.

Javidan, M. (2004). Performance Orientation. In R. J. House, P. J. Hanges, M. Javidan, P. W. Dorfman & V. Gupta (Eds.), *Culture, Leadership, and Organizations: The GLOBE Study of 62 Societies* (pp. 239–281). Thousand Oaks, CA: Sage Publications.

Jurik, N., & Cowgill, J. (2005). The Construction of Client Identities in a Post-Welfare Social Service Program: The Double Bind of Microenterprise Development. In A. L. Schneider & H. M. Ingram (Eds.), *Deserving and Entitled: Social Constructions and Public Policy* (pp. 173–196). Albany: State University of New York Press.

Karlan, D., & Morduch, J. (2009). *Access to Finance Handbook of Development Economics* (Vol. 5). Elsevier Science and Technology Books.

Kearns, K. P. (2000). *Private Sector Strategies for Social Sector Success: The Guide to Strategy and Planning for Public and Nonprofit Organizations*. San Francisco: Jossey-Bass Inc.

Kettl, D. F. (2007). *The Transformation of Governance: Public Administration for Twenty-First Century America*. Baltimore: The Johns Hopkins University Press.

Koenig-Archibugi, M. (2004). Transnational Corporations and Public Accountability. *Government and Opposition*, 39, 234–259.

Latortue, A., Littlefield, E., Siedek, H., & McKee, K. (2007). *Managing the Floodgates? Making the Most of International Flows of Microfinance Funding*. Washington, DC: Consultative Group to Assist the Poor.

Learning, S. T. O. (1960). *Atomic Energy Standard Treasury of Learning with Funk & Wangalls Dictionary for Young People* (Vol. 1, pp. 63–91). New York: Standard Reference Works Publishing Company, Inc.

Manalo, M. (2003). *Microfinance Institutions' Response in Conflict Environments*. Africa Region Working Paper Series. Washington, DC: The World Bank.

March, J. G. (1999). *The Pursuit of Organizational Intelligence*. Cambridge: Blackwell Business.

Meagher, P., Compos, P., Christen, R. P., Druschel, K., Gallardo, J., & Martowijoyo, S. (2006). *Microfinance Regulation in Seven Countries: A Comparative Study*. College Park: The IRIS Center at The University of Maryland.

Miamidian, E., & Khalaf, R. (2009, October). Restructuring of MITAF, memorandum to Kreditanstalt fur Wiederaufbau.

MITAF. (2006). Investment Committee Policies and Procedures Manual. Sierra Leone.

Mollenkamp, C. (2011, Tuesday, June 21). Lending Battle is Risky Business. *The Wall Street Journal*, pp. c1, 2.

Momo, S., Costa, L., Letho, M., Manzi, S., & Rebakis, J. (2011). *Post-Conflict Action & Microfinance in Sierra Leone*. The Hague: Spanda Publishing.

Nutt, P. C. (2010). On the Study of Process: Merging Qualitative and Quantitative Approaches. In P. C. Nutt & D. C. Wilson (Eds.), *Handbook of Decision Making* (pp. 581–618). West Sussex: John Wiley & Son, Ltd.

OECD. (2011). *Development Aid at a Glance: Statistics by Region Developing Countries*. Paris: Organization for Economic Co-operation and Development.

Ostrom, E. (2005). *Understanding Institutional Diversity*. Princeton, NJ: Princeton University Press.

Ostrom, E., Gibson, C., Shivakumar, S., & Andersson, K. (2002). *Aid, Incentives, and Sustainability: An Institutional Analysis of Development Cooperation* (D. f. E. a. I. Audit, Trans.). Stockholm: Swedish International Development Agency.

Oxfam. (2005). *Paying the Price: Why Rich Countries must Invest Now in a War on Poverty*. Oxford, UK: Oxfam International.

Pallage, S., & Robe, M. A. (2003). On the Welfare Cost of Economic Fluctuations in Developing Countries. *International Economic Review*, 44(2), 677–698.

Parsons, T. (Ed.). (1947). *Max Weber: The Theory of Social and Economic Organization*. New York: The Free Press.

Patton, A. (1996). *Physicians, Colonial Racism, and Diaspora in West Africa*. Gainesville: University Press of Florida.

Picard, L. A., & Buss, T. F. (2009). *A Fragile Balance; Re-examining the History of Foreign Aid, Security, and Diplomacy*. Sterling, VA: Kumarian Press.

Reed, I. (2009). *Sub-Saharan Africa the Other World: Issues and Politics of the Developing World* (pp. 147–209). New York: Pearson Education, Inc.

Reille, X., & Forster, S. (2008). *Foreign Capital Investment in Microfinance: Balancing Social and Finance Returns* (Vol. Focus Note 44). Washington, DC: CGAP.

Riggs, F. W. (2006). The Prismatic Model: Conceptualizing Transitional Societies. In E. E. Otenyo & N. S. Lind (Eds.), *Comparative Public Administration: The Essential Readings* (Vol. 15, pp. 17–60). San Diego: Elsevier Press.

Rosenberg, R. (2006). *Review of UNDP Microfinance Portfolio*. Washington, DC: CGAP.

RSL. (2002). *National Recovery Strategy, 2002–2003*. Freetown: Government of the Republic of Sierra Leone.

Salisu, M. (2005). The Role of Capital Flight and Remittances. In E. A. S. P. Division (Ed.), *Capital Flows and Current Account Sustainability in Africa*. New York: United Nations Economic Commission for Africa, 382–404.

Scott, R., & Davis, G. (2003). *Organizations and Organizing: Rational, Natural, and Open Systems Perspectives* (5th ed.). Upper Saddle River, NJ: Pearson Education, Inc.

Seers, D. (1972). What Are We Trying to Measure? *Journal of Development Studies*, 8(3), 21–36.

Simon, H. (1996). *The Sciences of the Artificial* (Third ed.). Cambridge, MA: The MIT Press.

Slim, H. (2002). By What Authority? The Legitimacy Accountability and Non-Governmental Organizations. Paper presented at the International Council of Human Rights Policy International Meeting on Global Trends and Human Rights–Before and after September 11, Geneva.

Smillie, I. (2009). *Freedom from Want: The Remarkable Success Story of BRAC, the Global Grassroots Organization That's Winning the Fight Against Poverty*. Sterling: Kumanian Press.

Snibbe, A. C. (2006). Drowning in Data. *Stanford Social Innovation Review* (Fall), 39–45.

Springer, C. G. (2011, August/September). Management of the New Demographics in the Workplace. *PA Times*, p. 11.

Stiglitz, J. (1988). Economic Organization, Information, and Development. In H. Chenery & T. N. Srinivasan (Eds.), *Handbook of Development Economics* (Vol. 1, pp. 93–160). Amsterdam: Elsevier Science.

Stiglitz, J. (1993). The Role of the State in Financial Markets. Paper presented at the Proceedings of the Conference on Development Economics, Washington, D.C.: The World Bank.

Strauss, A. L., & Corbin, J. (1998). *Basics of Qualitative Research: Techniques and Procedures for Developing Grounded Theory* (Second ed.). Thousand Oaks, CA: SAGE Publications.

The Economist. (2005, July 2). The $25 billion Question. *The Economist*, 24–26.

The World Bank. (2000). *Reforming Public Institutions and Strengthening Governance* (P. R. a. E. M. N. P. Public Sector Group, Trans.). Washington, DC: The World Bank.

The World Bank. (2004). *Making Services Work for the Poor World Development Report*. Washington, DC: World Bank.

Triplett, T. (2010). Survey Design of the Study of Congregational Giving for International Development and Relief Work [PowerPoint].

Tucker, J. (2011, March 24). [Personal Email].

UN-Sierra Leone. (2008). *Priority Plan for Peace Building Fund* (Revised July 2008 ed.). Freetown, Sierra Leone: Republic of Sierra Leone and United Nations-Sierra Leone.

UNCDF. (July 16, 2009). Sierra Leone: Inclusive Finance. Countries and Regions Retrieved January 2, 2010.

UNCDF. (2004a). *2003 Results-Oriented Annual Report of the United Nations Capital Development Fund.* New York: United Nations Capital Development Fund.

UNCDF. (2004b). Development of a Sustainable Pro-Poor Financial Sector in Sierra Leone (2004–2009). UNCDF Project Number: SIL/03/C01.

UNCDF. (2008). *United Nations Capital Development Fund 2007 Results-Oriented Annual Report.* New York: United Nations Capital Development Fund.

University, I. (2009, July 23). Common Framework Would Aid Cumulation of Isolated Knowledge [Press release], Bloomington: University of Indiana.

Van Slyke, D. M. (2005). Agents or Stewards: Using Theory to Understand the Government-Nonprofit. Social Service Contracting Relationship. *Journal of Public Administration Research and Theory*, 17, 157–187.

White, L. D. (1942). The Public Service of the Future. In L. D. White (Ed.), *The Future of Government in the United State: Essays in Honor of Charles E. Merriam* (pp. 192–217). Chicago: University of Chicago Press.

Wignaraja, K. (Ed.). (2009). *Capacity Development: A UNDP Primer.* New York: United Nations Development Programme.

Wilson, W. (1887). The Study of Administration. *Political Science Quarterly*, 2(2), 197–222.

Yong, E. (2016). *I Contain Multitudes: The Microbes within Us and a Grander View of Life*. New York: HarperCollins Publishers.

Yunus, H. (1999). *Banker to the Poor: Micro-Lending and the Battle Against World Poverty*. New York: PublicAffairs.

Zietlow, J. T., Hankin, J. A., & Seidner, A. G. (2007). *Financial Management for Nonprofit Organizations: Policies and Practices*. New York: John Wiley and Sons, Inc.

Index

Page references for figures are italicized.

About the Author

David Bell is a faculty member of the Paul H. O'Neill School of Public and Environmental Affairs. He earned his Ph.D. in public and international affairs from the University of Pittsburgh, where he also received his MPA with a focus on nonprofit management, specifically NGOs. At the undergraduate level, he studied public affairs management at Michigan State University. His research interests include leadership and accountability involving public organizations, entrepreneurship, and capital flow in developing countries, program evaluation, nonprofit management, organizational leadership, and cross-sector collaboration. Bell is a member of the American Society for Public Administration (ASPA), the Association for Research on Nonprofit Organizations and Voluntary Action (ARNOVA), the Conference of Minority Public Administrators (COMPA), and the Consortium for International Management, Policy and Development (CIMPAD). He has extensive management and executive experience at civil society organizations, including those that focus on human services and the banking industry.

www.ingramcontent.com/pod-product-compliance
Ingram Content Group UK Ltd.
Pitfield, Milton Keynes, MK11 3LW, UK
UKHW041843031026
15587UKWH00002B/970

9 781498 568944